WAID MOK FITZPATRICK

ARCHIE®

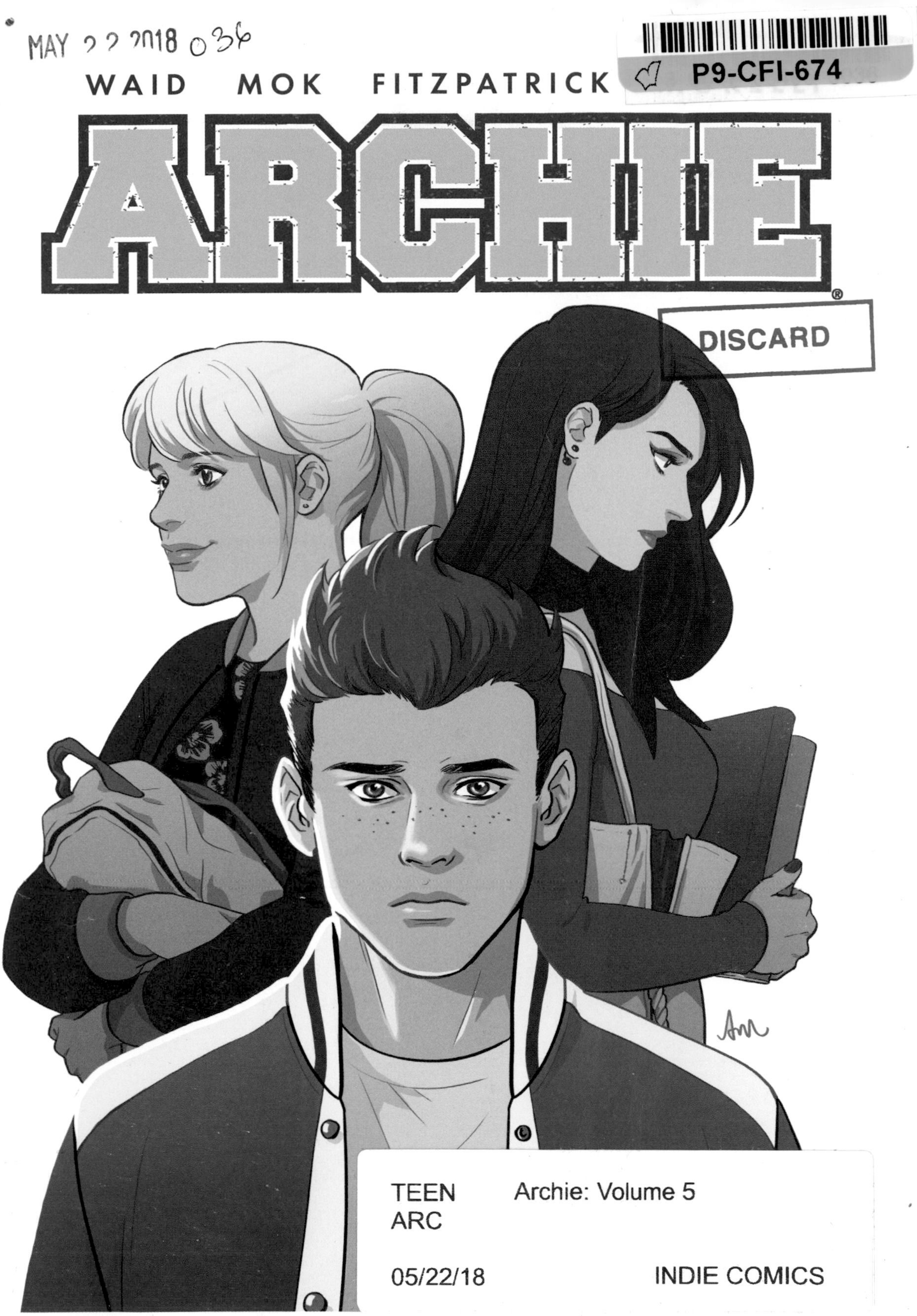

THE HEART OF RIVERDALE

STORY BY
MARK WAID

ART BY
AUDREY MOK

COLORS BY
KELLY FITZPATRICK

LETTERING BY
JACK MORELLI

EDITORIAL TEAM
MIKE PELLERITO
VINCENT LOVALLO
JAMIE LEE ROTANTE
STEPHEN OSWALD

GRAPHIC DESIGN BY
KARI McLACHLAN

EDITOR-IN-CHIEF
VICTOR GORELICK

PUBLISHER
JON GOLDWATER

PREVIOUSLY IN...

ARCHIE®

Archie Andrews finally completed working on his grandfather's 1969 Mach 1 Cobra Jet with his longtime friend Betty Cooper, something they had both been eagerly anticipating for years. Archie promised Betty she'd be the first to ride in the car, but he broke that promise in an attempt to save face in his relationship with Veronica Lodge, by taking up his nemesis Reggie Mantle's challenge to a race. Knowing that Archie was in over his head, Betty tried to put a stop to the race. Archie slammed on his brakes in time, but Reggie did not and Betty's car ending up driving off a cliff. Betty fell into a coma and the outlook was bleak—but ever the trooper, she came out of it. Unfortunately, upon waking she realized that she lost all feeling in her legs. With Betty's future uncertain, it's going to take the entire town of Riverdale to come together and help out everyone's favorite girl-next-door... both for Betty's sake and for the good of the entire town.

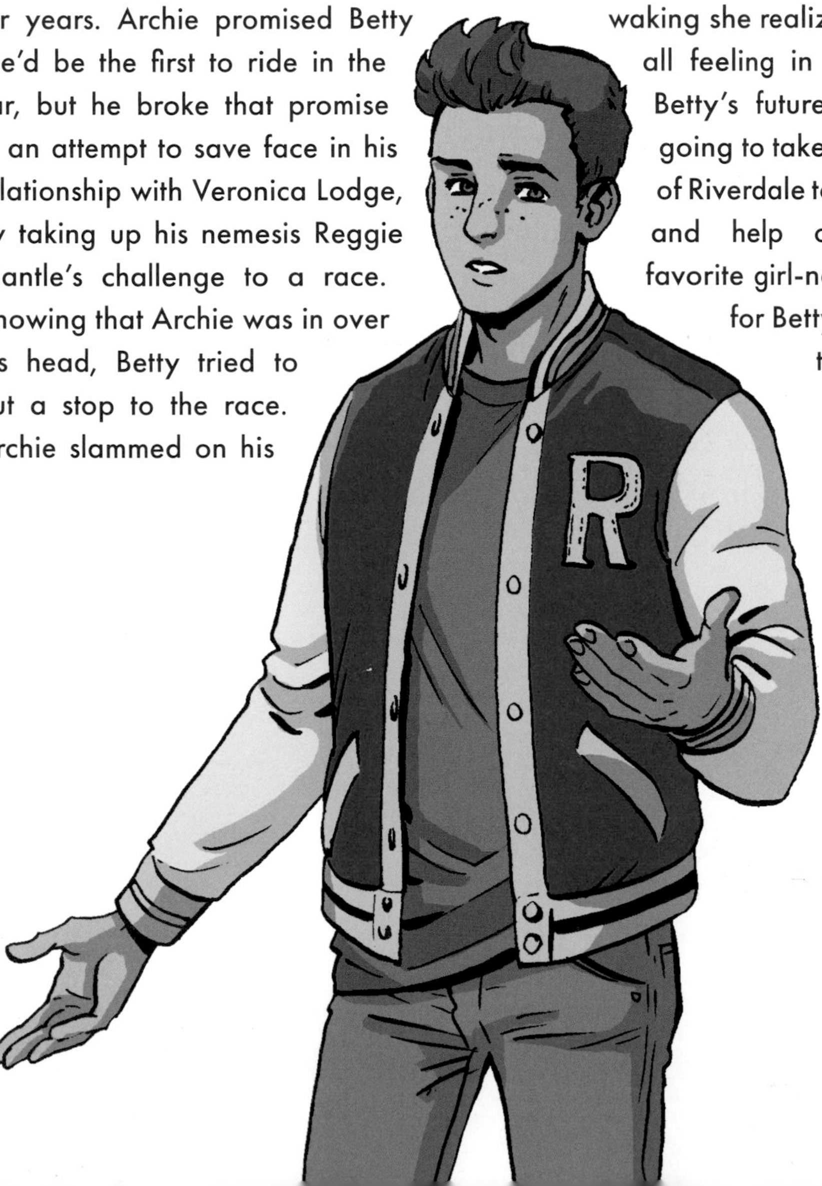
R

ISSUE TWENTY-THREE

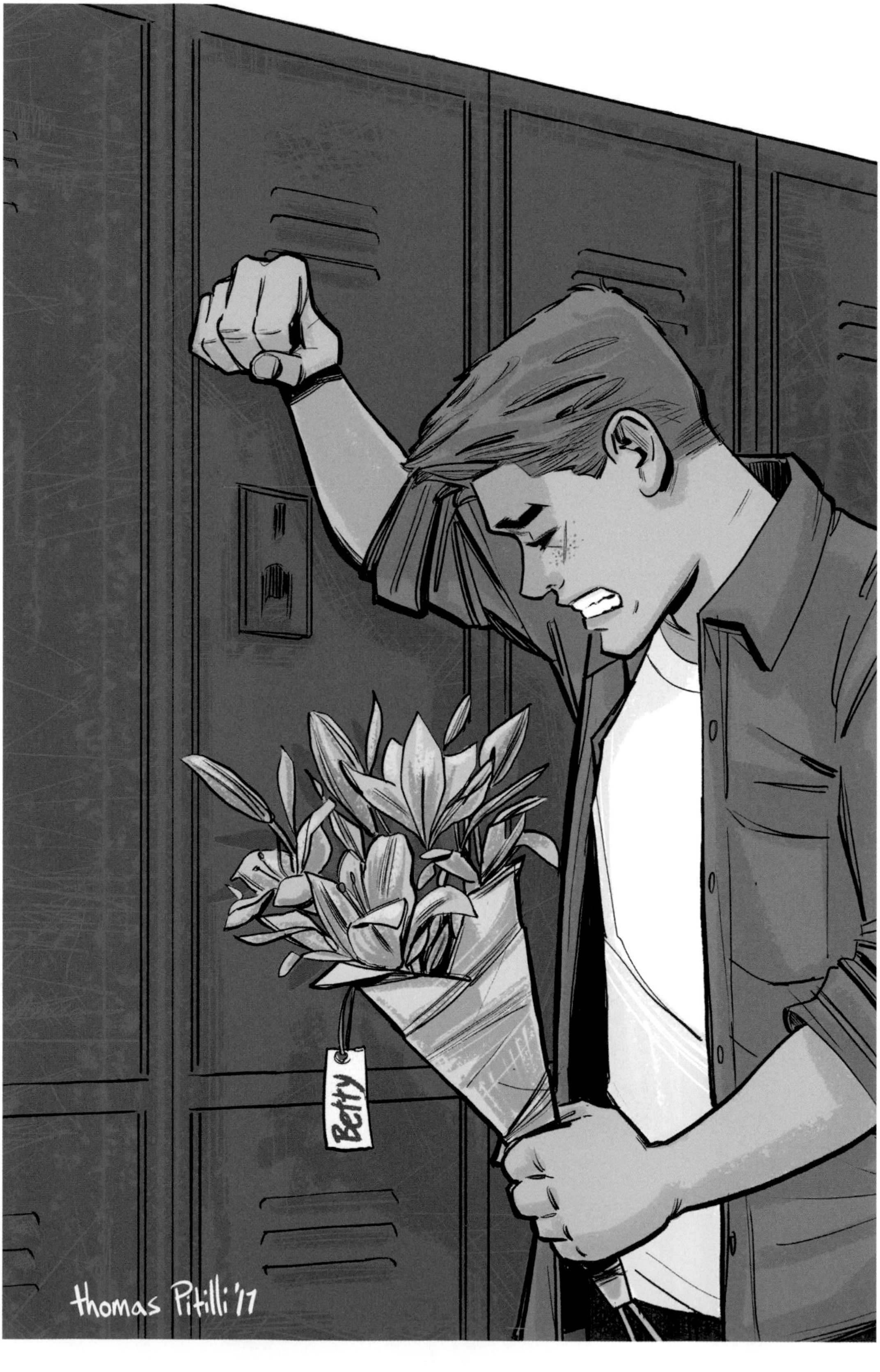

Betty
thomas Pitilli '17

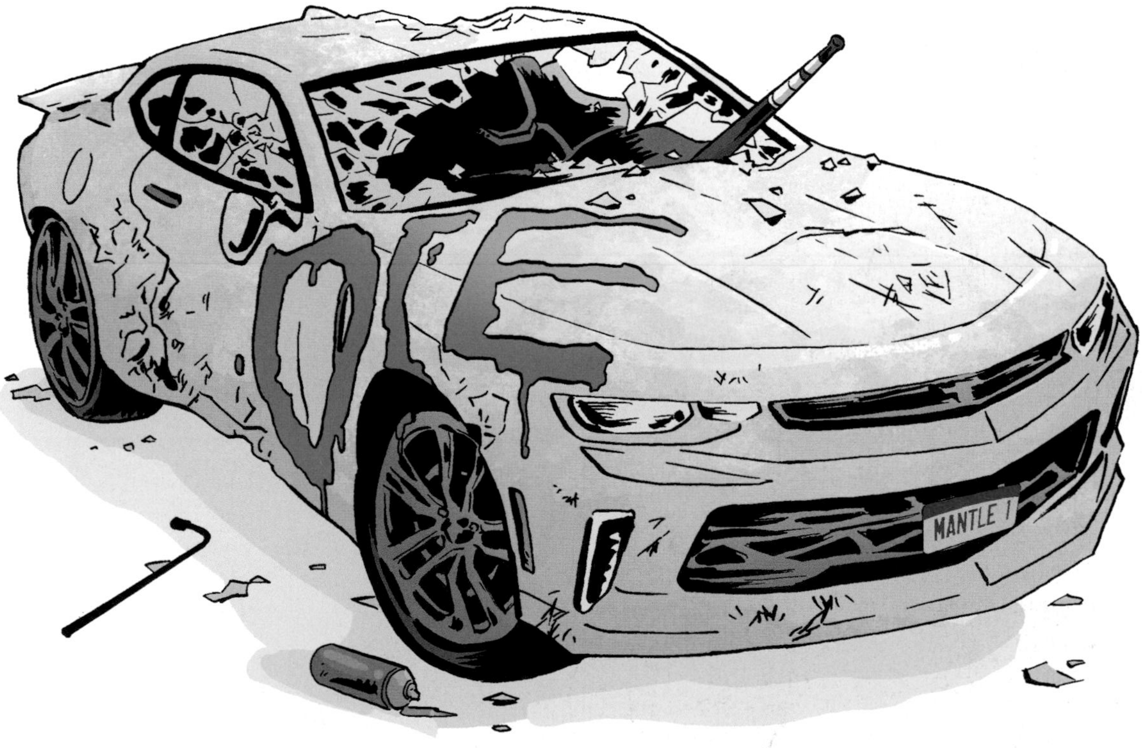
MANTLE 1

CHAPTER ONE: BRUISING

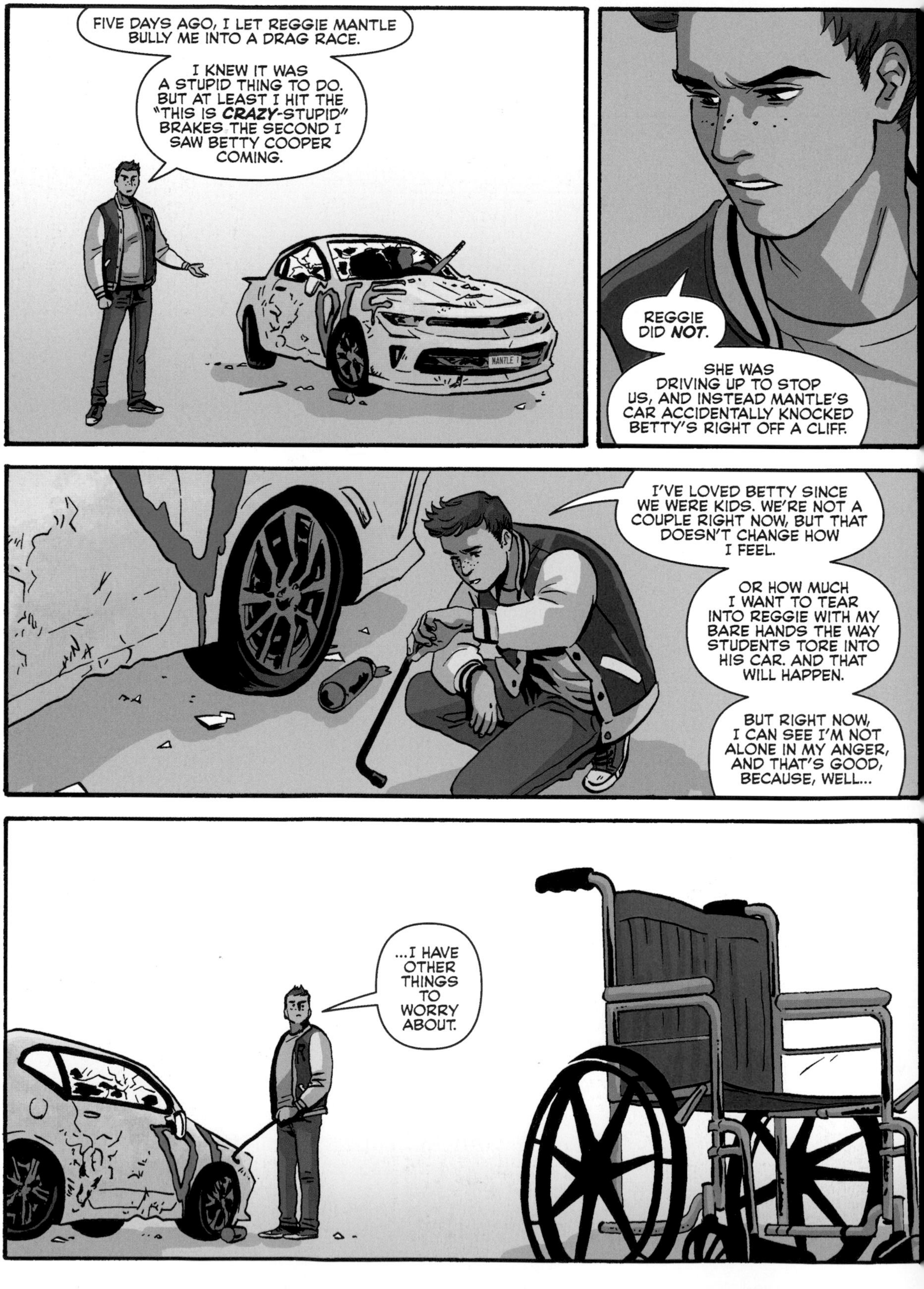
FIVE DAYS AGO, I LET REGGIE MANTLE BULLY ME INTO A DRAG RACE.
I KNEW IT WAS A STUPID THING TO DO. BUT AT LEAST I HIT THE "THIS IS *CRAZY*-STUPID" BRAKES THE SECOND I SAW BETTY COOPER COMING.
MANTLE 1
REGGIE DID ***NOT***.
SHE WAS DRIVING UP TO STOP US, AND INSTEAD MANTLE'S CAR ACCIDENTALLY KNOCKED BETTY'S RIGHT OFF A CLIFF.
I'VE LOVED BETTY SINCE WE WERE KIDS. WE'RE NOT A COUPLE RIGHT NOW, BUT THAT DOESN'T CHANGE HOW I FEEL.
OR HOW MUCH I WANT TO TEAR INTO REGGIE WITH MY BARE HANDS THE WAY STUDENTS TORE INTO HIS CAR. AND THAT WILL HAPPEN.
BUT RIGHT NOW, I CAN SEE I'M NOT ALONE IN MY ANGER, AND THAT'S GOOD, BECAUSE, WELL...
...I HAVE OTHER THINGS TO WORRY ABOUT.

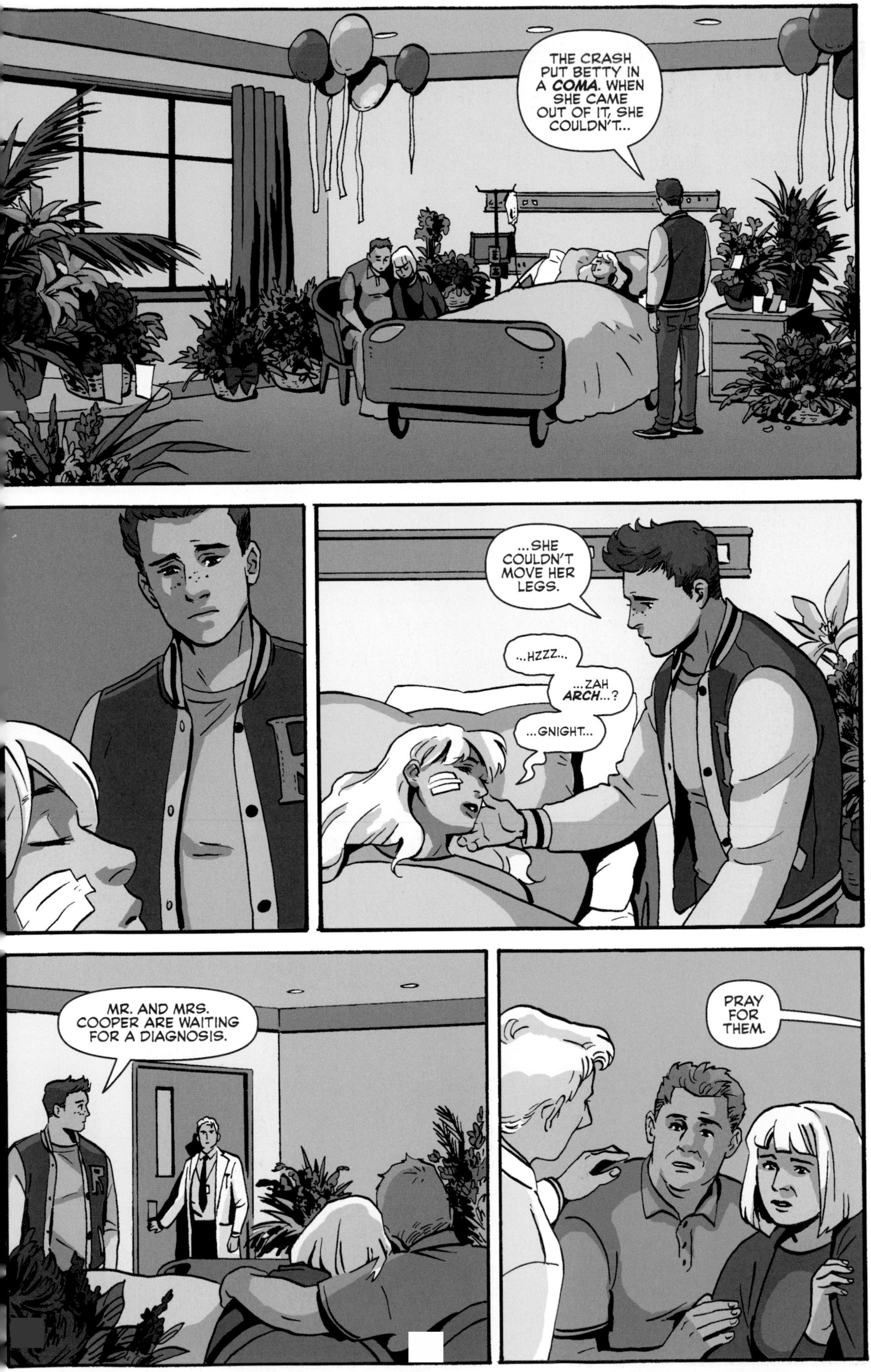
THE CRASH PUT BETTY IN A COMA. WHEN SHE CAME OUT OF IT, SHE COULDN'T...
...SHE COULDN'T MOVE HER LEGS.
...HZZZ...
...ZAH ARCH...?
...GNIGHT...
MR. AND MRS. COOPER ARE WAITING FOR A DIAGNOSIS.
PRAY FOR THEM.

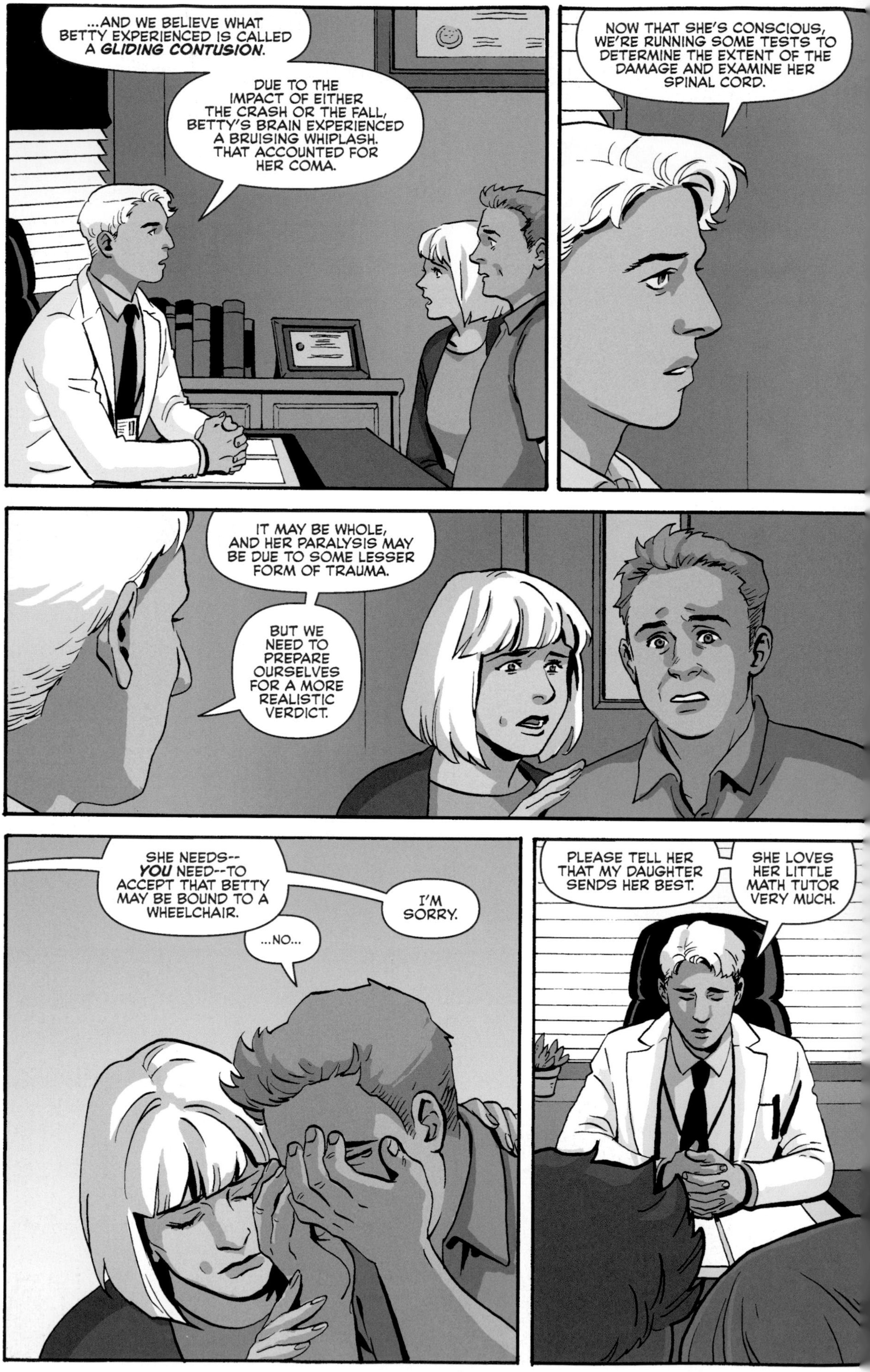
...AND WE BELIEVE WHAT BETTY EXPERIENCED IS CALLED A ***GLIDING CONTUSION***.
DUE TO THE IMPACT OF EITHER THE CRASH OR THE FALL, BETTY'S BRAIN EXPERIENCED A BRUISING WHIPLASH. THAT ACCOUNTED FOR HER COMA.
NOW THAT SHE'S CONSCIOUS, WE'RE RUNNING SOME TESTS TO DETERMINE THE EXTENT OF THE DAMAGE AND EXAMINE HER SPINAL CORD.
IT MAY BE WHOLE, AND HER PARALYSIS MAY BE DUE TO SOME LESSER FORM OF TRAUMA.
BUT WE NEED TO PREPARE OURSELVES FOR A MORE REALISTIC VERDICT.
SHE NEEDS-- ***YOU*** NEED--TO ACCEPT THAT BETTY MAY BE BOUND TO A WHEELCHAIR.
I'M SORRY.
...NO...
PLEASE TELL HER THAT MY DAUGHTER SENDS HER BEST.
SHE LOVES HER LITTLE MATH TUTOR VERY MUCH.

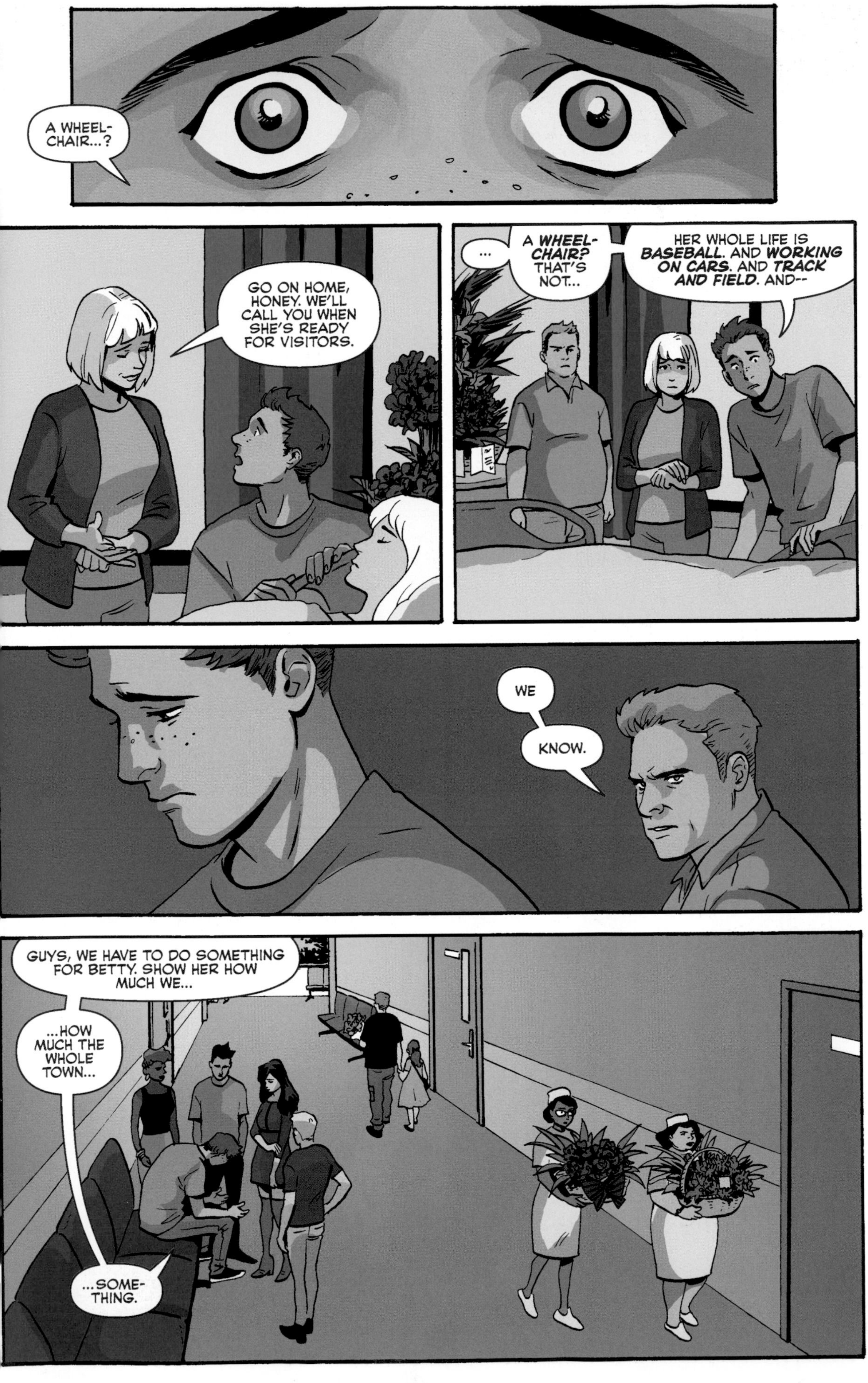
A WHEEL-
CHAIR...?
GO ON HOME, HONEY. WE'LL CALL YOU WHEN SHE'S READY FOR VISITORS.
...
A WHEEL-CHAIR? THAT'S NOT...
HER WHOLE LIFE IS BASEBALL. AND WORKING ON CARS. AND TRACK AND FIELD. AND--
WE
KNOW.
GUYS, WE HAVE TO DO SOMETHING FOR BETTY. SHOW HER HOW MUCH WE...
...HOW MUCH THE WHOLE TOWN...
...SOME-THING.

CHAPTER TWO: LIKE e-MAILS

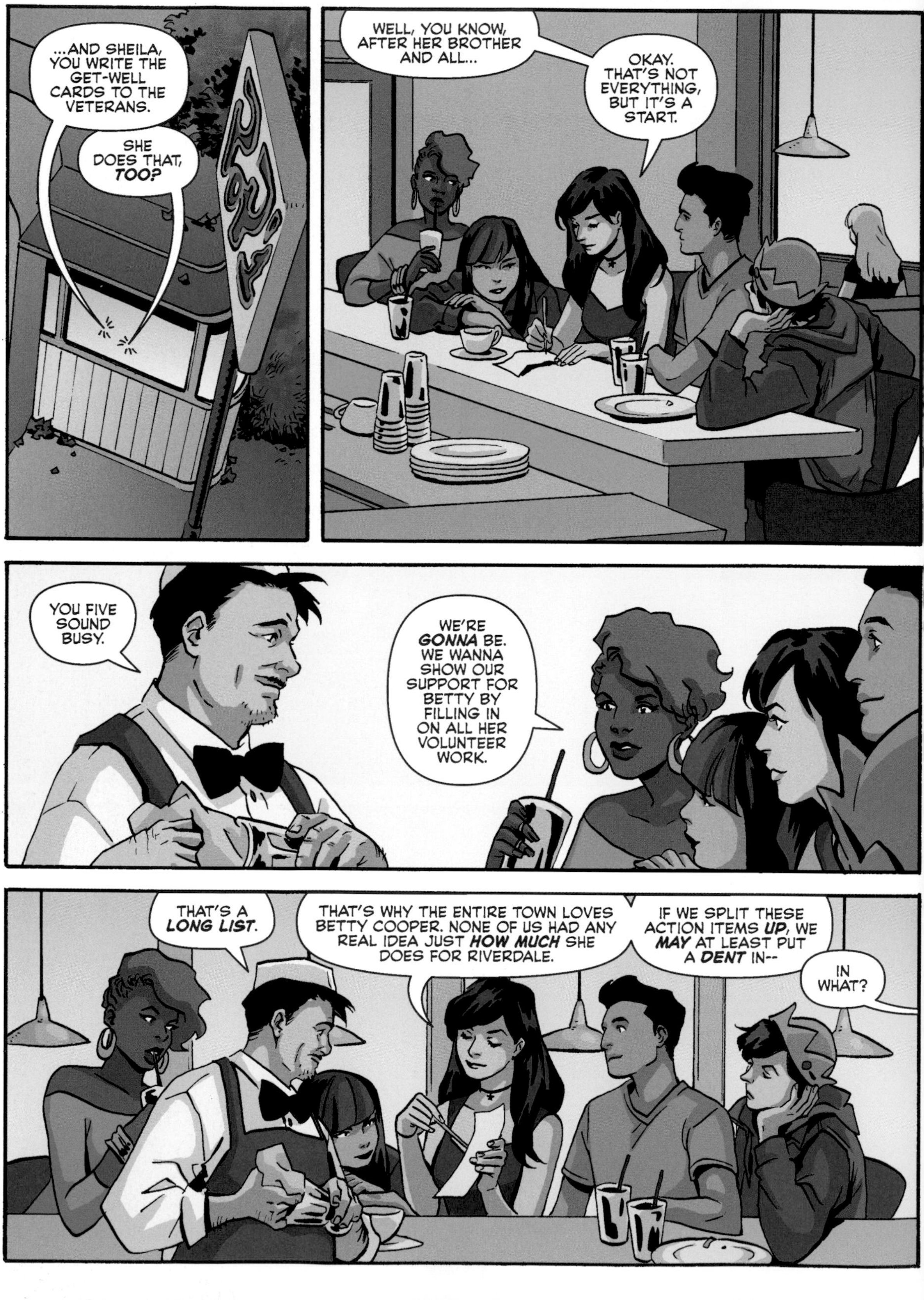

...AND SHEILA, YOU WRITE THE GET-WELL CARDS TO THE VETERANS.
SHE DOES THAT, *TOO?*
WELL, YOU KNOW, AFTER HER BROTHER AND ALL...
OKAY. THAT'S NOT EVERYTHING, BUT IT'S A START.
YOU FIVE SOUND BUSY.
WE'RE *GONNA* BE. WE WANNA SHOW OUR SUPPORT FOR BETTY BY FILLING IN ON ALL HER VOLUNTEER WORK.
THAT'S A *LONG LIST*.
THAT'S WHY THE ENTIRE TOWN LOVES BETTY COOPER. NONE OF US HAD ANY REAL IDEA JUST *HOW MUCH* SHE DOES FOR RIVERDALE.
IF WE SPLIT THESE ACTION ITEMS *UP*, WE *MAY* AT LEAST PUT A *DENT* IN--
IN WHAT?

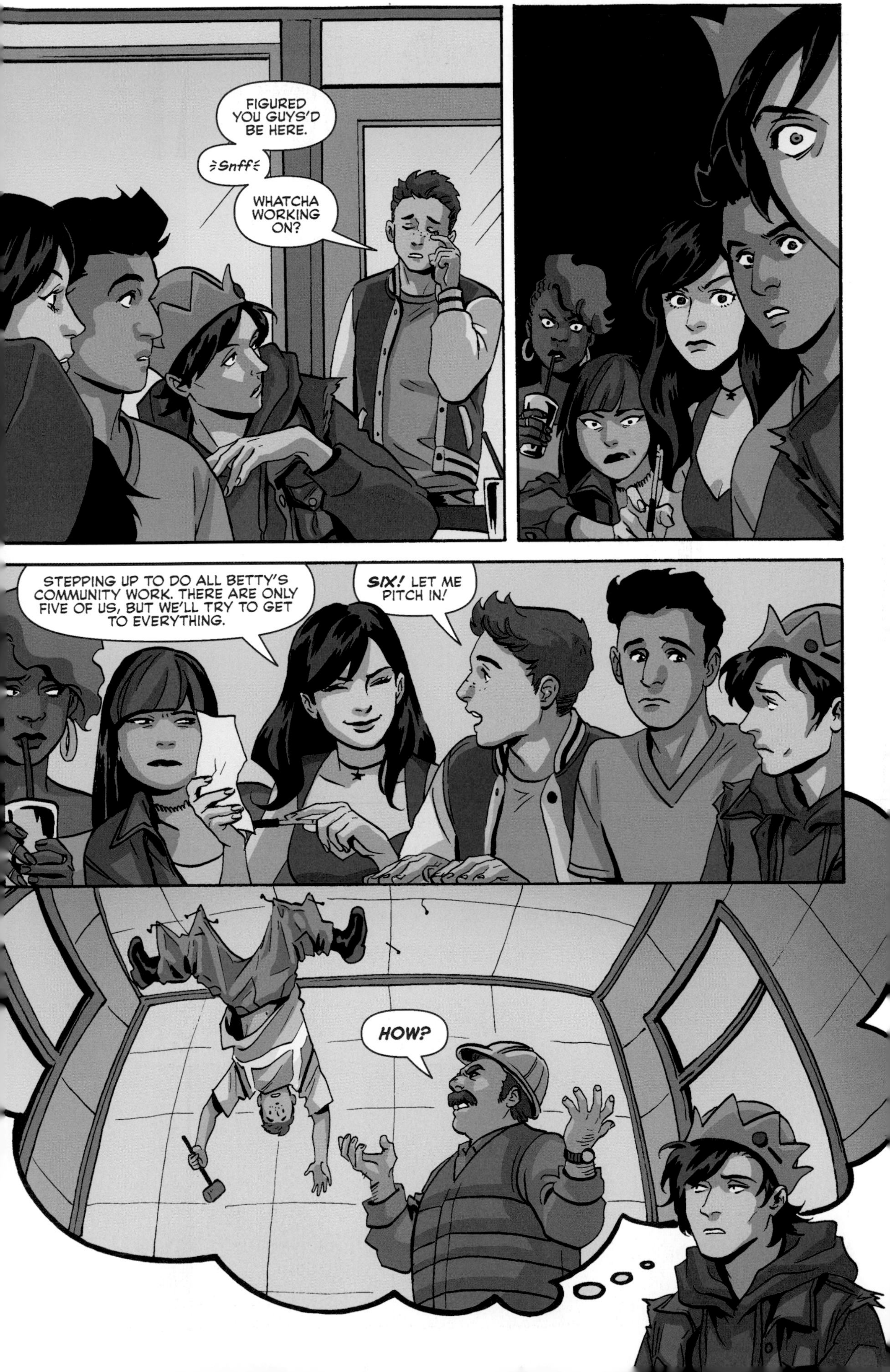
FIGURED YOU GUYS'D BE HERE.
≷Snff≶
WHATCHA WORKING ON?
STEPPING UP TO DO ALL BETTY'S COMMUNITY WORK. THERE ARE ONLY FIVE OF US, BUT WE'LL TRY TO GET TO EVERYTHING.
SIX! LET ME PITCH IN!
HOW?

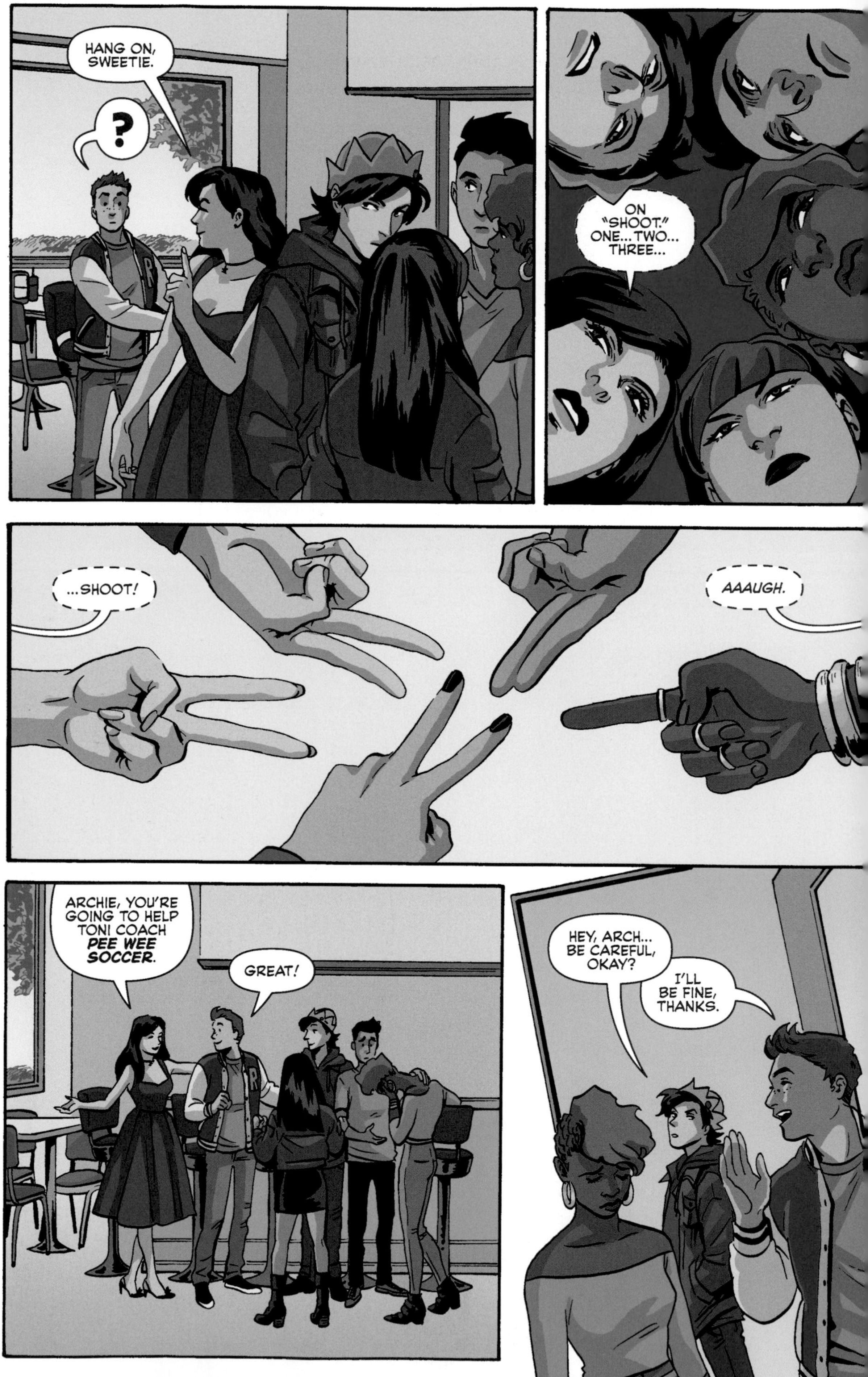
HANG ON, SWEETIE.
?
ON "SHOOT." ONE...TWO... THREE...
...SHOOT!
AAAUGH.
ARCHIE, YOU'RE GOING TO HELP TONI COACH PEE WEE SOCCER.
GREAT!
HEY, ARCH... BE CAREFUL, OKAY?
I'LL BE FINE, THANKS.

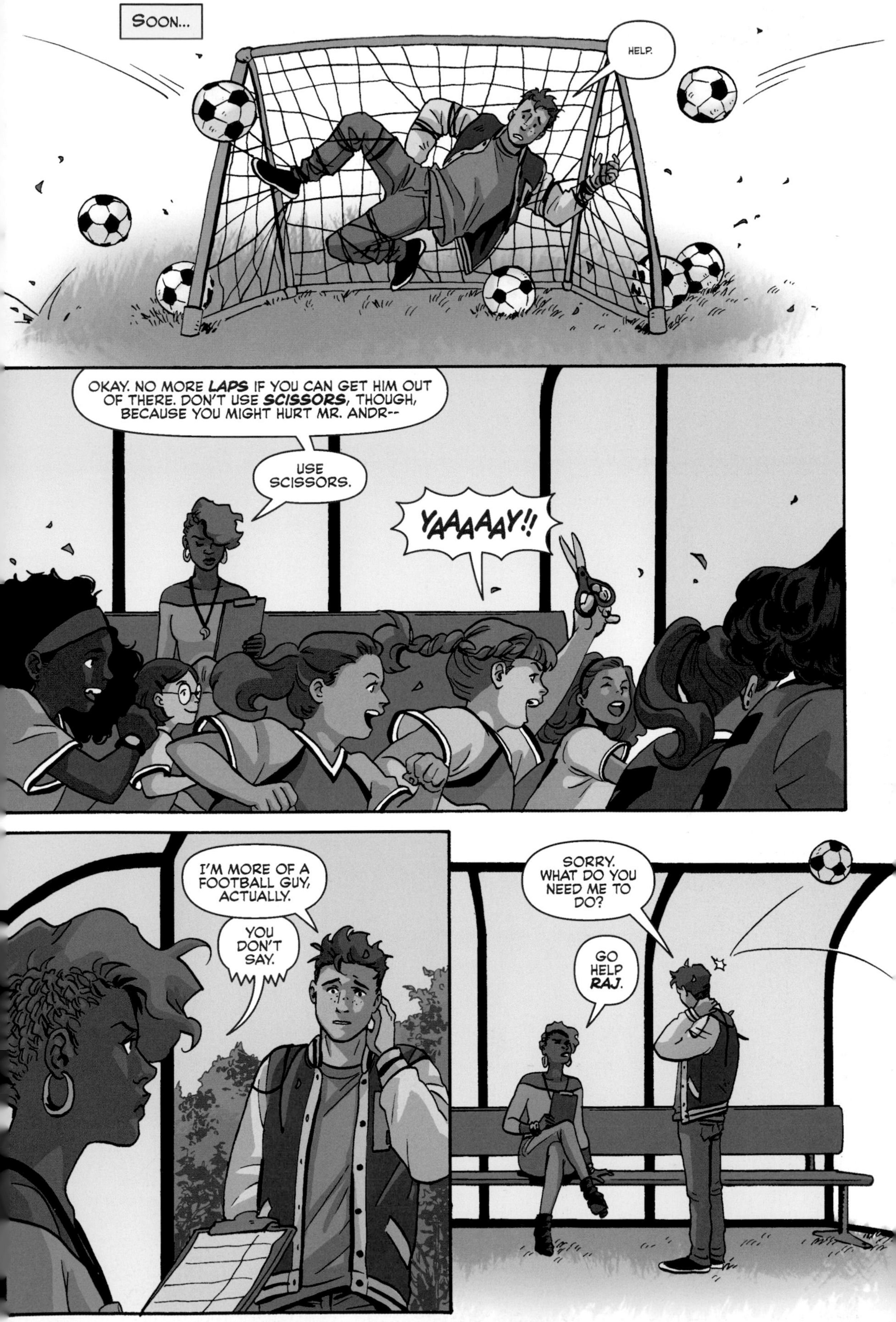
SOON...
HELP.
OKAY. NO MORE LAPS IF YOU CAN GET HIM OUT OF THERE. DON'T USE SCISSORS, THOUGH, BECAUSE YOU MIGHT HURT MR. ANDR--
USE SCISSORS.
YAAAAAY!!
I'M MORE OF A FOOTBALL GUY, ACTUALLY.
YOU DON'T SAY.
SORRY. WHAT DO YOU NEED ME TO DO?
GO HELP RAJ.

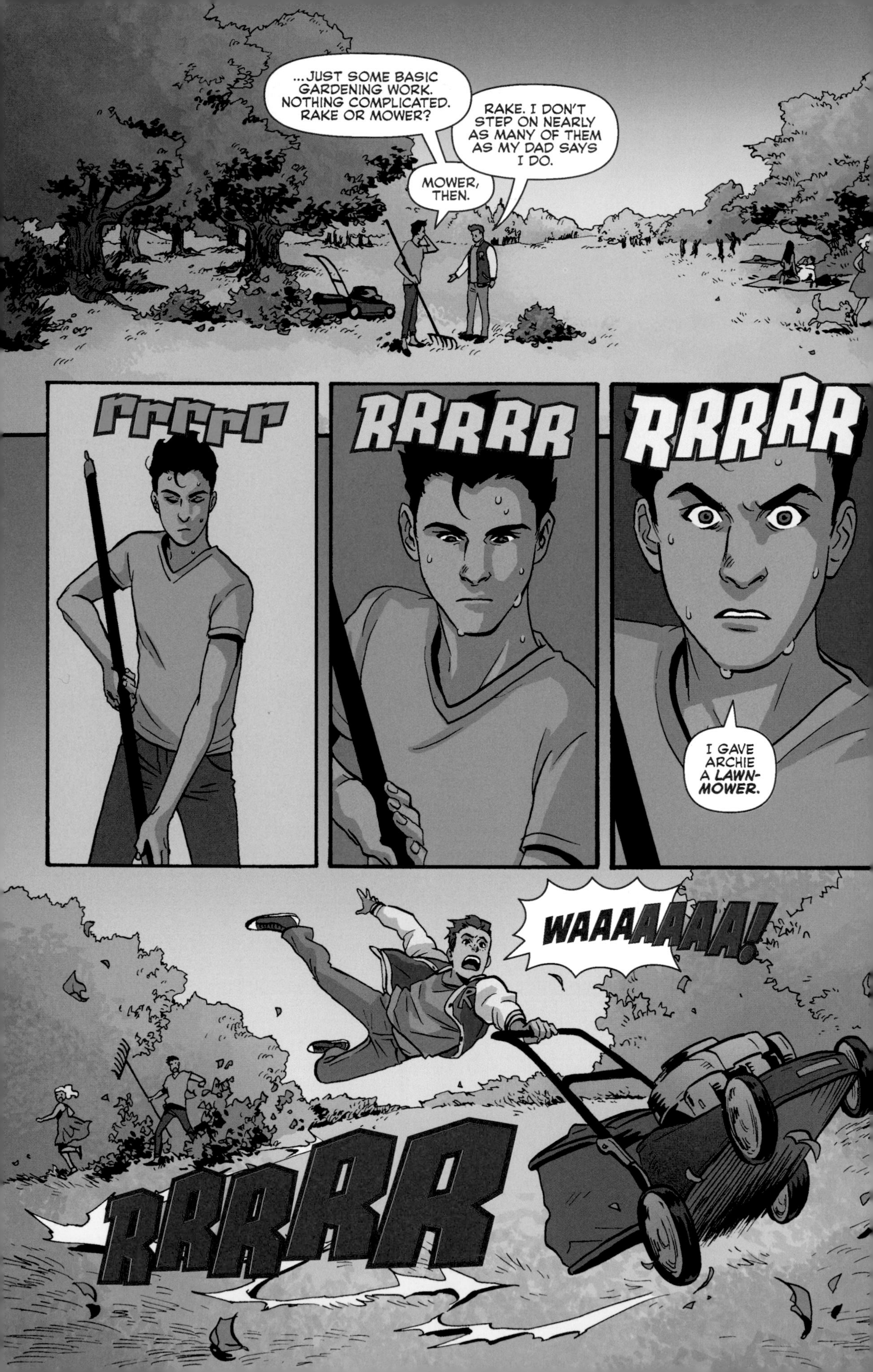
...JUST SOME BASIC GARDENING WORK. NOTHING COMPLICATED. RAKE OR MOWER?
RAKE. I DON'T STEP ON NEARLY AS MANY OF THEM AS MY DAD SAYS I DO.
MOWER, THEN.
rrrrr
RRRRR
RRRRR
I GAVE ARCHIE A *LAWN-MOWER.*
WAAAAAAA!
RRRRR

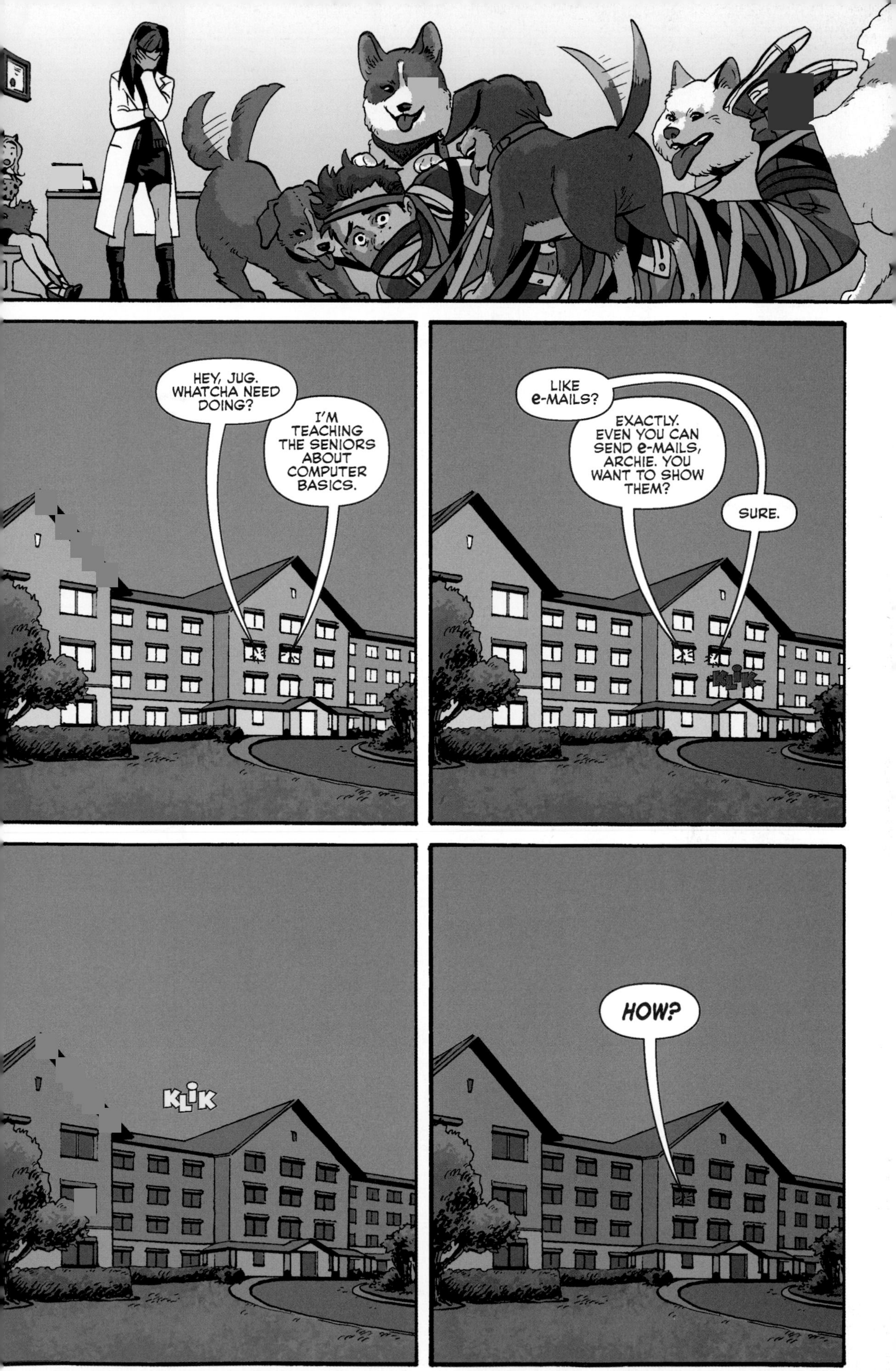
HEY, JUG. WHATCHA NEED DOING?
I'M TEACHING THE SENIORS ABOUT COMPUTER BASICS.
LIKE e-MAILS?
EXACTLY. EVEN YOU CAN SEND e-MAILS, ARCHIE. YOU WANT TO SHOW THEM?
SURE.
KLIK
KLIK
HOW?

CHAPTER THREE: HURRY.

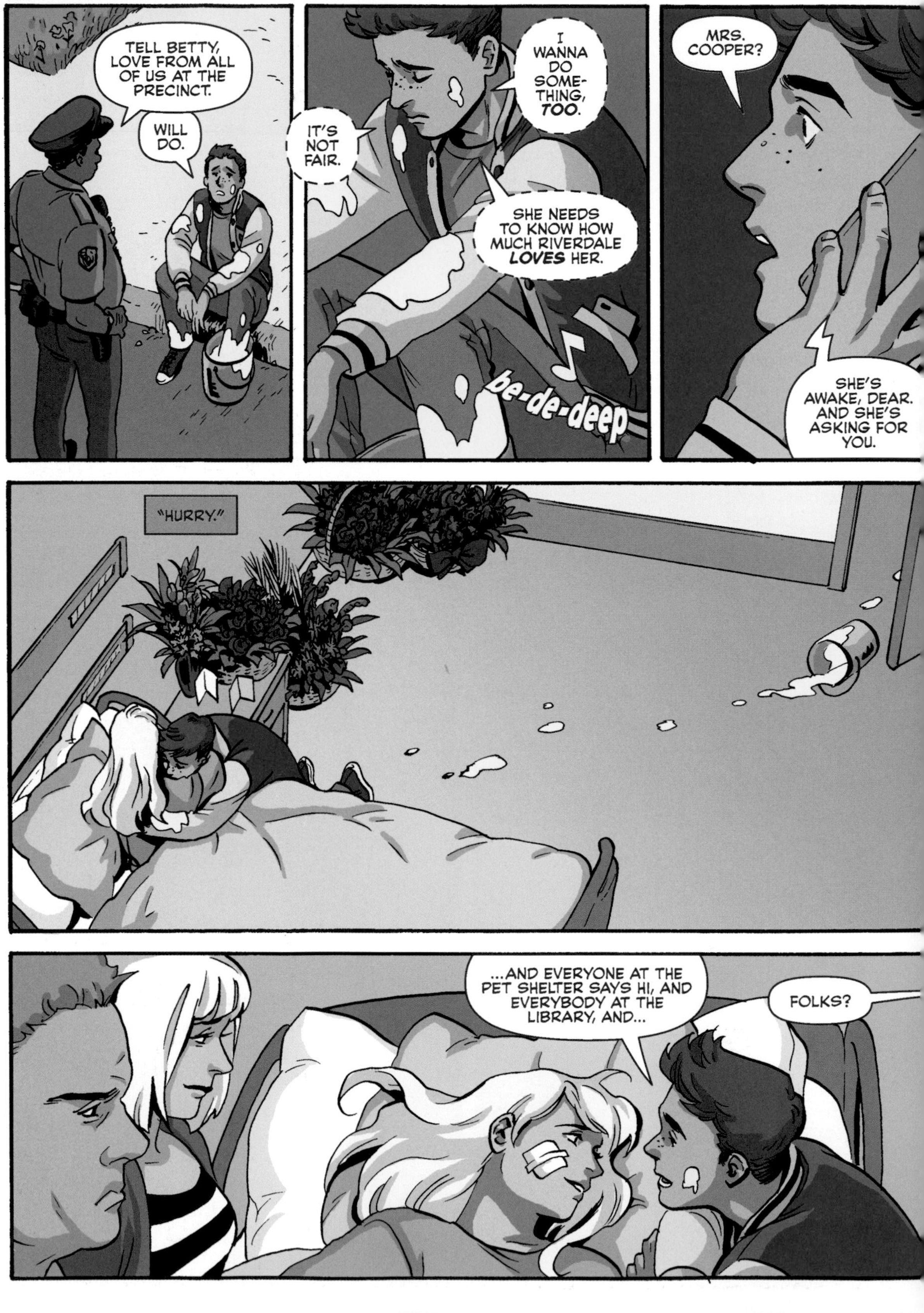

TELL BETTY, LOVE FROM ALL OF US AT THE PRECINCT.
WILL DO.
IT'S NOT FAIR.
I WANNA DO SOME-THING, TOO.
SHE NEEDS TO KNOW HOW MUCH RIVERDALE LOVES HER.
be-de-deep
MRS. COOPER?
SHE'S AWAKE, DEAR. AND SHE'S ASKING FOR YOU.
"HURRY."
...AND EVERYONE AT THE PET SHELTER SAYS HI, AND EVERYBODY AT THE LIBRARY, AND...
FOLKS?

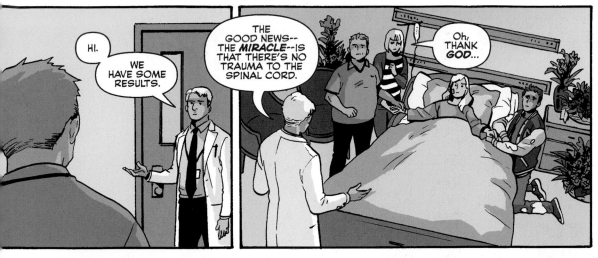

HI.

WE HAVE SOME RESULTS.

THE GOOD NEWS-- THE *MIRACLE*--IS THAT THERE'S NO TRAUMA TO THE SPINAL CORD.

Oh, THANK *GOD*...

HOWEVER.

I'VE CONSULTED WITH SOME COLLEAGUES, AND WE BELIEVE THE CONTUSIONS TO YOUR BRAIN ARE THE PROBLEM.

THAT DOESN'T ALLOW MUCH TREATMENT. ALL WE CAN REALLY DO RIGHT NOW IS WAIT AND SEE IF YOUR BRAIN HEALS BY ITSELF. THAT COULD TAKE MONTHS.

I'M BEING PERFECTLY HONEST WITH YOU. YOU'RE GOING TO NEED A WHEELCHAIR, AND THE ODDS OF YOU GETTING *OUT* OF IT ARE A THOUSAND TO ONE.

I'LL TAKE THOSE ODDS.

CHAPTER FOUR: MEANWHILE... Dilton & MOOSE

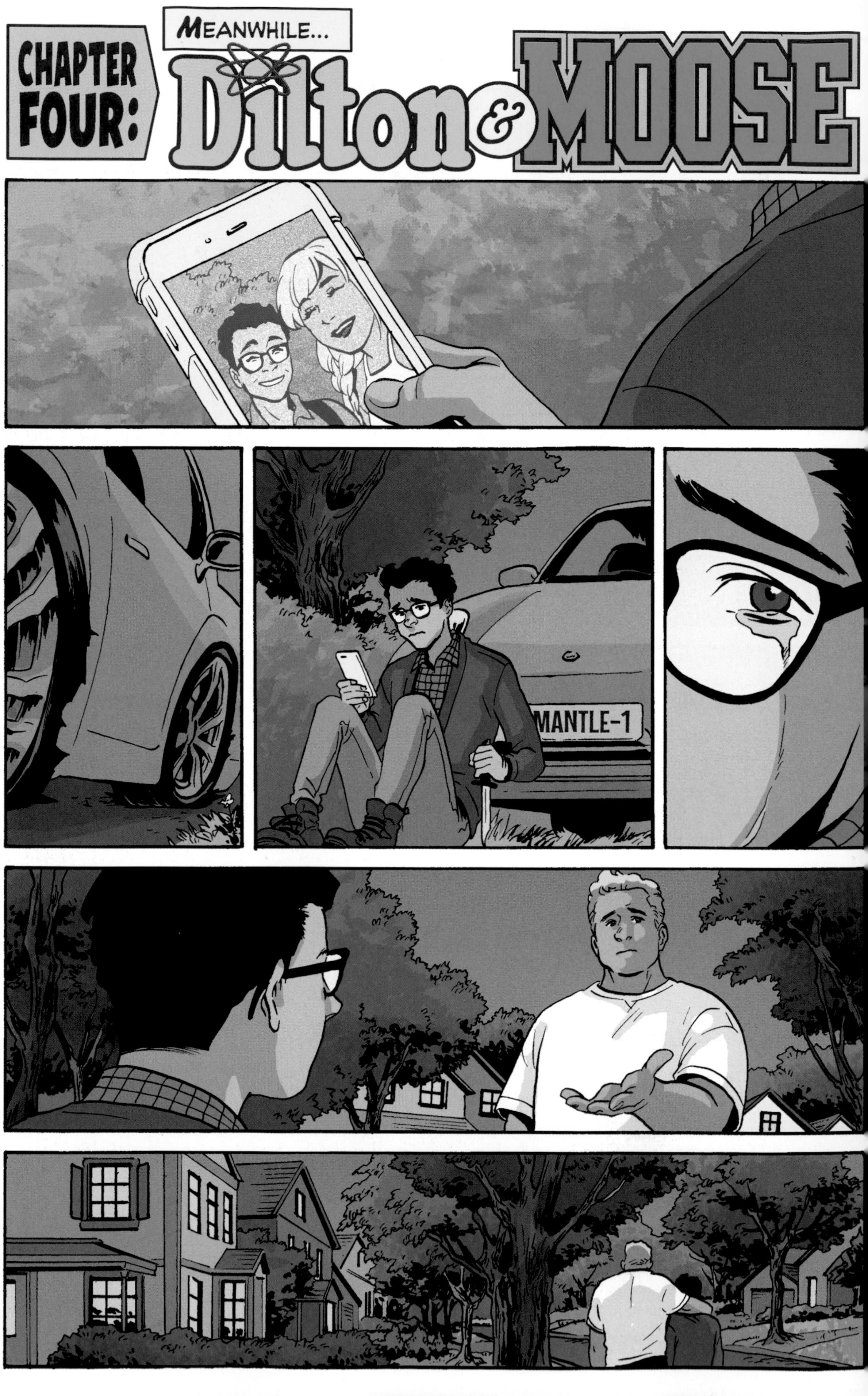
MANTLE-1

CHAPTER FIVE: THE HEART OF RIVERDALE

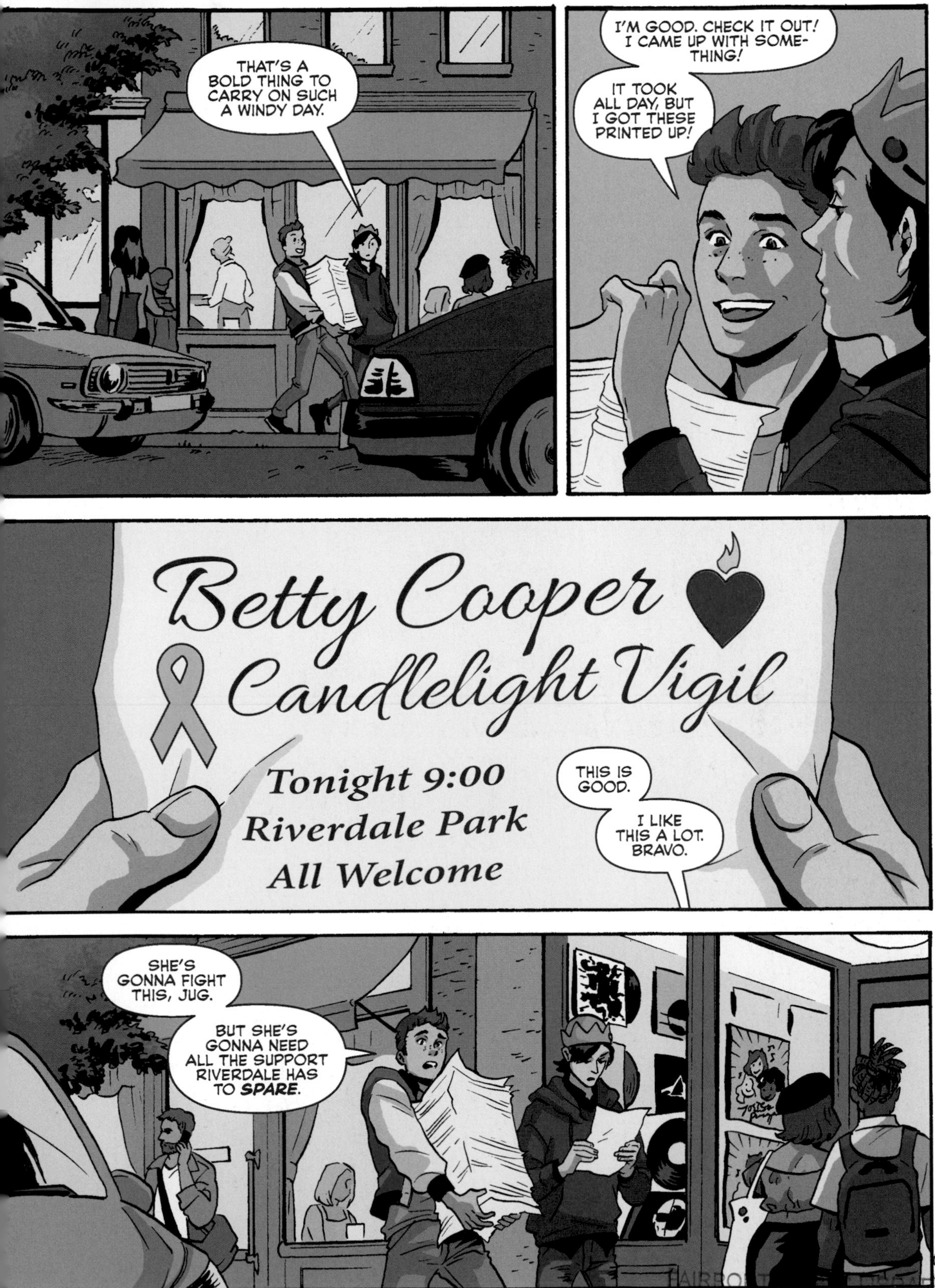
THAT'S A BOLD THING TO CARRY ON SUCH A WINDY DAY.
I'M GOOD. CHECK IT OUT! I CAME UP WITH SOME-THING!
IT TOOK ALL DAY, BUT I GOT THESE PRINTED UP!
Betty Cooper Candlelight Vigil
Tonight 9:00
Riverdale Park
All Welcome
THIS IS GOOD.
I LIKE THIS A LOT. BRAVO.
SHE'S GONNA FIGHT THIS, JUG.
BUT SHE'S GONNA NEED ALL THE SUPPORT RIVERDALE HAS TO *SPARE*.

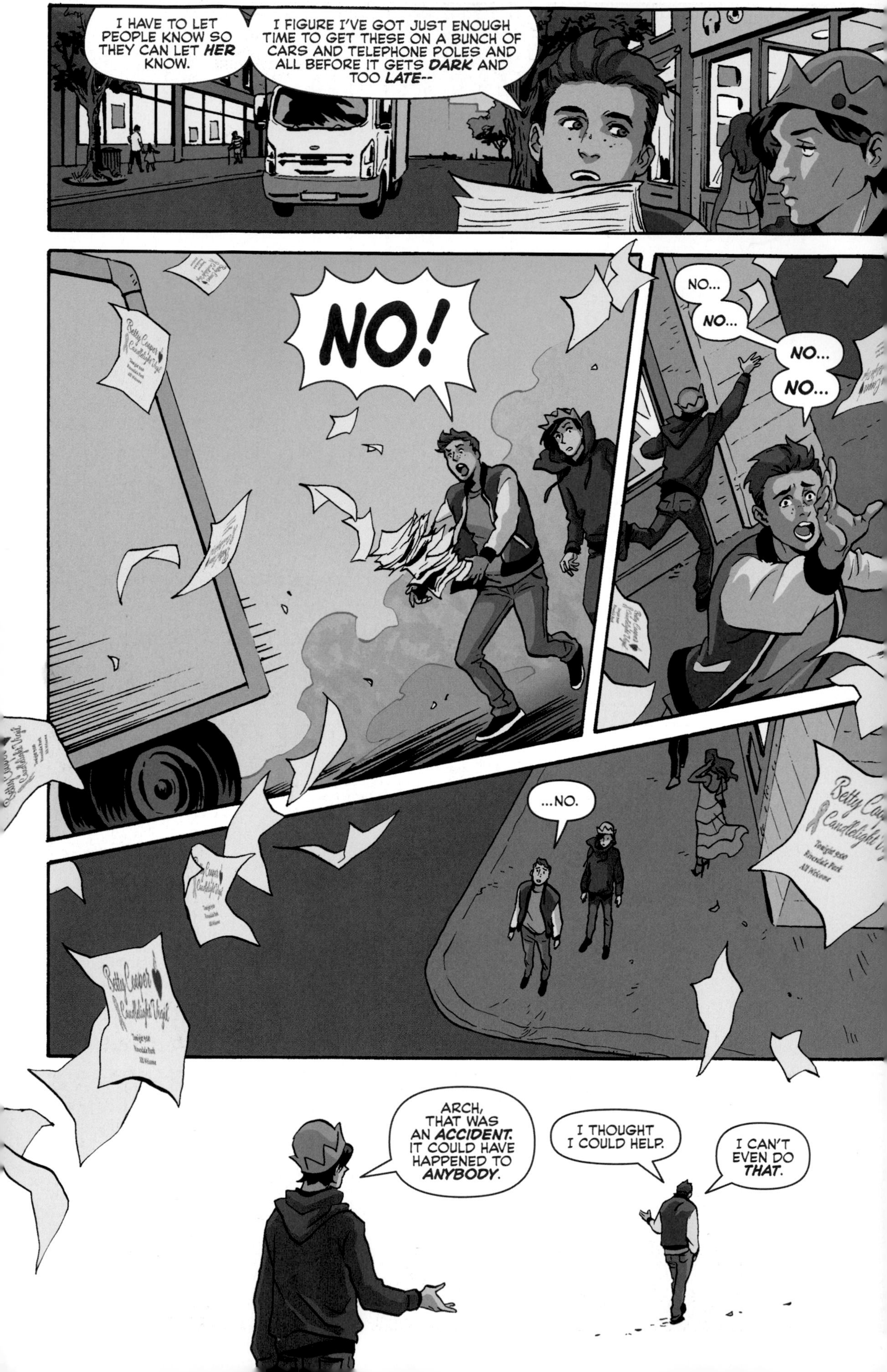

I HAVE TO LET PEOPLE KNOW SO THEY CAN LET *HER* KNOW.
I FIGURE I'VE GOT JUST ENOUGH TIME TO GET THESE ON A BUNCH OF CARS AND TELEPHONE POLES AND ALL BEFORE IT GETS *DARK* AND TOO *LATE*--
NO!
NO...
NO...
NO...
NO...
...NO.
ARCH, THAT WAS AN *ACCIDENT.* IT COULD HAVE HAPPENED TO *ANYBODY*.
I THOUGHT I COULD HELP.
I CAN'T EVEN DO *THAT*.

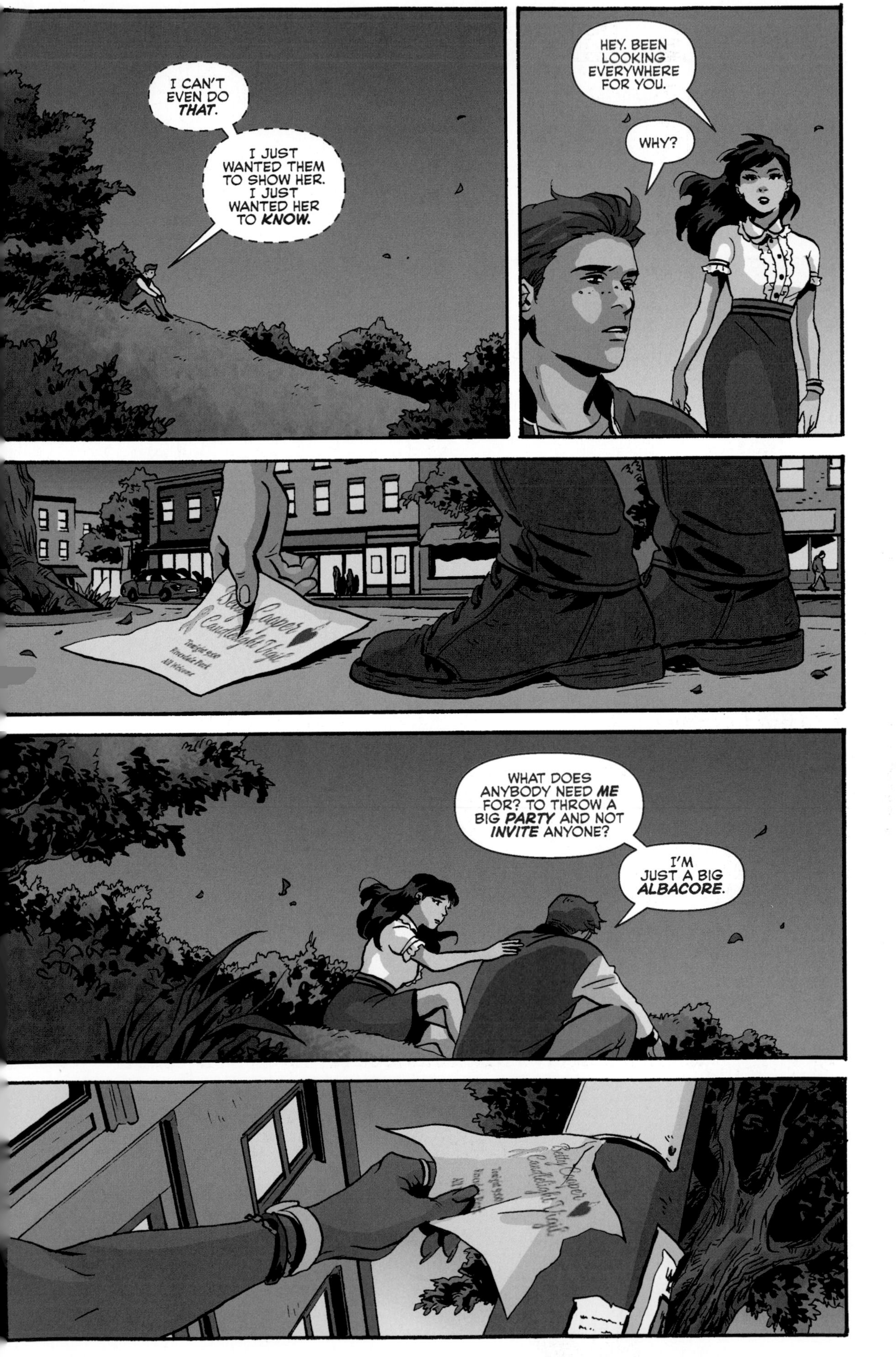
I CAN'T EVEN DO ***THAT***.
I JUST WANTED THEM TO SHOW HER. I JUST WANTED HER TO ***KNOW***.
HEY. BEEN LOOKING EVERYWHERE FOR YOU.
WHY?
WHAT DOES ANYBODY NEED ***ME*** FOR? TO THROW A BIG ***PARTY*** AND NOT ***INVITE*** ANYONE?
I'M JUST A BIG ***ALBACORE***.

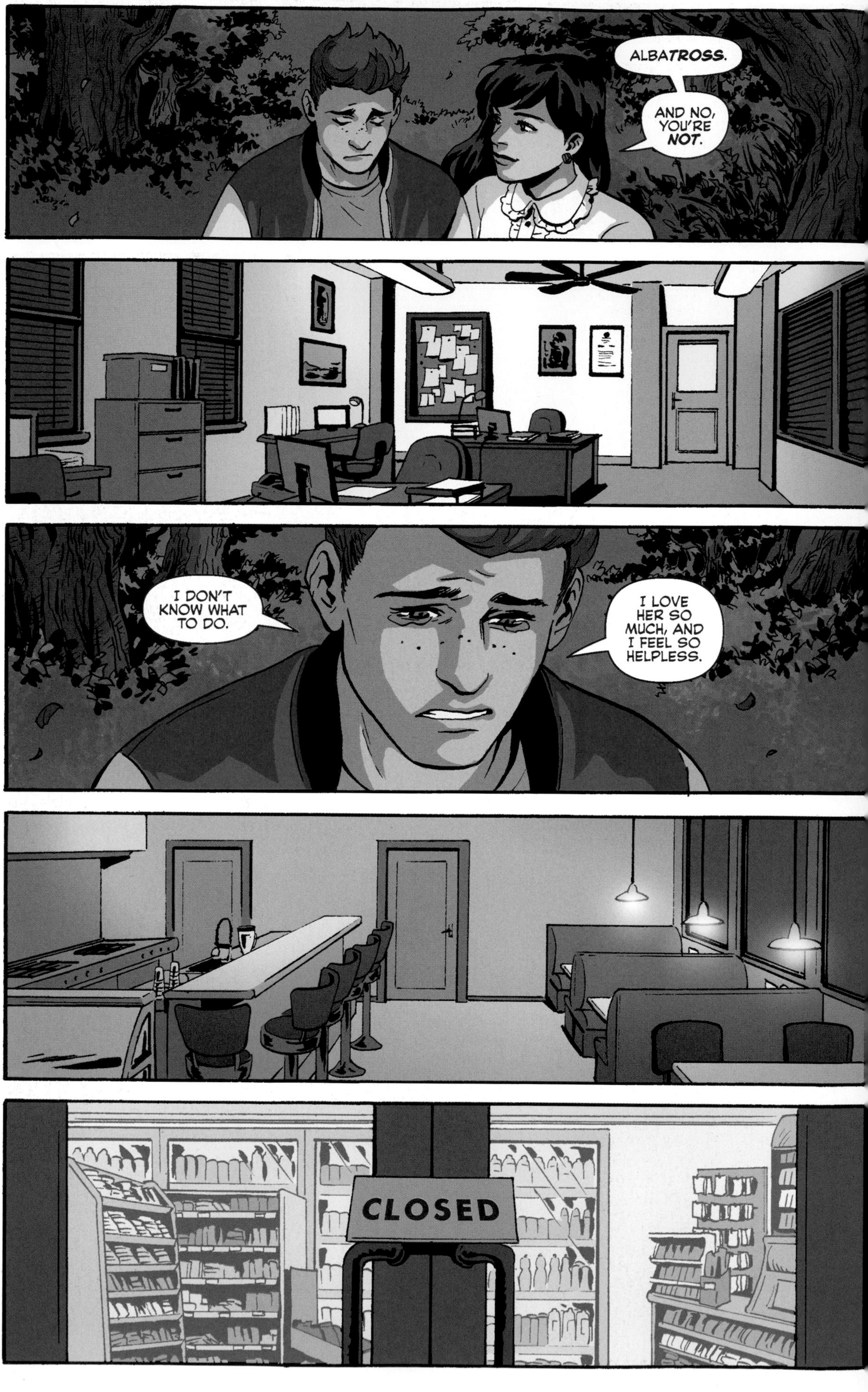
ALBATROSS.
AND NO, YOU'RE NOT.
I DON'T KNOW WHAT TO DO.
I LOVE HER SO MUCH, AND I FEEL SO HELPLESS.
CLOSED

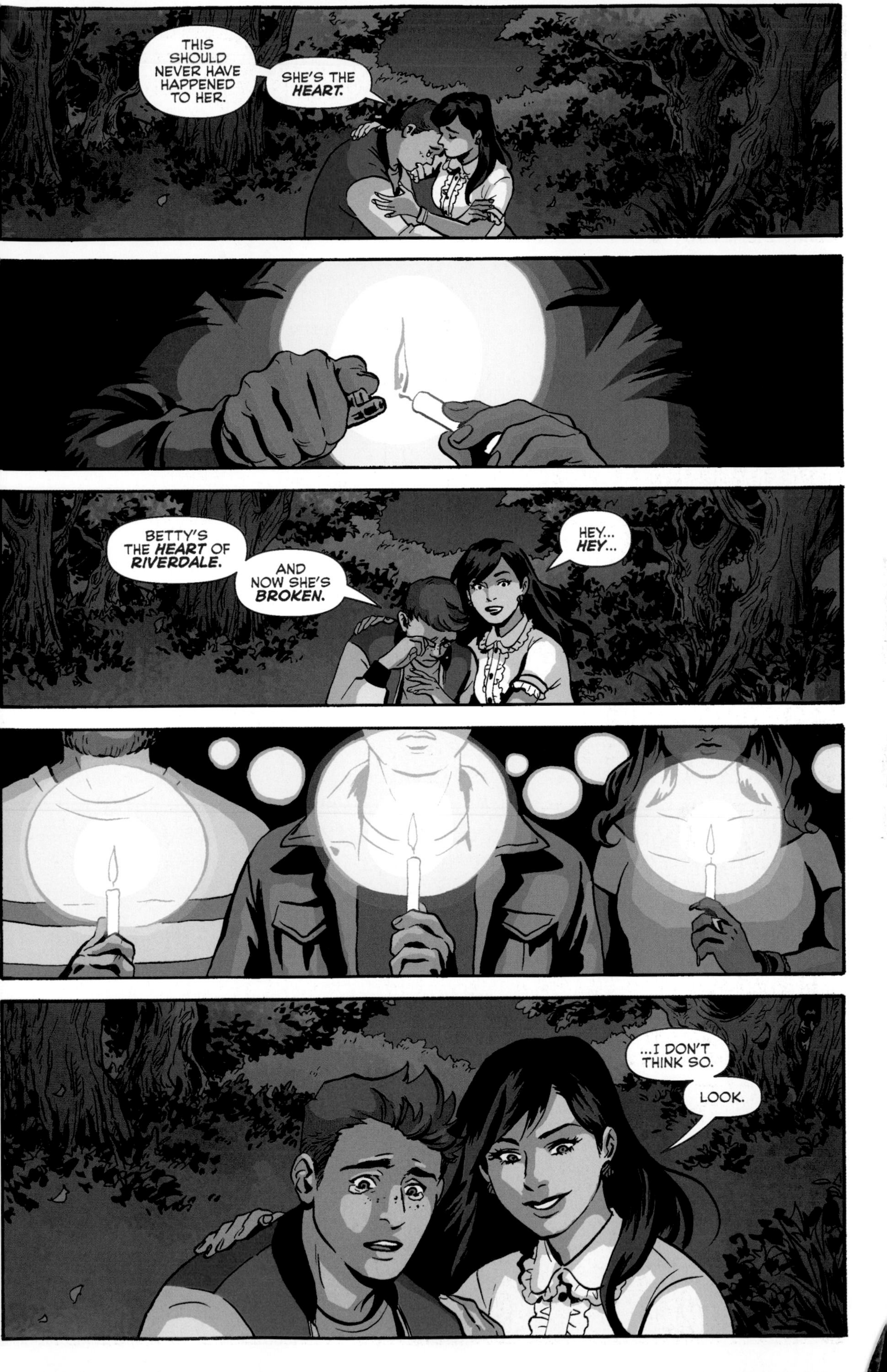
THIS SHOULD NEVER HAVE HAPPENED TO HER.
SHE'S THE *HEART.*
BETTY'S THE *HEART* OF *RIVERDALE.*
AND NOW SHE'S *BROKEN.*
HEY... *HEY*...
...I DON'T THINK SO.
LOOK.

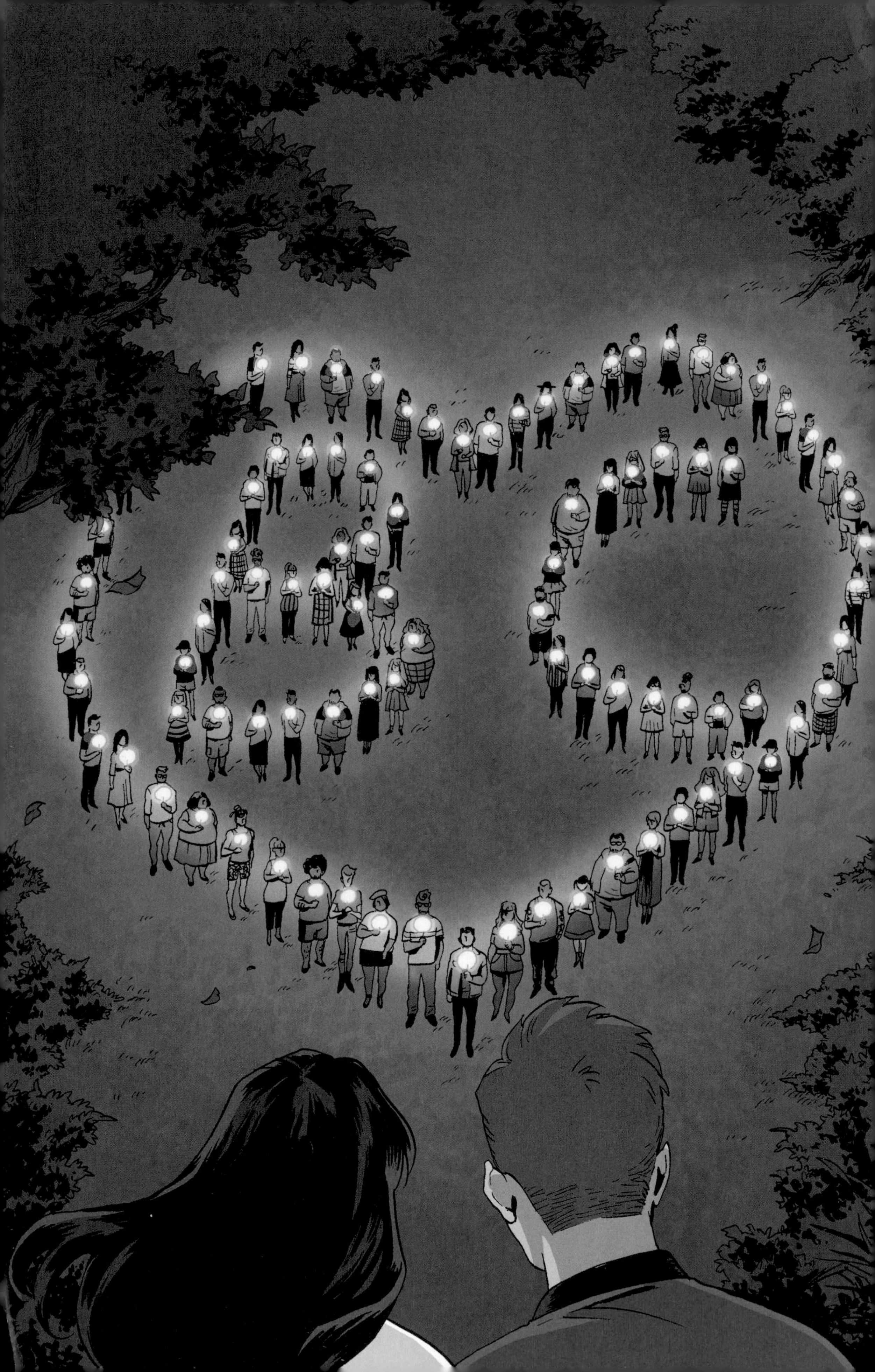

TO BE CONTINUED...

ISSUE TWENTY-FOUR

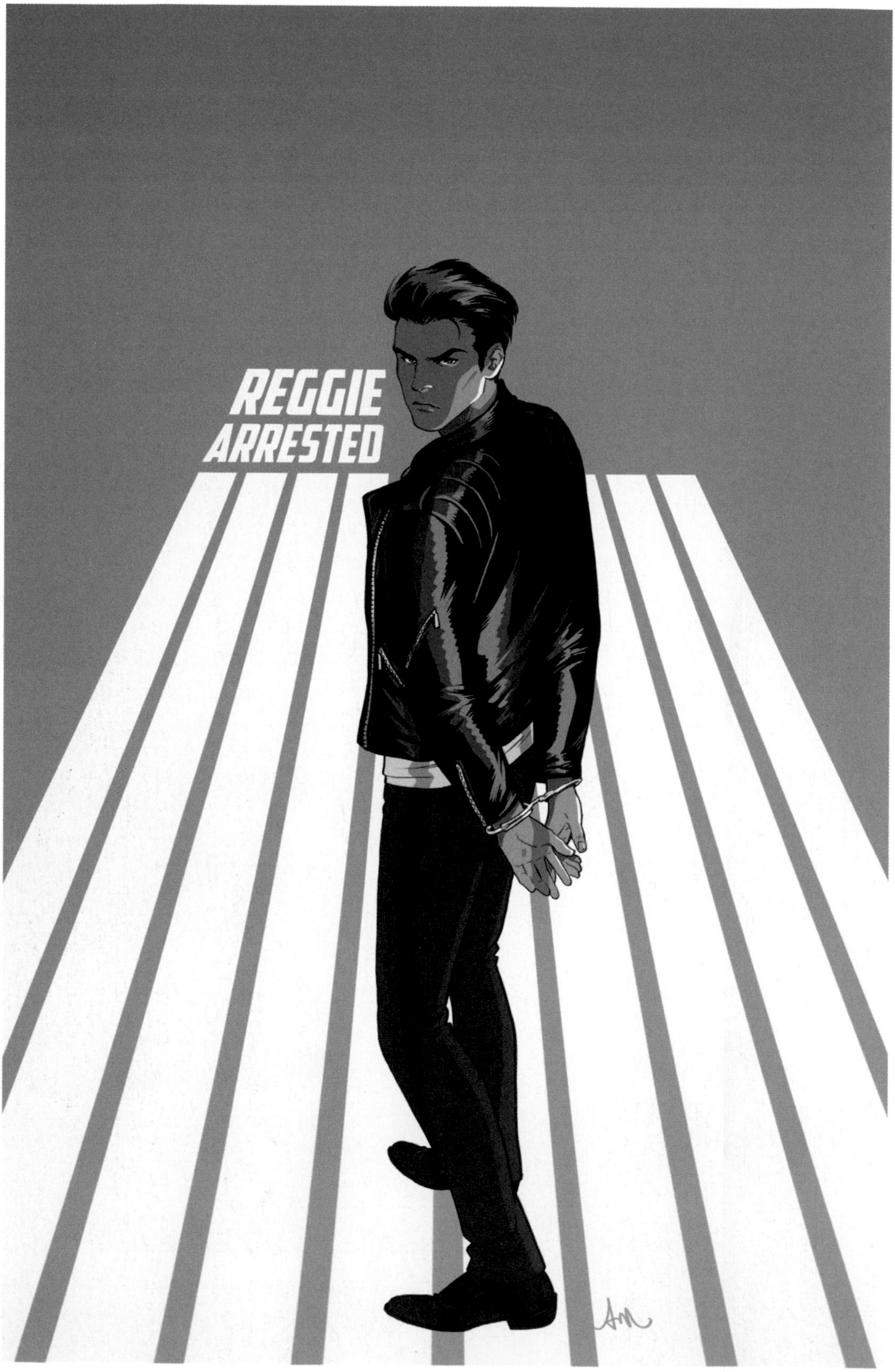
REGGIE
ARRESTED

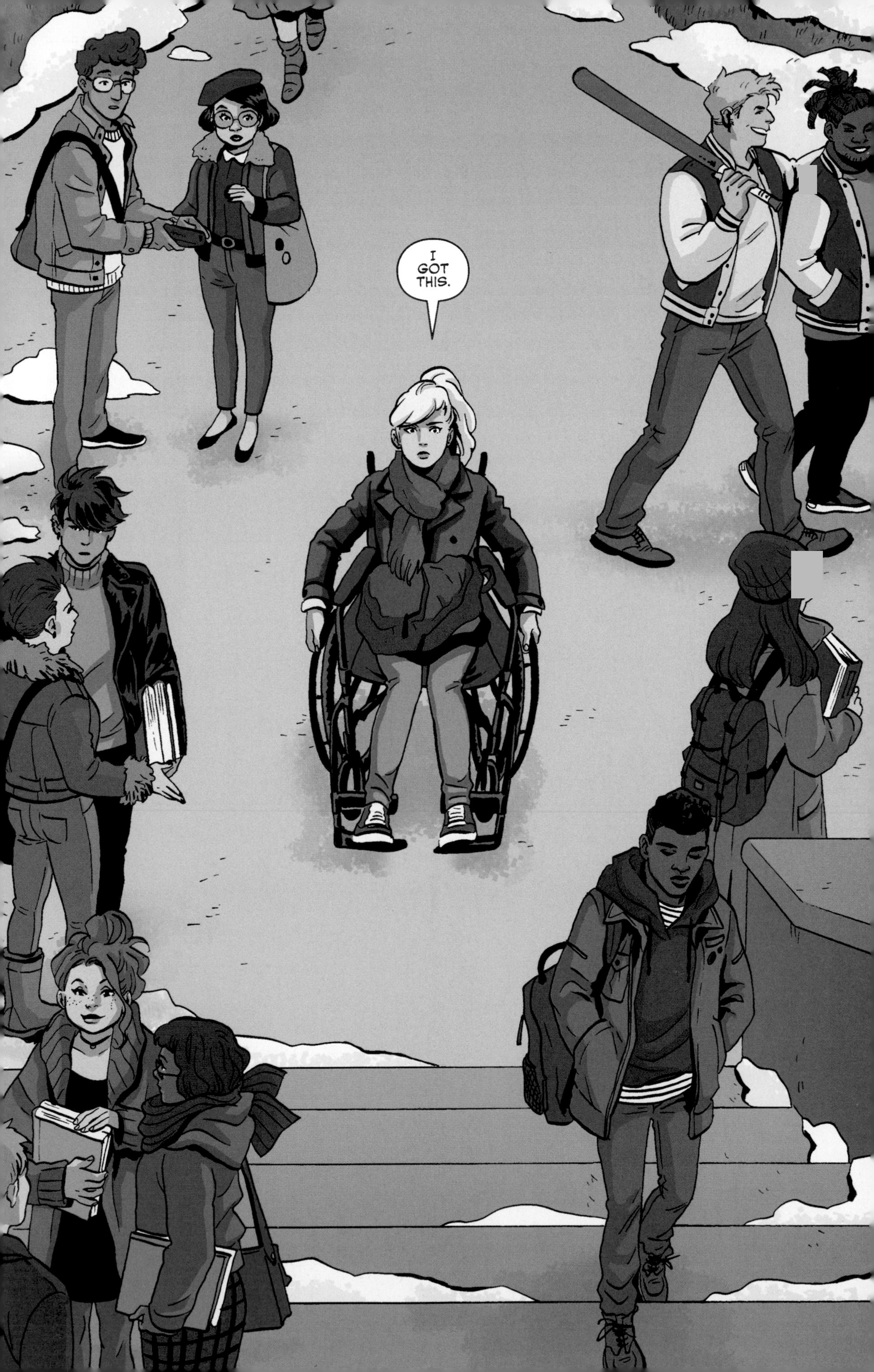
I GOT THIS.

CHAPTER ONE: SOUNDS EXPENSIVE

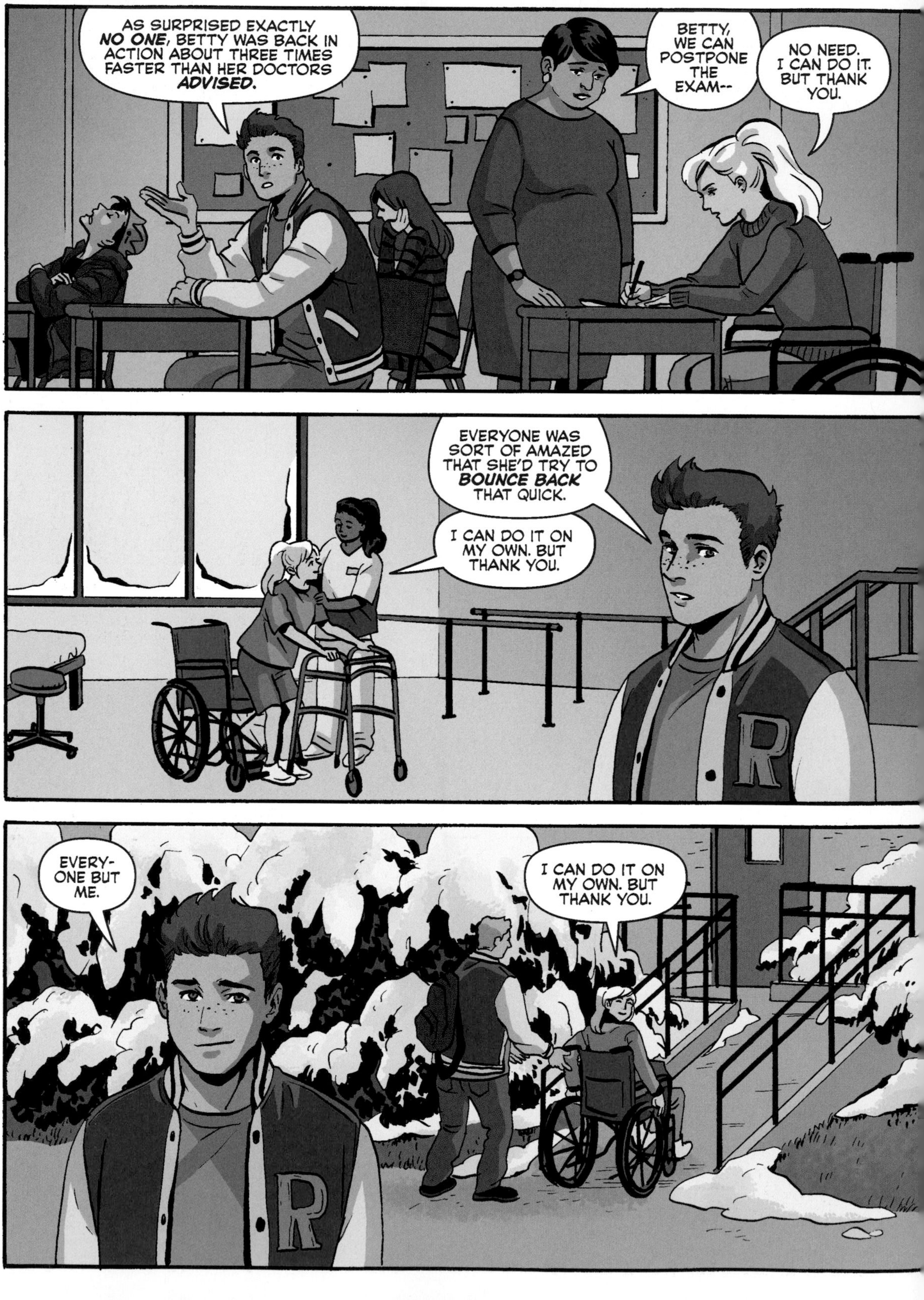
AS SURPRISED EXACTLY NO ONE, BETTY WAS BACK IN ACTION ABOUT THREE TIMES FASTER THAN HER DOCTORS ADVISED.
BETTY, WE CAN POSTPONE THE EXAM--
NO NEED. I CAN DO IT. BUT THANK YOU.
EVERYONE WAS SORT OF AMAZED THAT SHE'D TRY TO BOUNCE BACK THAT QUICK.
I CAN DO IT ON MY OWN. BUT THANK YOU.
EVERY-ONE BUT ME.
I CAN DO IT ON MY OWN. BUT THANK YOU.

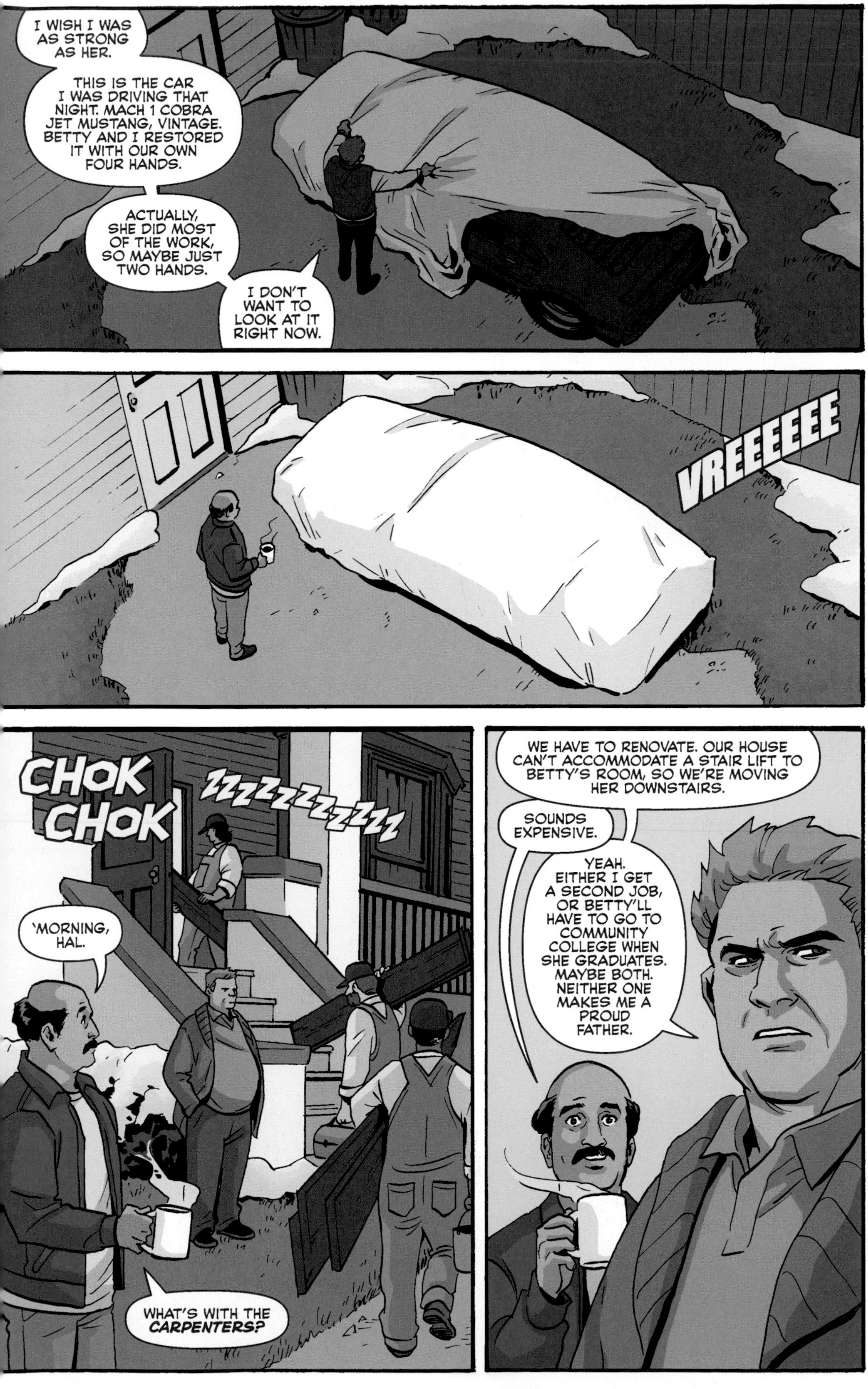

I WISH I WAS AS STRONG AS HER.
THIS IS THE CAR I WAS DRIVING THAT NIGHT. MACH 1 COBRA JET MUSTANG, VINTAGE. BETTY AND I RESTORED IT WITH OUR OWN FOUR HANDS.
ACTUALLY, SHE DID MOST OF THE WORK, SO MAYBE JUST TWO HANDS.
I DON'T WANT TO LOOK AT IT RIGHT NOW.
VREEEEEE
CHOK CHOK
ZZZZZZZZZZZ
'MORNING, HAL.
WHAT'S WITH THE *CARPENTERS?*
WE HAVE TO RENOVATE. OUR HOUSE CAN'T ACCOMMODATE A STAIR LIFT TO BETTY'S ROOM, SO WE'RE MOVING HER DOWNSTAIRS.
SOUNDS EXPENSIVE.
YEAH. EITHER I GET A SECOND JOB, OR BETTY'LL HAVE TO GO TO COMMUNITY COLLEGE WHEN SHE GRADUATES. MAYBE BOTH. NEITHER ONE MAKES ME A PROUD FATHER.

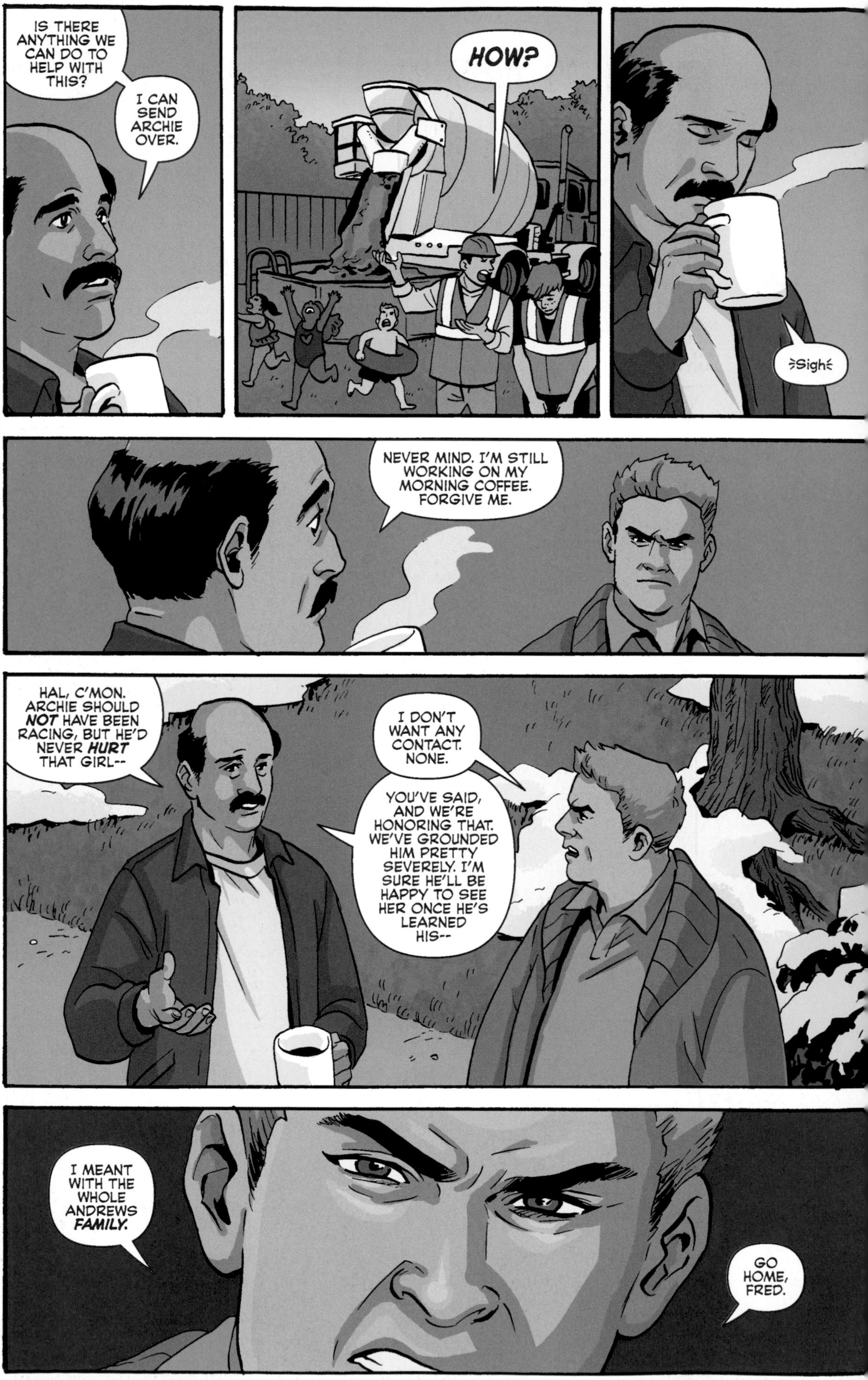
IS THERE ANYTHING WE CAN DO TO HELP WITH THIS?
I CAN SEND ARCHIE OVER.
HOW?
Sigh
NEVER MIND. I'M STILL WORKING ON MY MORNING COFFEE. FORGIVE ME.
I DON'T WANT ANY CONTACT. NONE.
HAL, C'MON. ARCHIE SHOULD NOT HAVE BEEN RACING, BUT HE'D NEVER HURT THAT GIRL--
YOU'VE SAID, AND WE'RE HONORING THAT. WE'VE GROUNDED HIM PRETTY SEVERELY. I'M SURE HE'LL BE HAPPY TO SEE HER ONCE HE'S LEARNED HIS--
I MEANT WITH THE WHOLE ANDREWS FAMILY.
GO HOME, FRED.

CHAPTER TWO: REGGIE IS A GOOD BOY

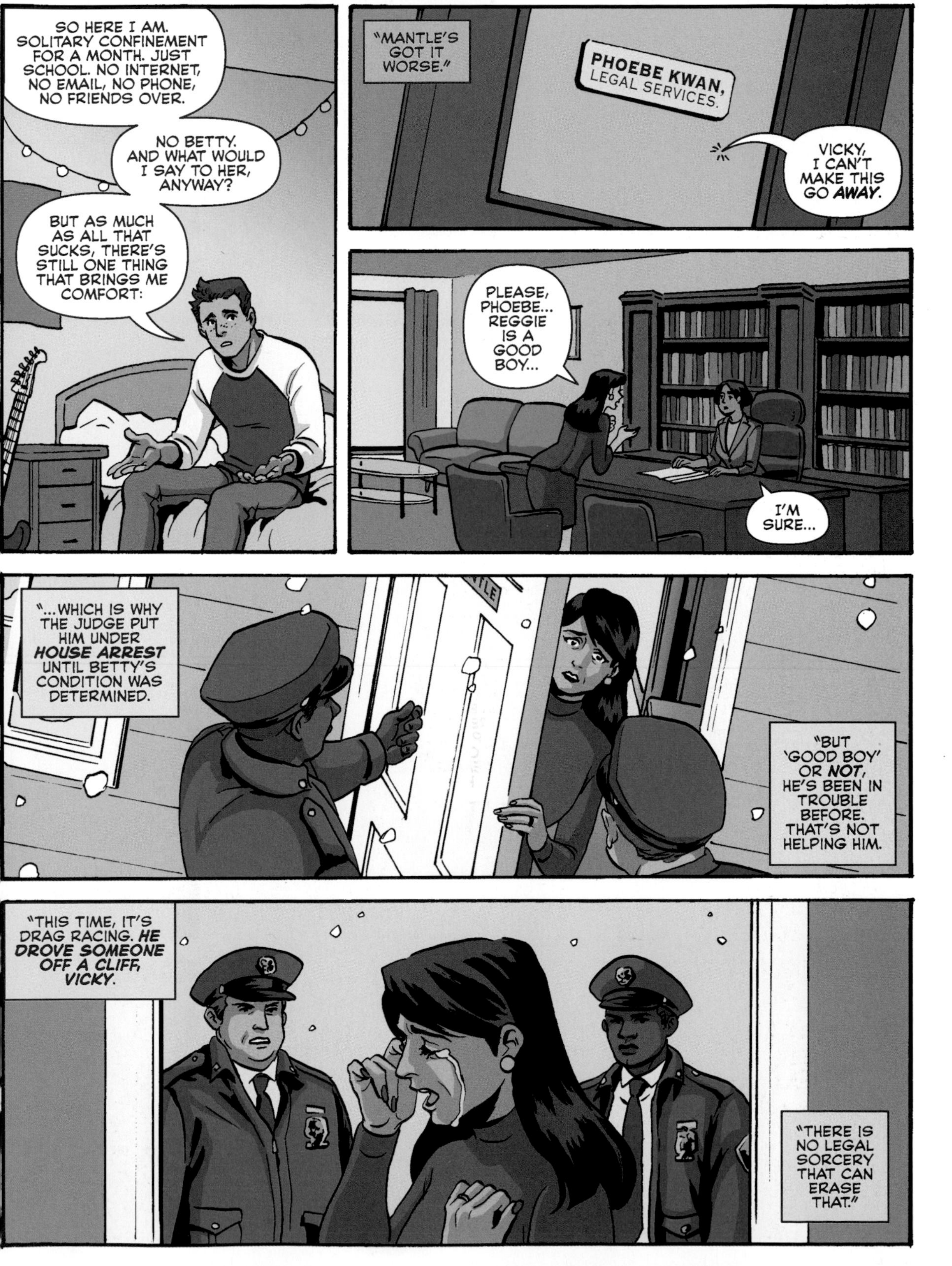

SO HERE I AM. SOLITARY CONFINEMENT FOR A MONTH. JUST SCHOOL. NO INTERNET, NO EMAIL, NO PHONE, NO FRIENDS OVER.
NO BETTY. AND WHAT WOULD I SAY TO HER, ANYWAY?
BUT AS MUCH AS ALL THAT SUCKS, THERE'S STILL ONE THING THAT BRINGS ME COMFORT:
"MANTLE'S GOT IT WORSE."
PHOEBE KWAN, LEGAL SERVICES.
VICKY, I CAN'T MAKE THIS GO *AWAY*.
PLEASE, PHOEBE... REGGIE IS A GOOD BOY...
I'M SURE...
"...WHICH IS WHY THE JUDGE PUT HIM UNDER ***HOUSE ARREST*** UNTIL BETTY'S CONDITION WAS DETERMINED.
"BUT 'GOOD BOY' OR ***NOT***, HE'S BEEN IN TROUBLE BEFORE. THAT'S NOT HELPING HIM.
"THIS TIME, IT'S DRAG RACING. ***HE DROVE SOMEONE OFF A CLIFF, VICKY***.
"THERE IS NO LEGAL SORCERY THAT CAN ERASE THAT."

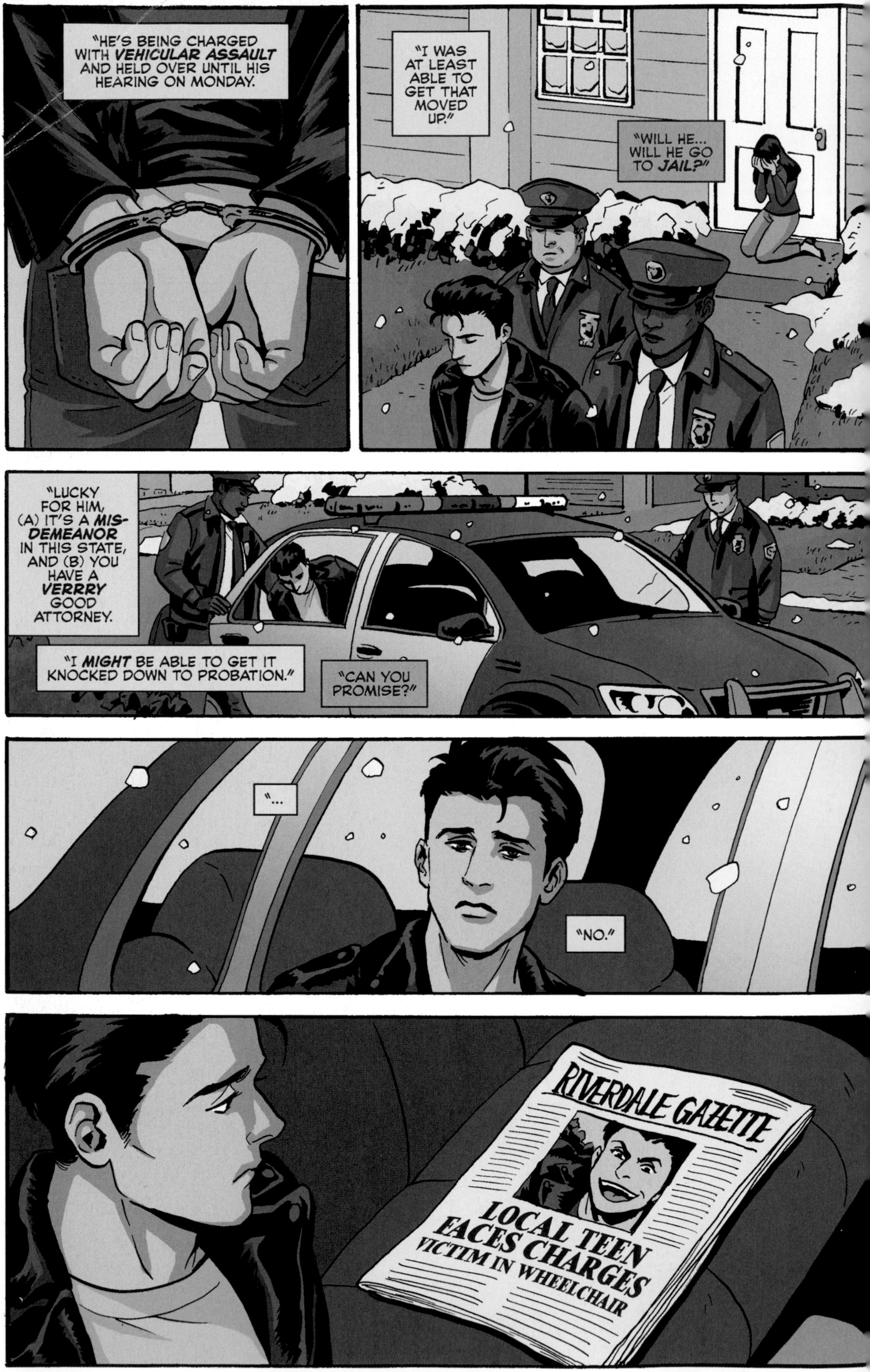
"HE'S BEING CHARGED WITH VEHICULAR ASSAULT AND HELD OVER UNTIL HIS HEARING ON MONDAY.
"I WAS AT LEAST ABLE TO GET THAT MOVED UP."
"WILL HE... WILL HE GO TO JAIL?"
"LUCKY FOR HIM, (A) IT'S A MISDEMEANOR IN THIS STATE, AND (B) YOU HAVE A VERRRY GOOD ATTORNEY.
"I MIGHT BE ABLE TO GET IT KNOCKED DOWN TO PROBATION."
"CAN YOU PROMISE?"
"...
"NO."
RIVERDALE GAZETTE
LOCAL TEEN FACES CHARGES
VICTIM IN WHEELCHAIR

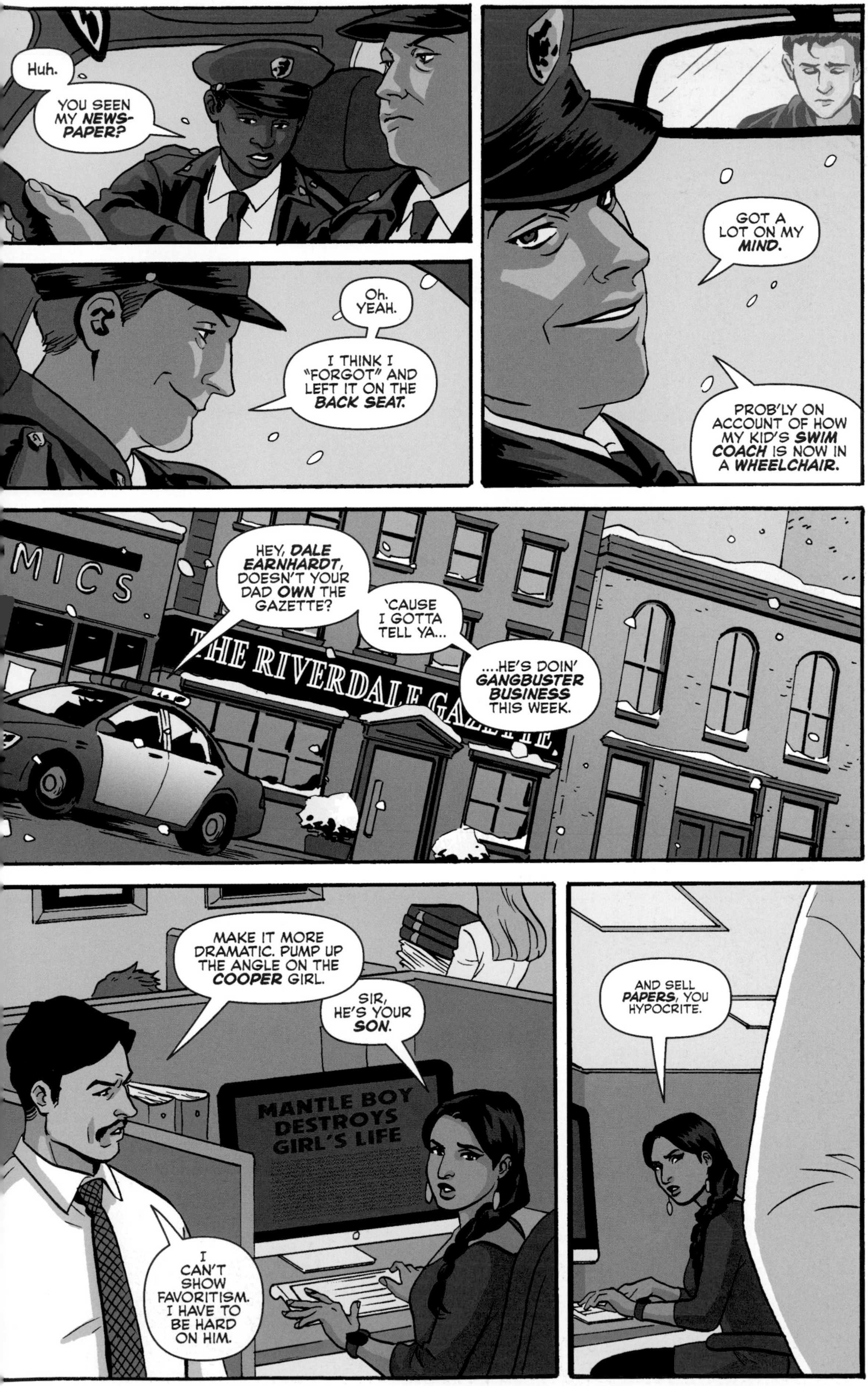
Huh.
YOU SEEN MY NEWS-PAPER?
GOT A LOT ON MY MIND.
Oh. YEAH.
I THINK I "FORGOT" AND LEFT IT ON THE BACK SEAT.
PROB'LY ON ACCOUNT OF HOW MY KID'S SWIM COACH IS NOW IN A WHEELCHAIR.
MICS
HEY, DALE EARNHARDT, DOESN'T YOUR DAD OWN THE GAZETTE?
'CAUSE I GOTTA TELL YA...
....HE'S DOIN' GANGBUSTER BUSINESS THIS WEEK.
THE RIVERDALE GAZETTE
MAKE IT MORE DRAMATIC. PUMP UP THE ANGLE ON THE COOPER GIRL.
SIR, HE'S YOUR SON.
MANTLE BOY DESTROYS GIRL'S LIFE
I CAN'T SHOW FAVORITISM. I HAVE TO BE HARD ON HIM.
AND SELL PAPERS, YOU HYPOCRITE.

CHAPTER THREE: But Thank You

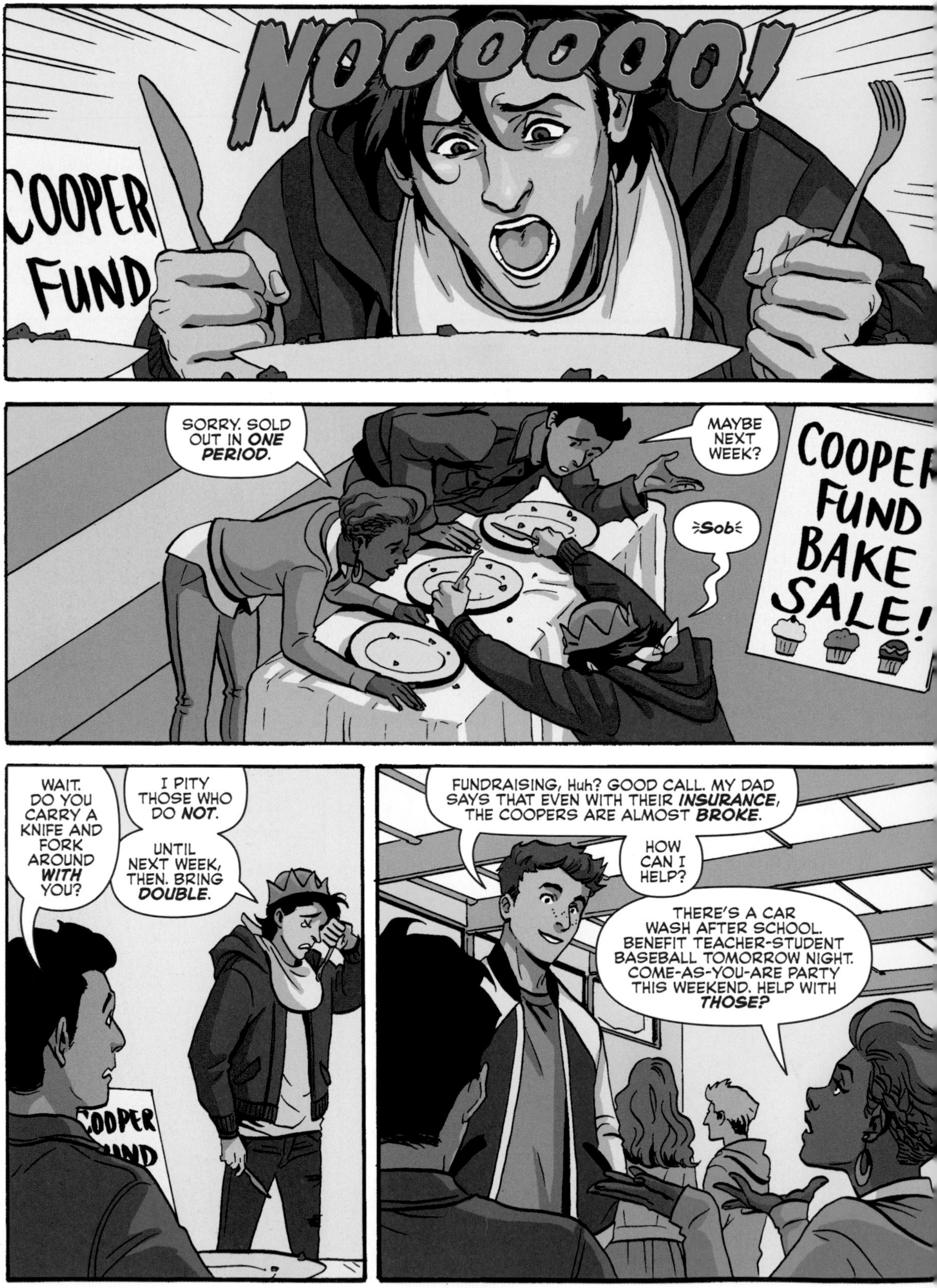
NOOOOOO!
COOPER FUND
SORRY. SOLD OUT IN *ONE PERIOD*.
MAYBE NEXT WEEK?
Sob
COOPER FUND BAKE SALE!
WAIT. DO YOU CARRY A KNIFE AND FORK AROUND *WITH* YOU?
I PITY THOSE WHO DO *NOT*.
UNTIL NEXT WEEK, THEN. BRING *DOUBLE*.
FUNDRAISING, Huh? GOOD CALL. MY DAD SAYS THAT EVEN WITH THEIR *INSURANCE*, THE COOPERS ARE ALMOST *BROKE*.
HOW CAN I HELP?
THERE'S A CAR WASH AFTER SCHOOL. BENEFIT TEACHER-STUDENT BASEBALL TOMORROW NIGHT. COME-AS-YOU-ARE PARTY THIS WEEKEND. HELP WITH *THOSE?*

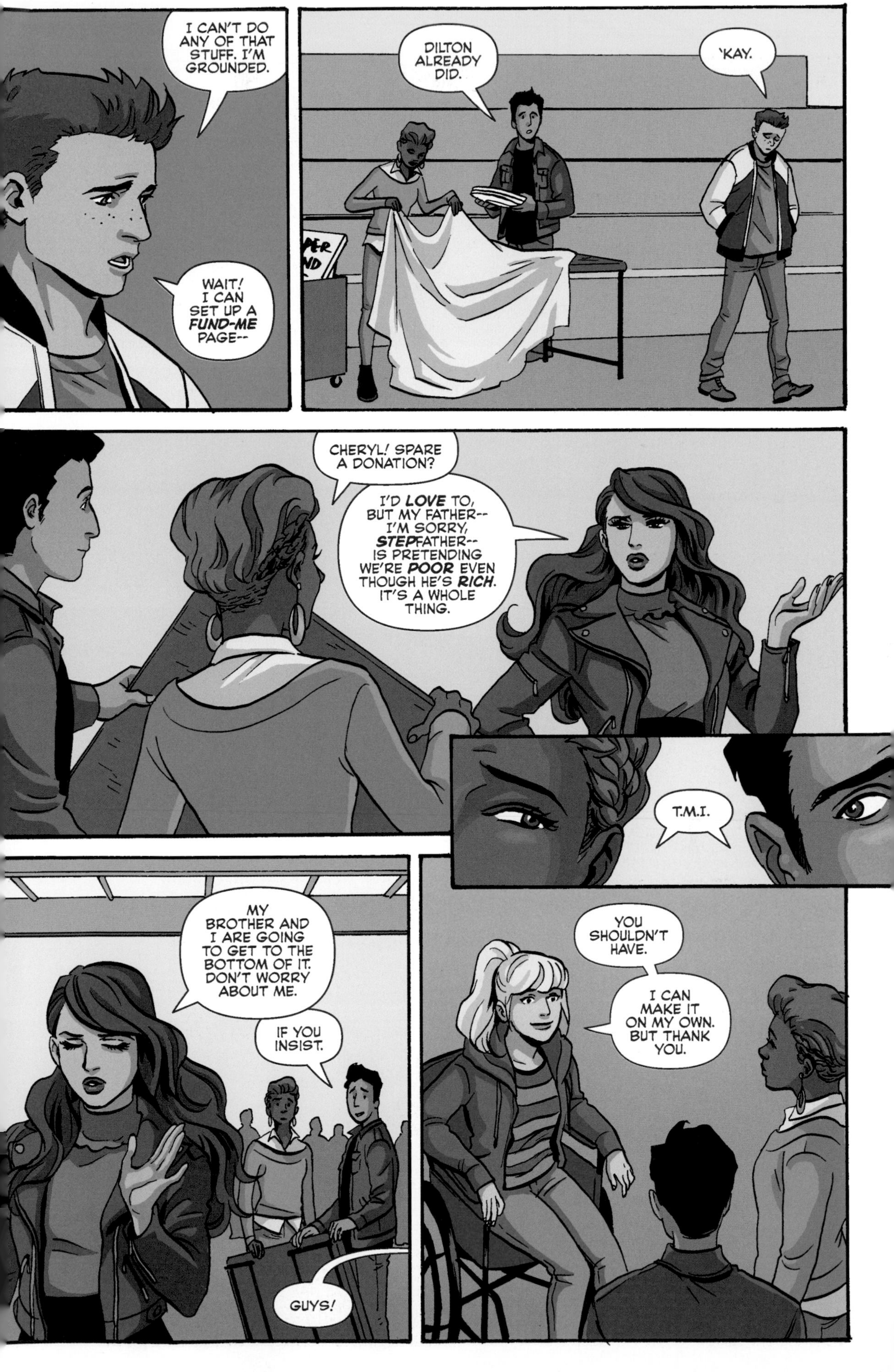
I CAN'T DO ANY OF THAT STUFF. I'M GROUNDED.
WAIT! I CAN SET UP A FUND-ME PAGE--
DILTON ALREADY DID.
'KAY.
CHERYL! SPARE A DONATION?
I'D LOVE TO, BUT MY FATHER-- I'M SORRY, STEPFATHER-- IS PRETENDING WE'RE POOR EVEN THOUGH HE'S RICH. IT'S A WHOLE THING.
T.M.I.
MY BROTHER AND I ARE GOING TO GET TO THE BOTTOM OF IT. DON'T WORRY ABOUT ME.
IF YOU INSIST.
GUYS!
YOU SHOULDN'T HAVE.
I CAN MAKE IT ON MY OWN. BUT THANK YOU.

WE KNOW. BUT WE *LOVE* YOU, COOPS.

THANK *YOU* FOR BEING *YOU*.

DILTON!

HI! HEY! I'M STILL COMING OVER TONIGHT TO HELP YOU CATCH UP ON *CHEMISTRY*, RIGHT?

AND ALGEBRA? AND FRENCH?

DILTON...SWEETIE... I THINK WE MAYBE NEED TO PUT THINGS ON PAUSE RIGHT NOW, OKAY?

BUT--

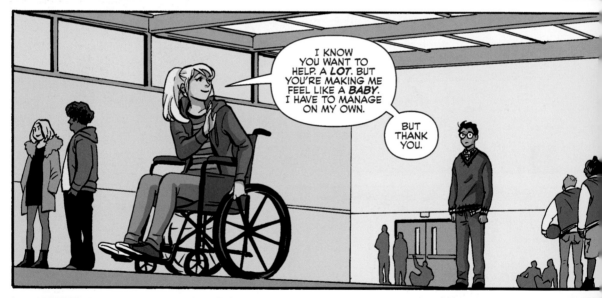

I KNOW YOU WANT TO HELP. A *LOT*. BUT YOU'RE MAKING ME FEEL LIKE A *BABY*. I HAVE TO MANAGE ON MY OWN.

BUT THANK YOU.

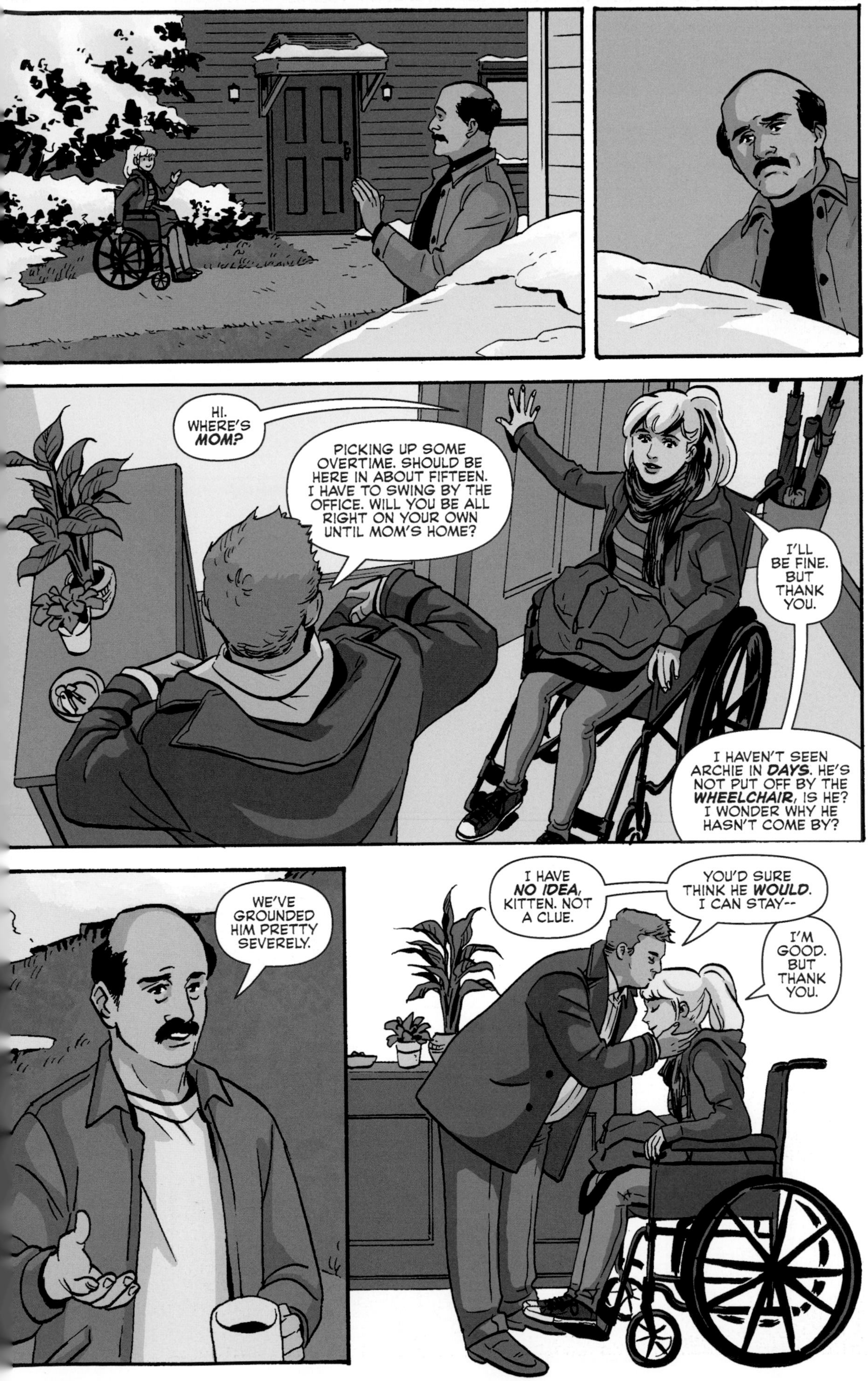
HI. WHERE'S *MOM?*
PICKING UP SOME OVERTIME. SHOULD BE HERE IN ABOUT FIFTEEN. I HAVE TO SWING BY THE OFFICE. WILL YOU BE ALL RIGHT ON YOUR OWN UNTIL MOM'S HOME?
I'LL BE FINE. BUT THANK YOU.
I HAVEN'T SEEN ARCHIE IN *DAYS*. HE'S NOT PUT OFF BY THE *WHEELCHAIR*, IS HE? I WONDER WHY HE HASN'T COME BY?
WE'VE GROUNDED HIM PRETTY SEVERELY.
I HAVE *NO IDEA*, KITTEN. NOT A CLUE.
YOU'D SURE THINK HE *WOULD*. I CAN STAY--
I'M GOOD. BUT THANK YOU.

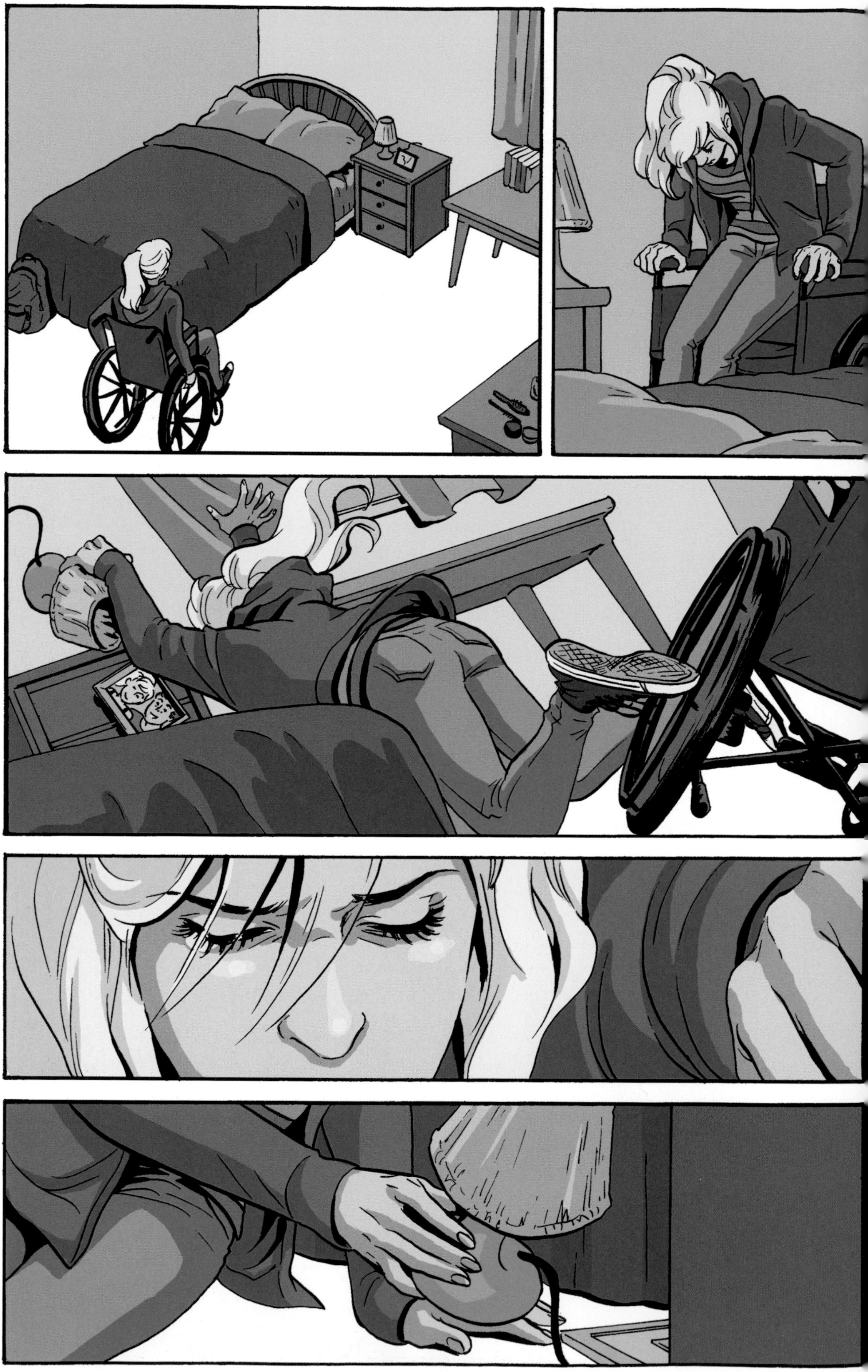

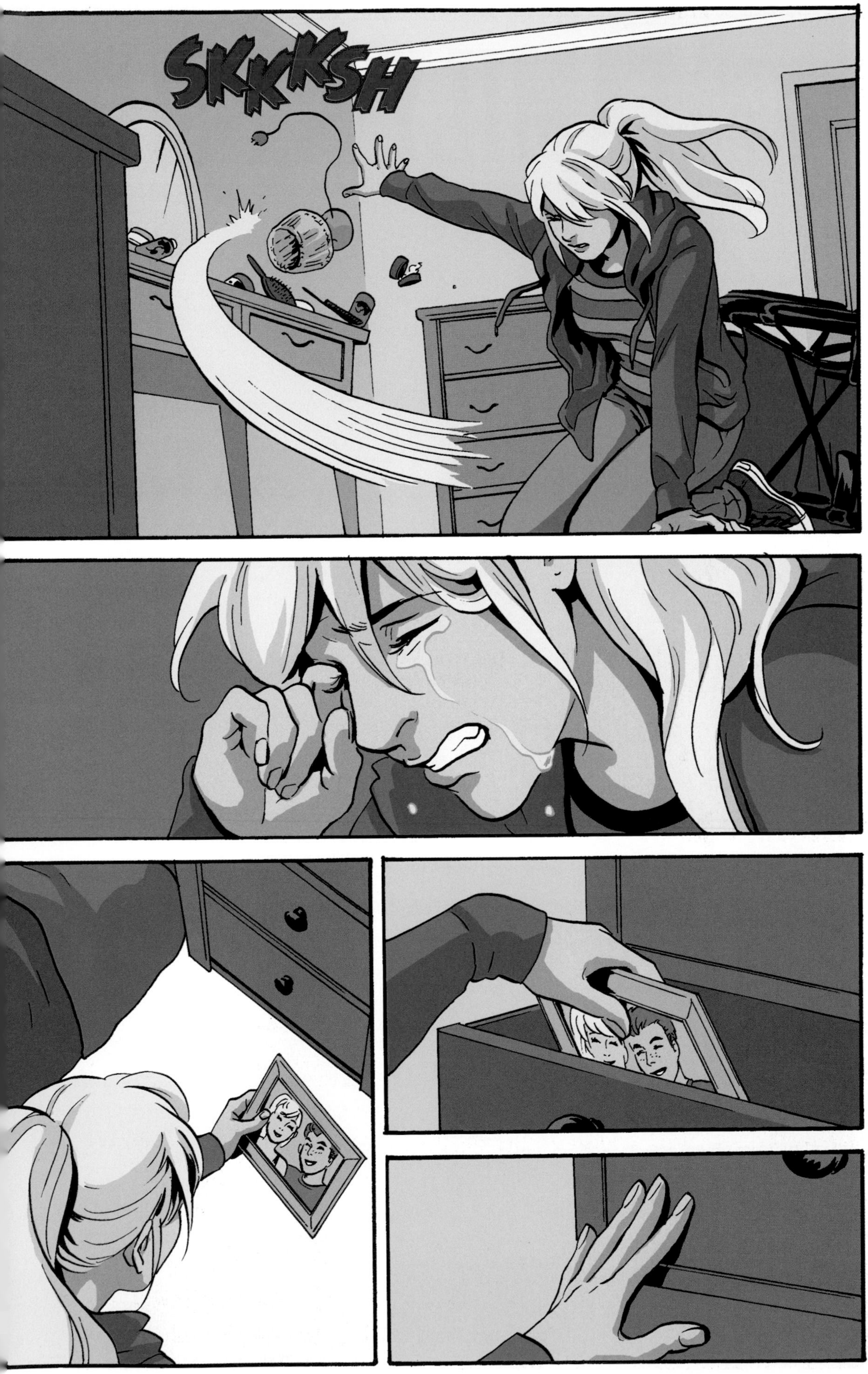
SKKKSH

CHAPTER FOUR: FAMILY MEETING

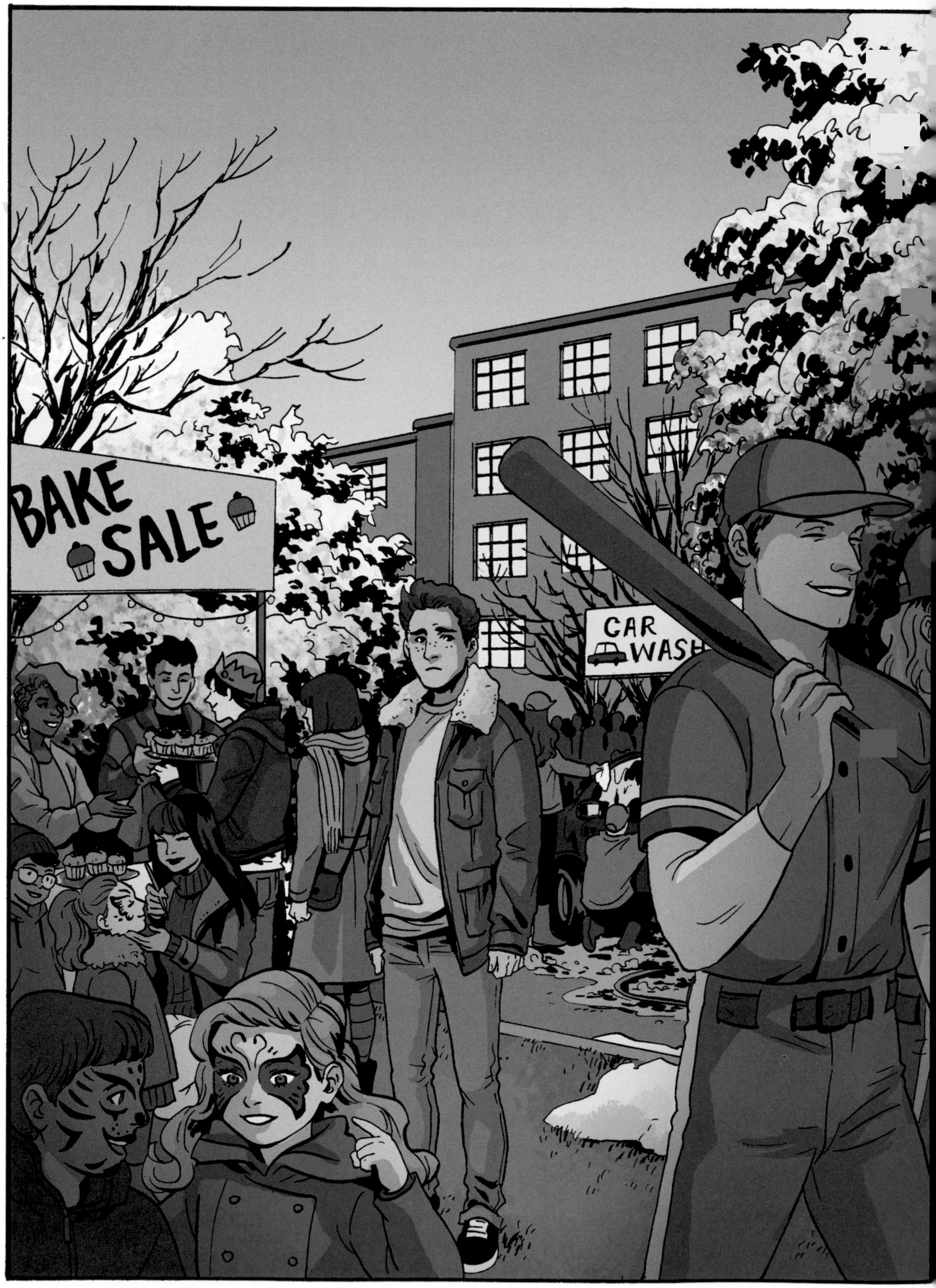

BAKE SALE
CAR WASH

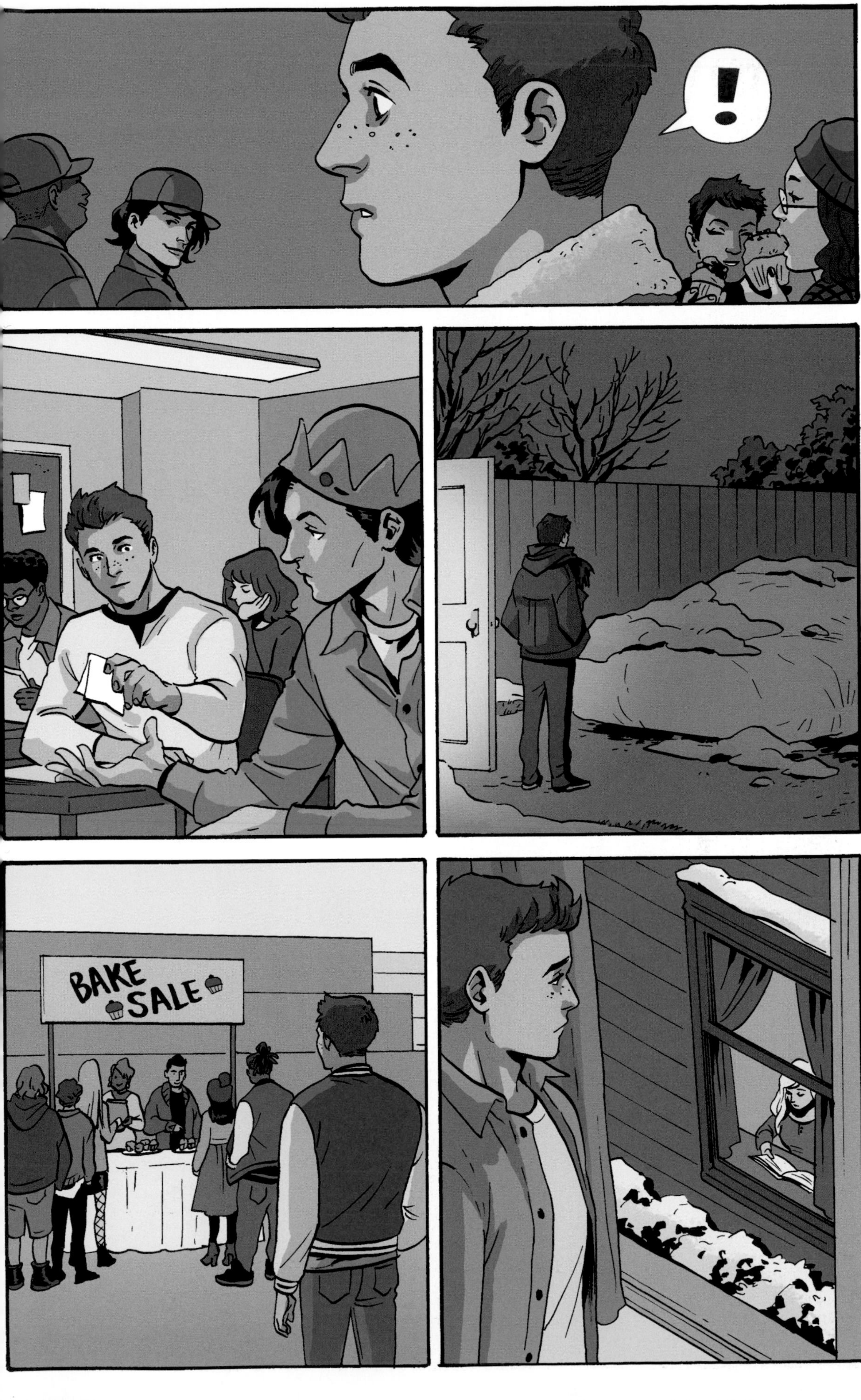
!
BAKE SALE

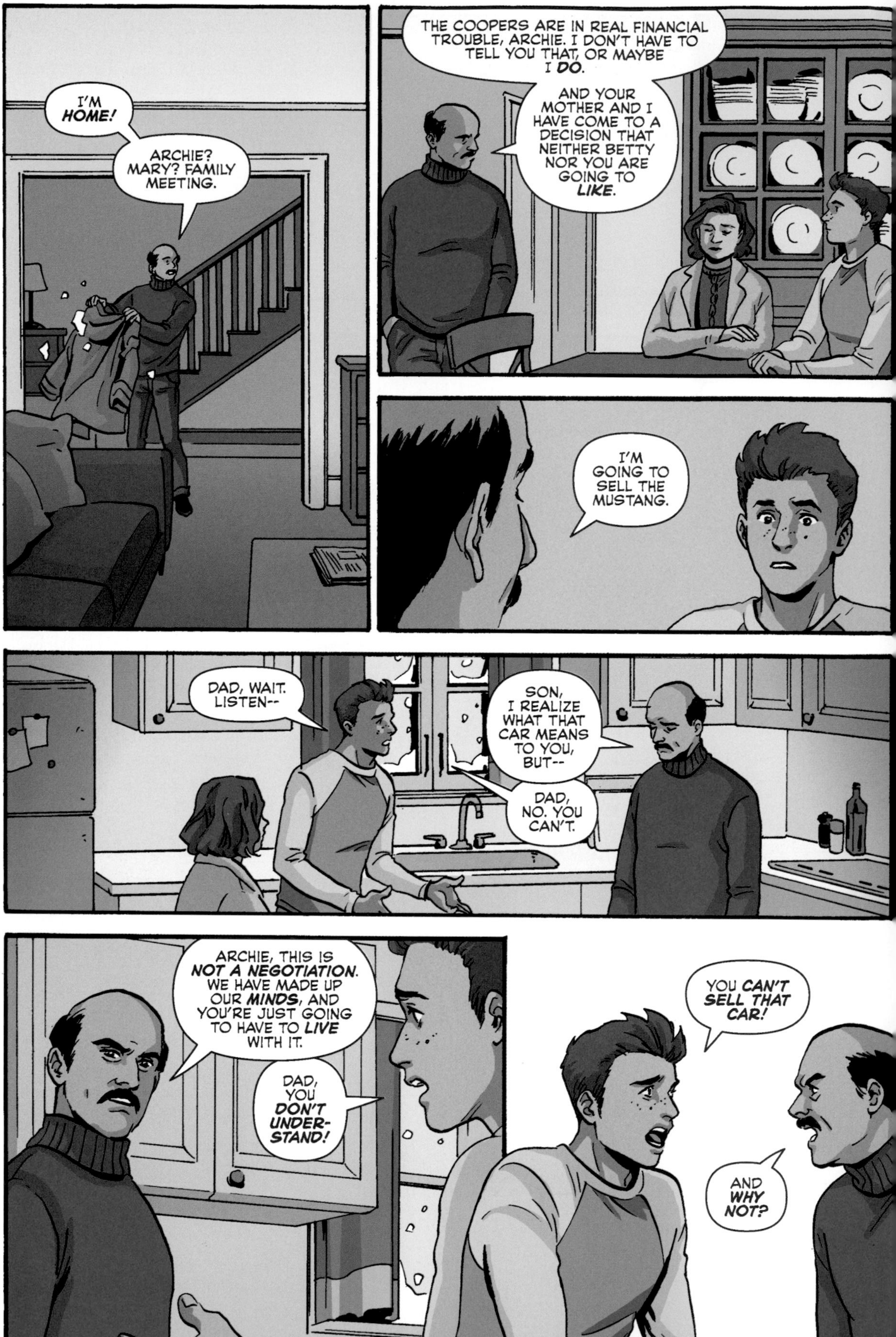
I'M HOME!
ARCHIE? MARY? FAMILY MEETING.
THE COOPERS ARE IN REAL FINANCIAL TROUBLE, ARCHIE. I DON'T HAVE TO TELL YOU THAT, OR MAYBE I DO.
AND YOUR MOTHER AND I HAVE COME TO A DECISION THAT NEITHER BETTY NOR YOU ARE GOING TO LIKE.
I'M GOING TO SELL THE MUSTANG.
DAD, WAIT. LISTEN--
SON, I REALIZE WHAT THAT CAR MEANS TO YOU, BUT--
DAD, NO. YOU CAN'T.
ARCHIE, THIS IS NOT A NEGOTIATION. WE HAVE MADE UP OUR MINDS, AND YOU'RE JUST GOING TO HAVE TO LIVE WITH IT.
DAD, YOU DON'T UNDER-STAND!
YOU CAN'T SELL THAT CAR!
AND WHY NOT?

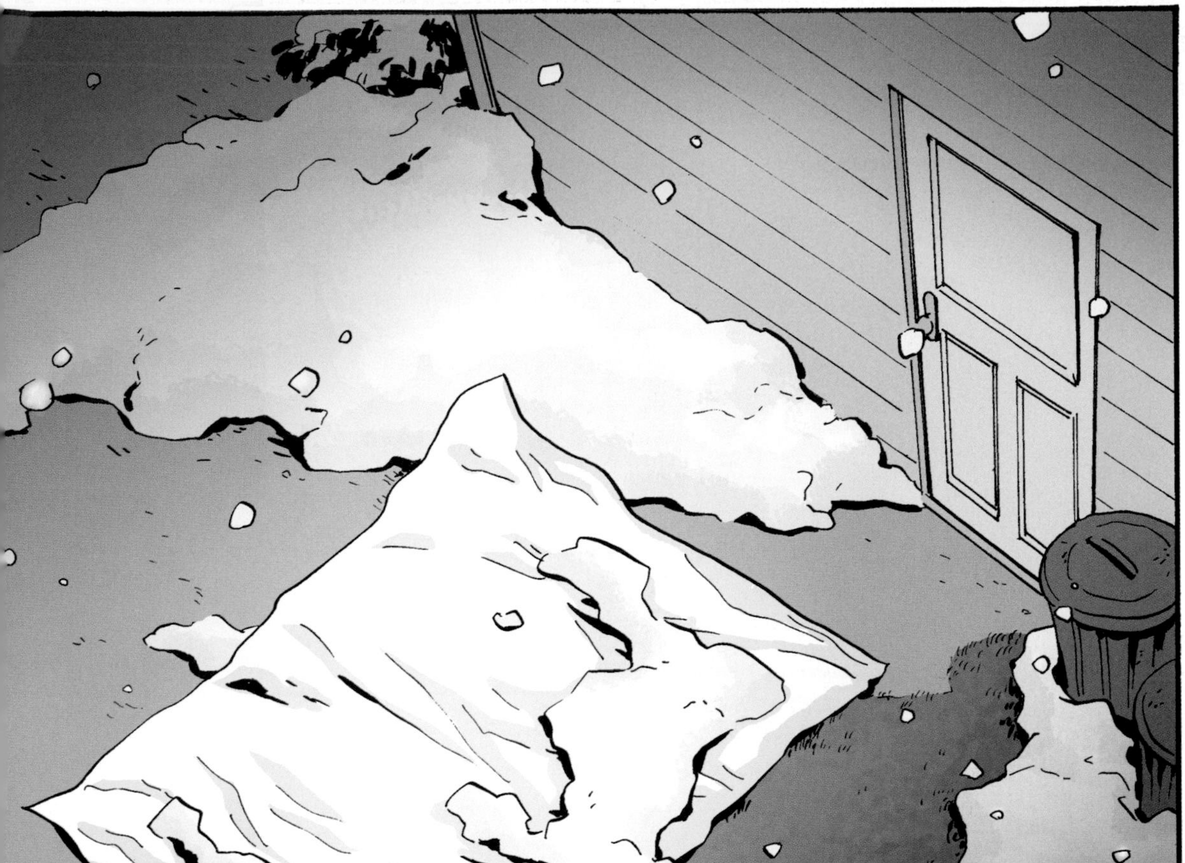

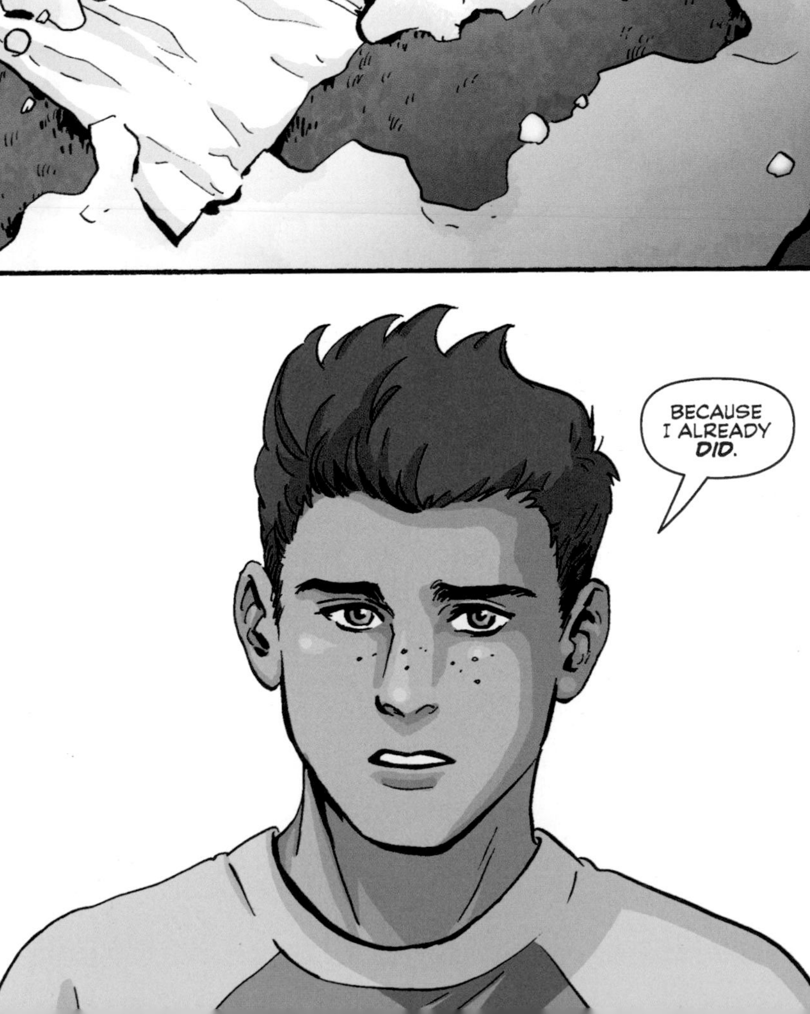
BECAUSE I ALREADY **DID**.

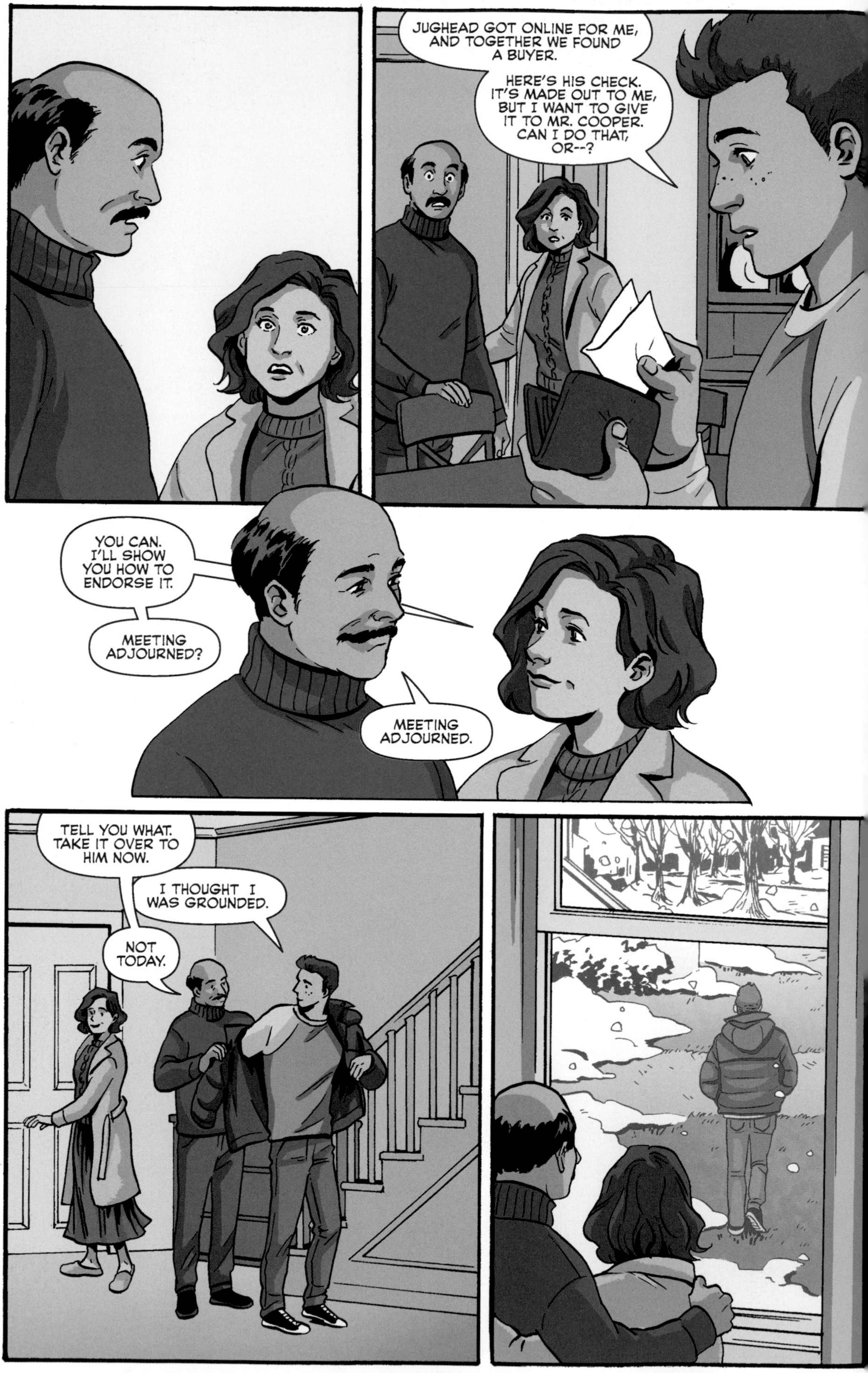
JUGHEAD GOT ONLINE FOR ME, AND TOGETHER WE FOUND A BUYER.
HERE'S HIS CHECK. IT'S MADE OUT TO ME, BUT I WANT TO GIVE IT TO MR. COOPER. CAN I DO THAT, OR--?
YOU CAN. I'LL SHOW YOU HOW TO ENDORSE IT.
MEETING ADJOURNED?
MEETING ADJOURNED.
TELL YOU WHAT. TAKE IT OVER TO HIM NOW.
I THOUGHT I WAS GROUNDED.
NOT TODAY.

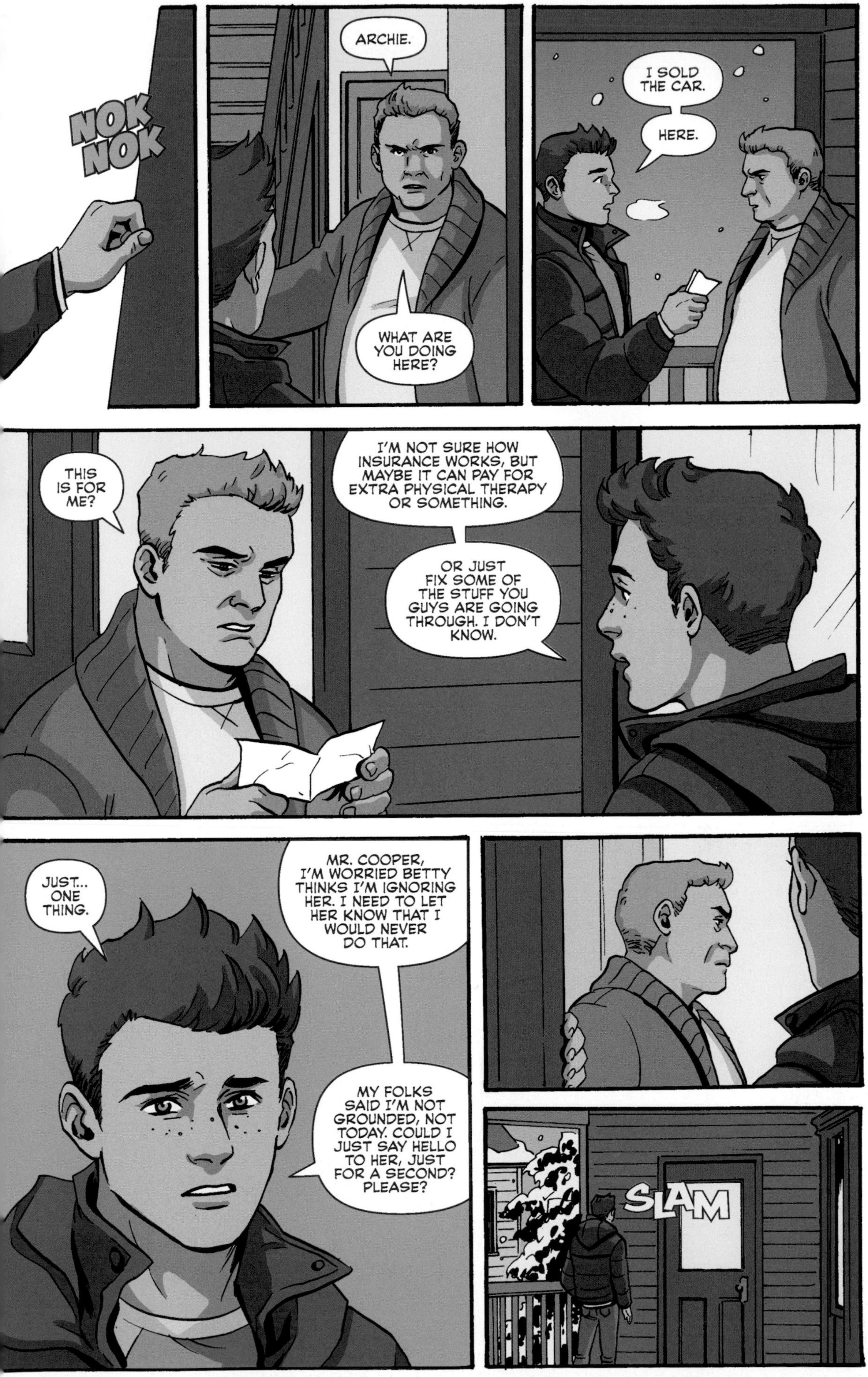
NOK NOK
ARCHIE.
WHAT ARE YOU DOING HERE?
I SOLD THE CAR.
HERE.
THIS IS FOR ME?
I'M NOT SURE HOW INSURANCE WORKS, BUT MAYBE IT CAN PAY FOR EXTRA PHYSICAL THERAPY OR SOMETHING.
OR JUST FIX SOME OF THE STUFF YOU GUYS ARE GOING THROUGH. I DON'T KNOW.
JUST... ONE THING.
MR. COOPER, I'M WORRIED BETTY THINKS I'M IGNORING HER. I NEED TO LET HER KNOW THAT I WOULD NEVER DO THAT.
MY FOLKS SAID I'M NOT GROUNDED, NOT TODAY. COULD I JUST SAY HELLO TO HER, JUST FOR A SECOND? PLEASE?
SLAM

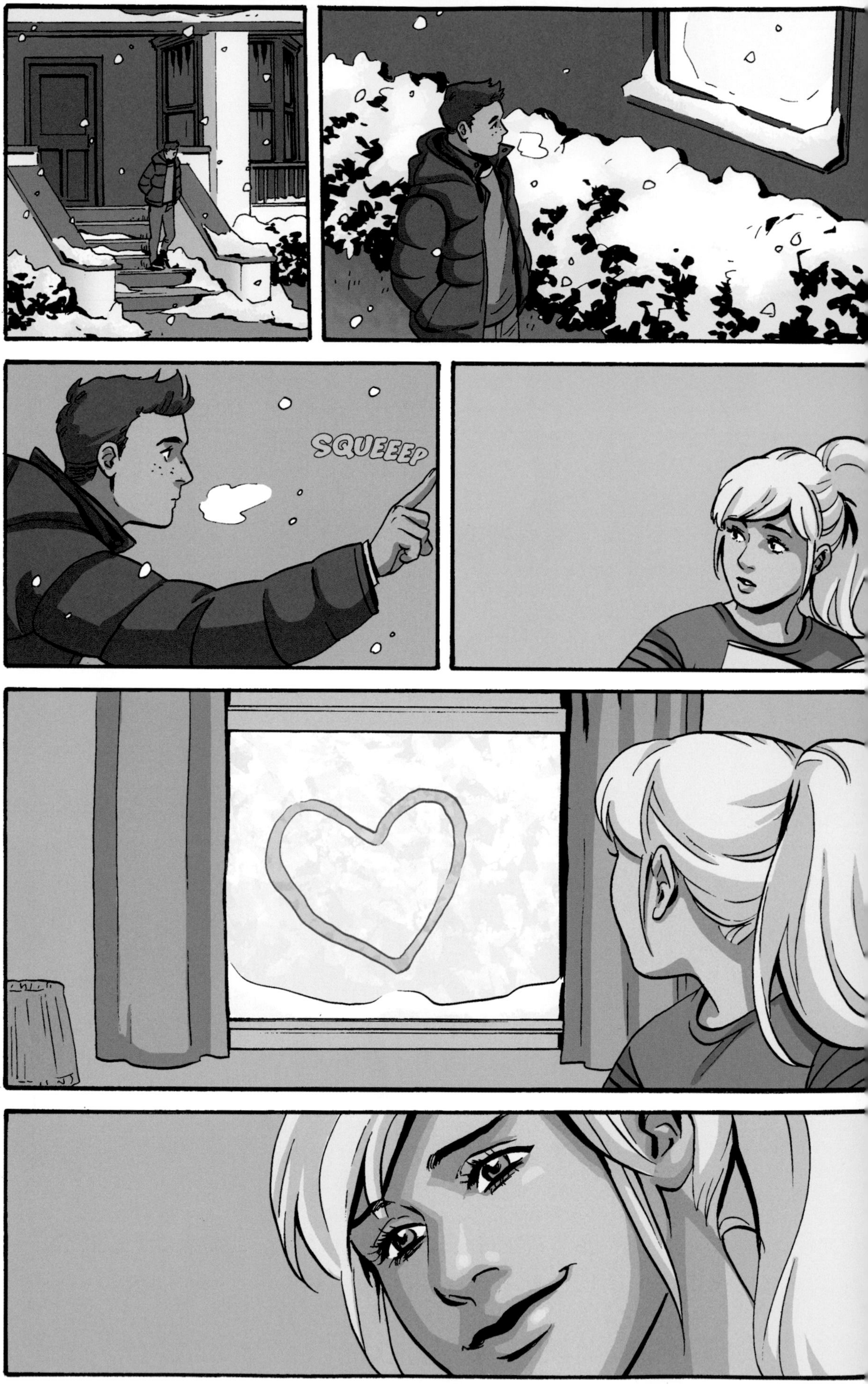
SQUEEEP

TO BE CONTINUED...

ISSUE TWENTY-FIVE

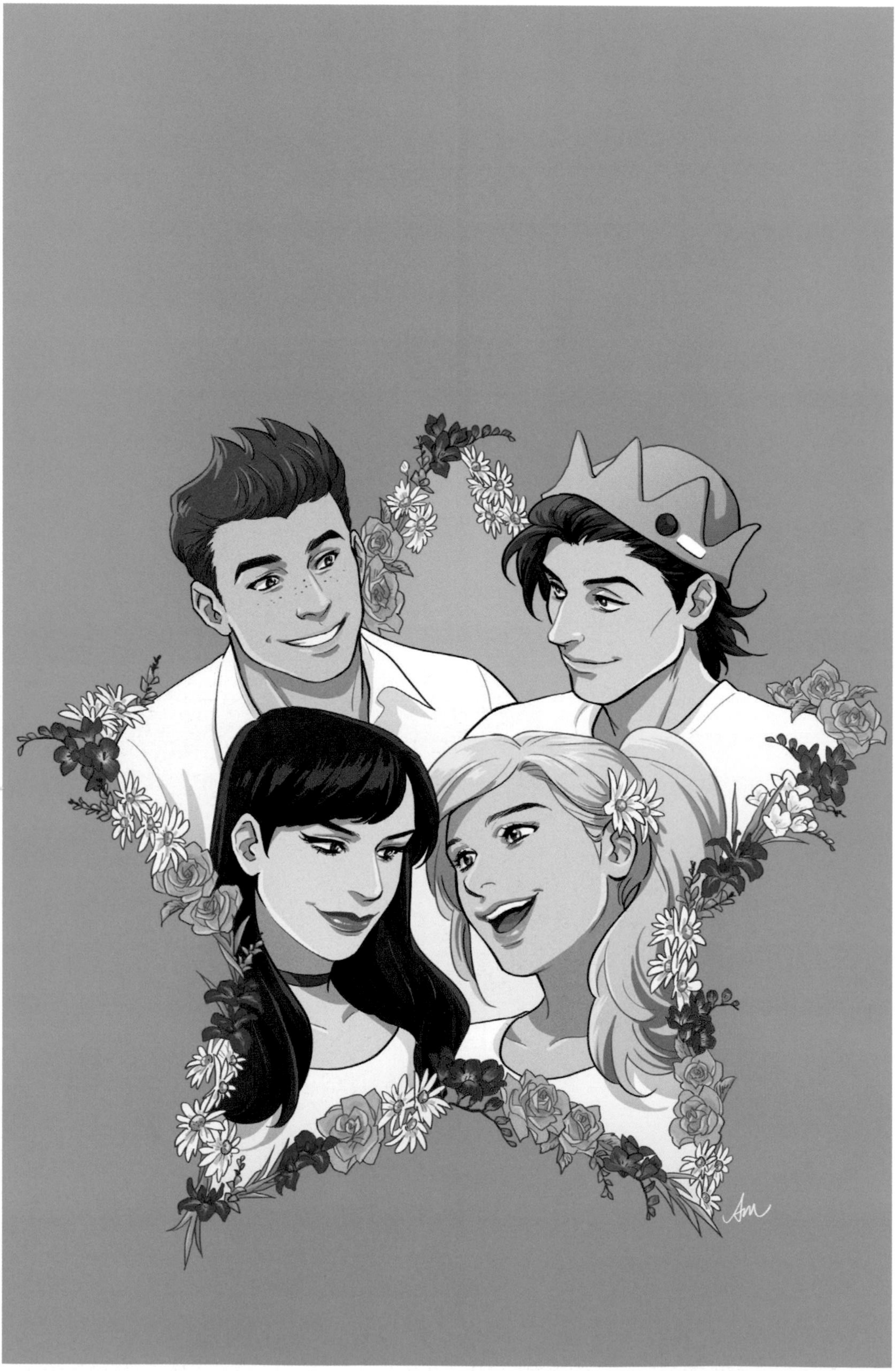

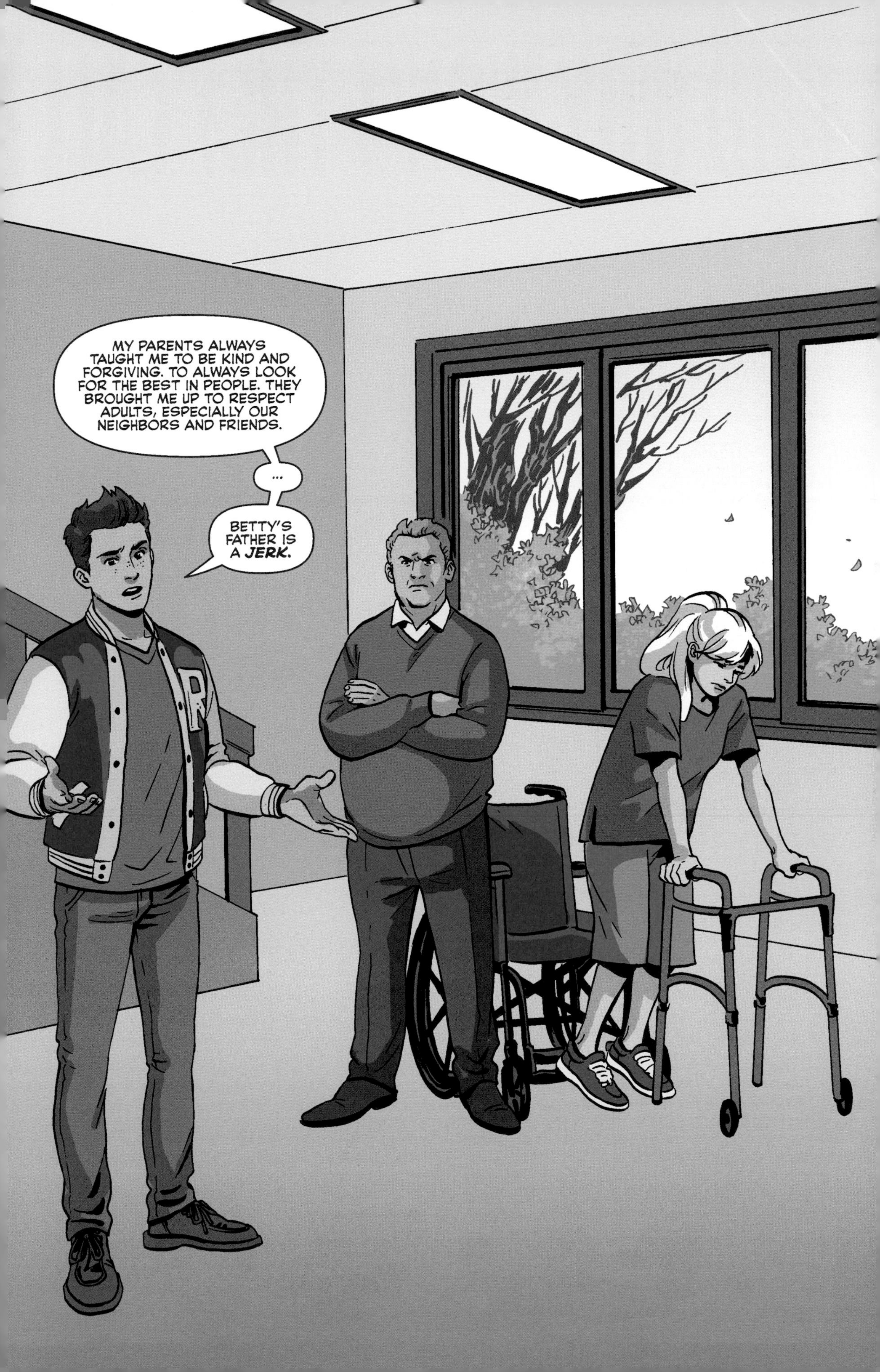
MY PARENTS ALWAYS TAUGHT ME TO BE KIND AND FORGIVING. TO ALWAYS LOOK FOR THE BEST IN PEOPLE. THEY BROUGHT ME UP TO RESPECT ADULTS, ESPECIALLY OUR NEIGHBORS AND FRIENDS.
...
BETTY'S FATHER IS A *JERK.*

CHAPTER ONE: WHY WON'T THEY CALL?

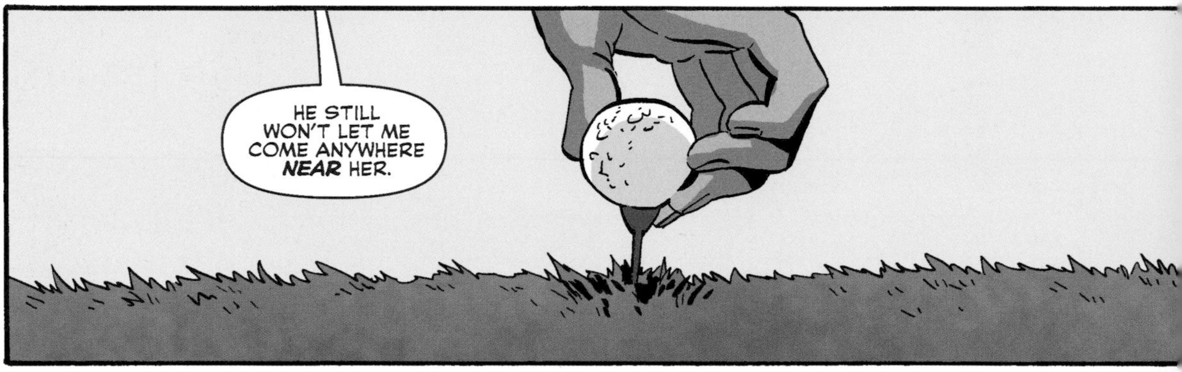
HE STILL WON'T LET ME COME ANYWHERE NEAR HER.

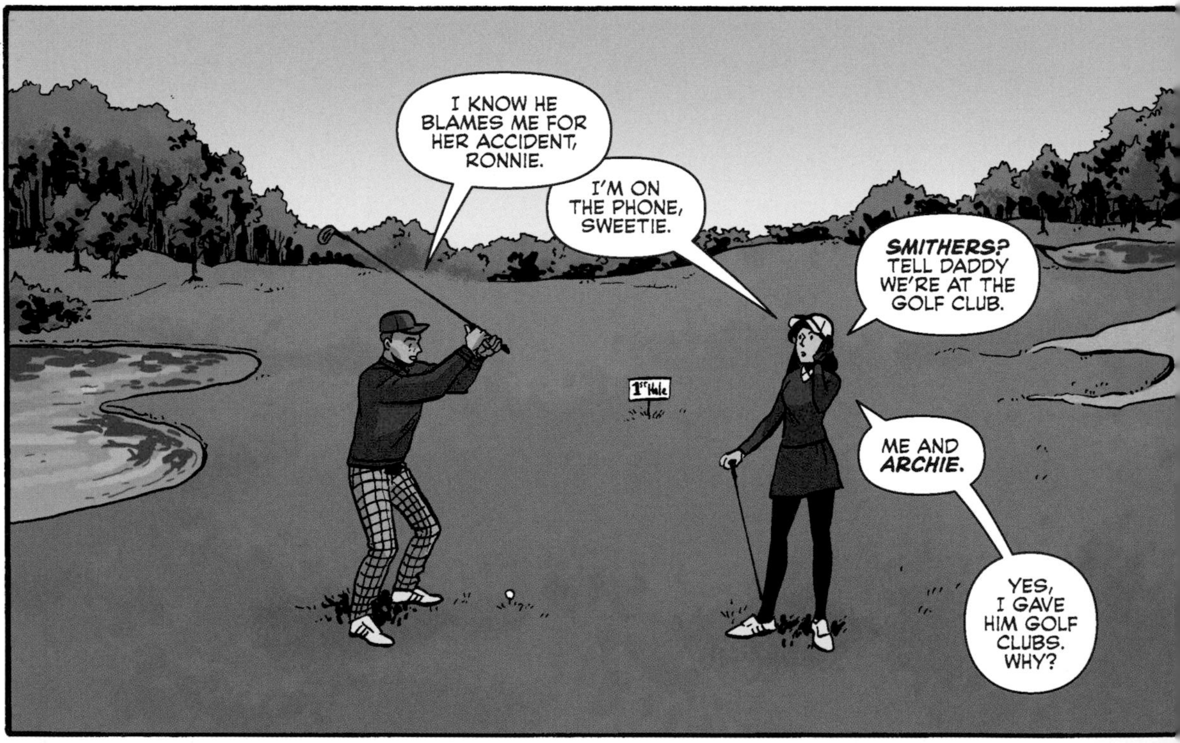
I KNOW HE BLAMES ME FOR HER ACCIDENT, RONNIE.
I'M ON THE PHONE, SWEETIE.
SMITHERS? TELL DADDY WE'RE AT THE GOLF CLUB.
1st Hole
ME AND ARCHIE.
YES, I GAVE HIM GOLF CLUBS. WHY?

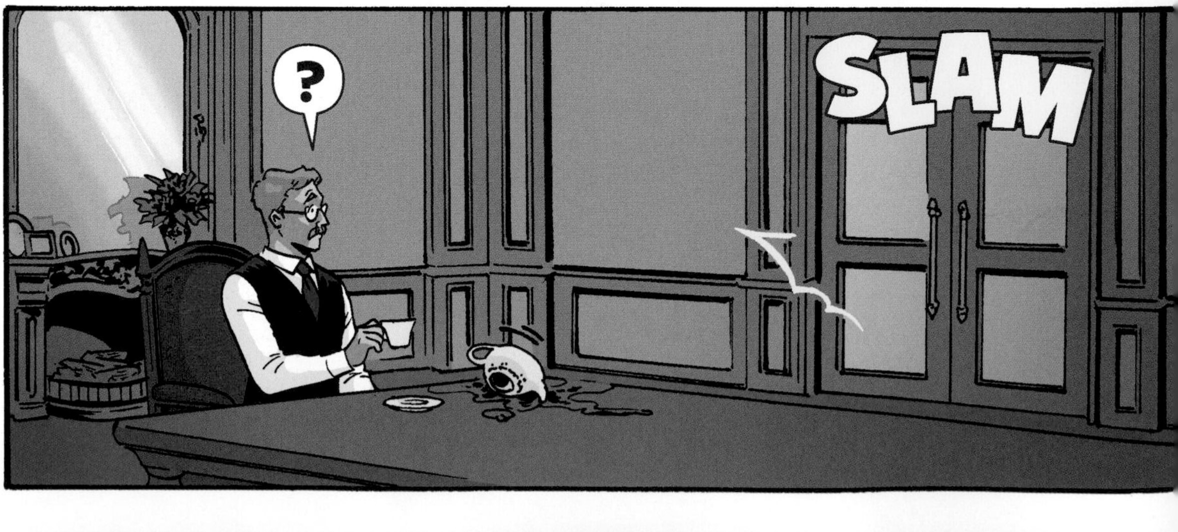
?
SLAM

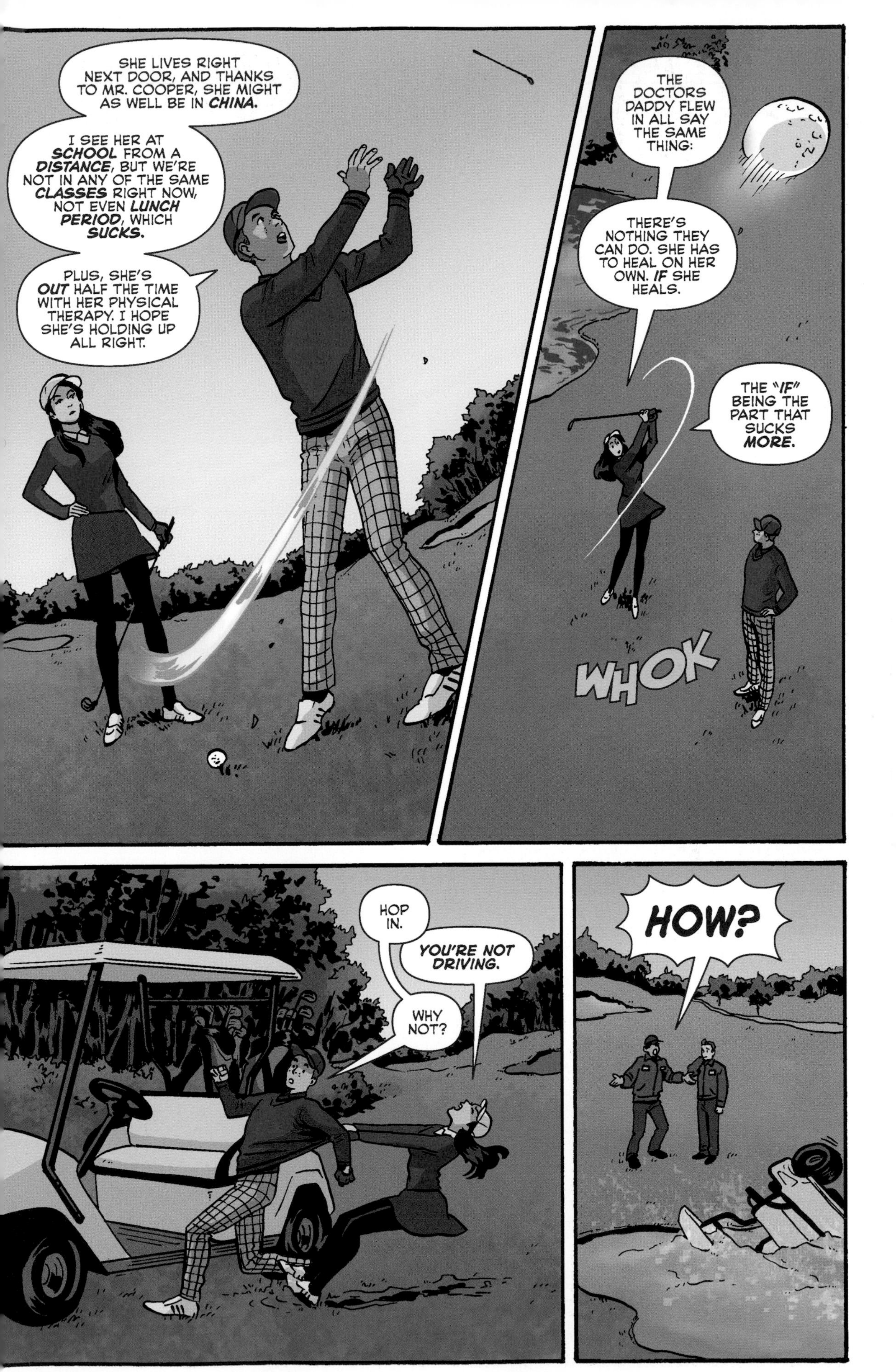
SHE LIVES RIGHT NEXT DOOR, AND THANKS TO MR. COOPER, SHE MIGHT AS WELL BE IN CHINA.
I SEE HER AT SCHOOL FROM A DISTANCE, BUT WE'RE NOT IN ANY OF THE SAME CLASSES RIGHT NOW, NOT EVEN LUNCH PERIOD, WHICH SUCKS.
PLUS, SHE'S OUT HALF THE TIME WITH HER PHYSICAL THERAPY. I HOPE SHE'S HOLDING UP ALL RIGHT.
THE DOCTORS DADDY FLEW IN ALL SAY THE SAME THING:
THERE'S NOTHING THEY CAN DO. SHE HAS TO HEAL ON HER OWN. IF SHE HEALS.
THE "IF" BEING THE PART THAT SUCKS MORE.
WHOK
HOP IN.
YOU'RE NOT DRIVING.
WHY NOT?
HOW?

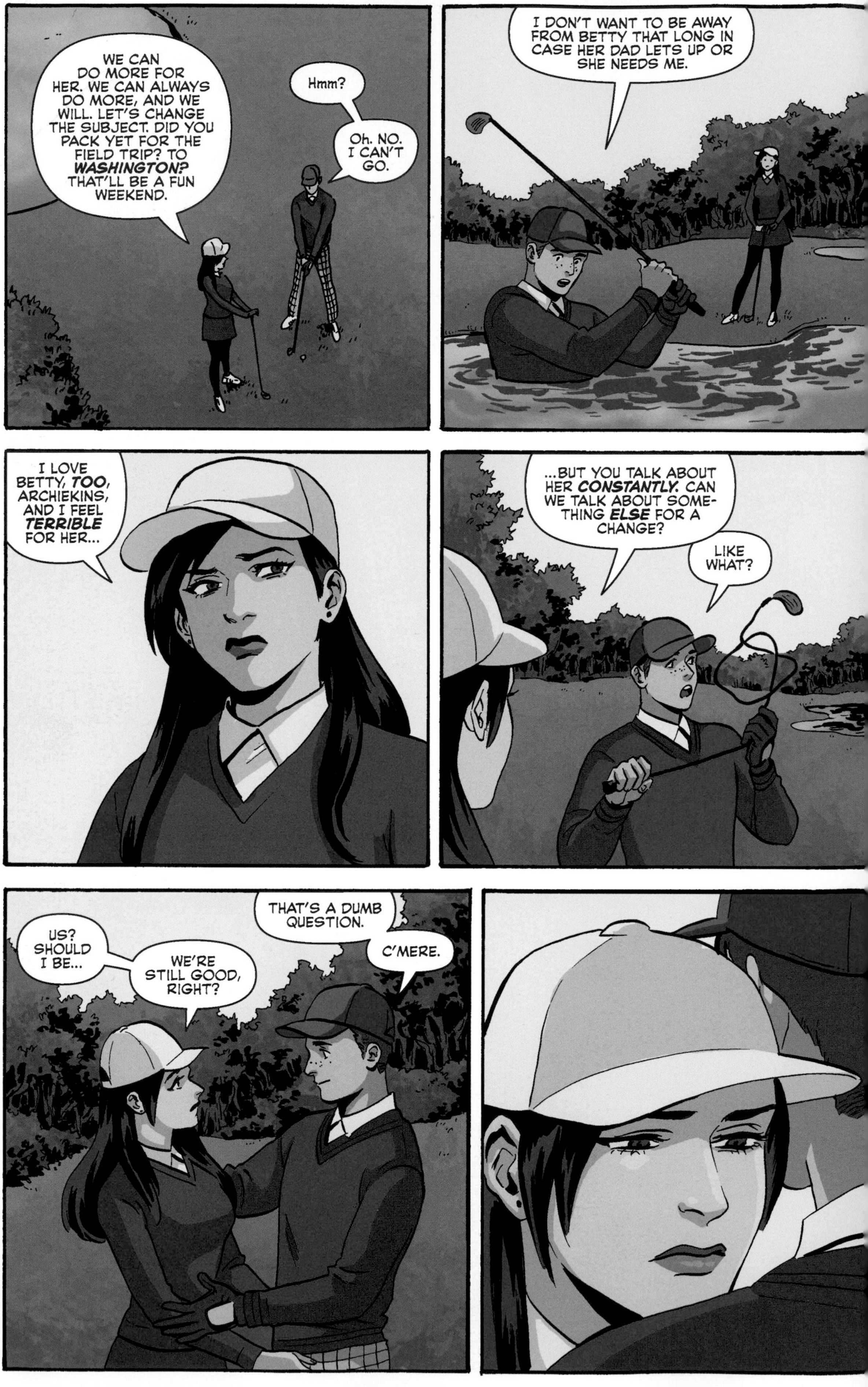
WE CAN DO MORE FOR HER. WE CAN ALWAYS DO MORE, AND WE WILL. LET'S CHANGE THE SUBJECT. DID YOU PACK YET FOR THE FIELD TRIP? TO WASHINGTON? THAT'LL BE A FUN WEEKEND.
Hmm?
Oh. NO. I CAN'T GO.
I DON'T WANT TO BE AWAY FROM BETTY THAT LONG IN CASE HER DAD LETS UP OR SHE NEEDS ME.
I LOVE BETTY, TOO, ARCHIEKINS, AND I FEEL TERRIBLE FOR HER...
...BUT YOU TALK ABOUT HER CONSTANTLY. CAN WE TALK ABOUT SOME-THING ELSE FOR A CHANGE?
LIKE WHAT?
US? SHOULD I BE...
WE'RE STILL GOOD, RIGHT?
THAT'S A DUMB QUESTION.
C'MERE.

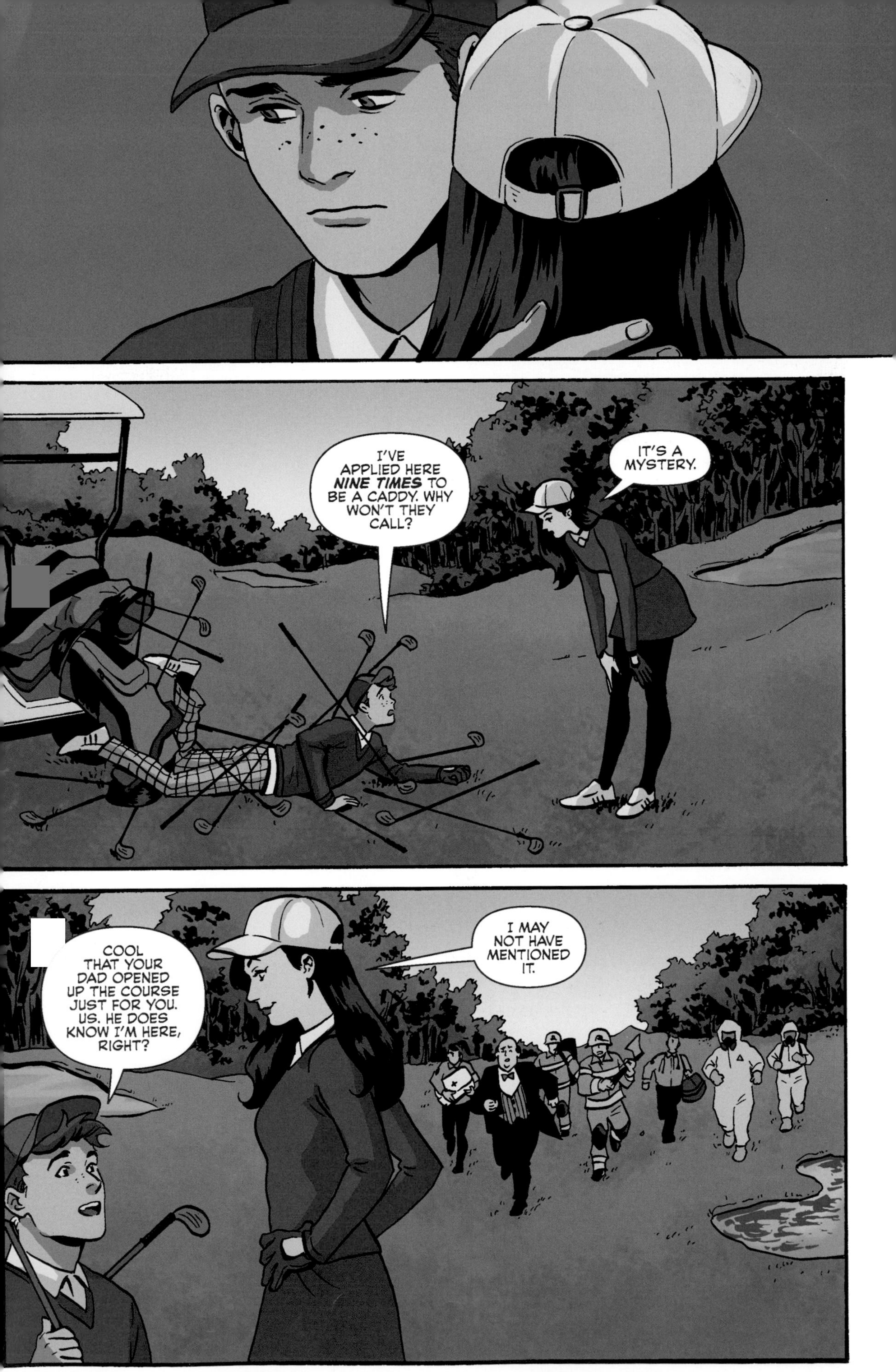
I'VE APPLIED HERE *NINE TIMES* TO BE A CADDY. WHY WON'T THEY CALL?
IT'S A MYSTERY.
COOL THAT YOUR DAD OPENED UP THE COURSE JUST FOR YOU. US. HE DOES KNOW I'M HERE, RIGHT?
I MAY NOT HAVE MENTIONED IT.

CHAPTER TWO: MATCHING HATS

HOT DOG! WHO'S A GOOD BOY? YOU ARE! YES, YOU ARE!

THERE **IS** A **DOG** INSIDE THERE, ISN'T THERE?

SOMETHING FARTS EVERY TWENTY MINUTES. YOU WANT **CHEESE?**

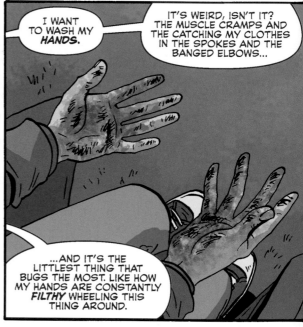

I WANT TO WASH MY **HANDS.**

IT'S WEIRD, ISN'T IT? THE MUSCLE CRAMPS AND THE CATCHING MY CLOTHES IN THE SPOKES AND THE BANGED ELBOWS...

...AND IT'S THE LITTLEST THING THAT BUGS THE MOST. LIKE HOW MY HANDS ARE CONSTANTLY **FILTHY** WHEELING THIS THING AROUND.

WOW. DO YOU **ALWAYS** HAVE WETNAPS ON YOU?

YOU NEVER KNOW WHEN **RIBS** MIGHT COME YOUR WAY.

YOU CRACK ME UP. YOU ALWAYS HAVE. WHEN DID WE BECOME SUCH GOOD FRIENDS?

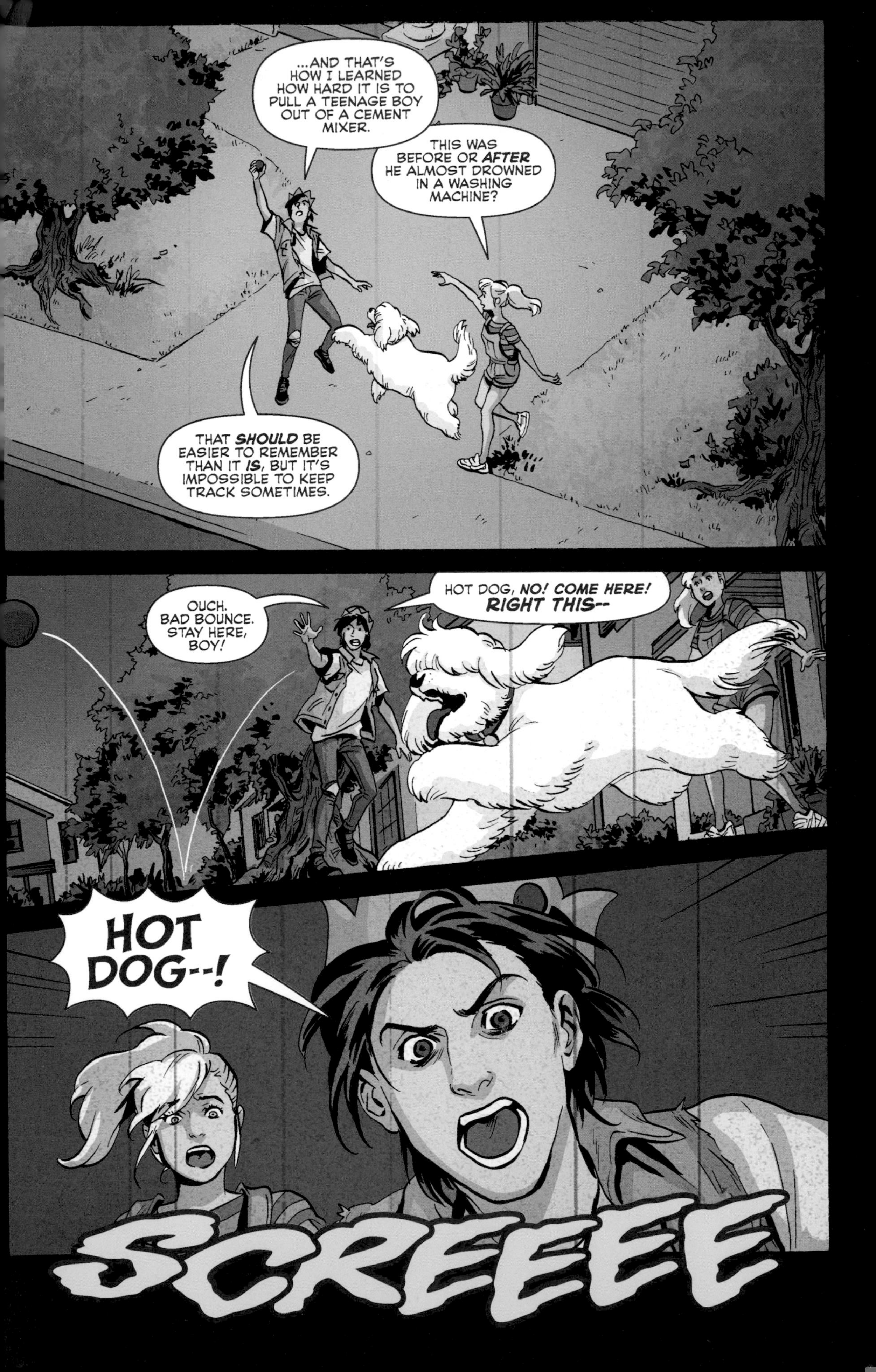
...AND THAT'S HOW I LEARNED HOW HARD IT IS TO PULL A TEENAGE BOY OUT OF A CEMENT MIXER.
THIS WAS BEFORE OR AFTER HE ALMOST DROWNED IN A WASHING MACHINE?
THAT SHOULD BE EASIER TO REMEMBER THAN IT IS, BUT IT'S IMPOSSIBLE TO KEEP TRACK SOMETIMES.
OUCH. BAD BOUNCE. STAY HERE, BOY!
HOT DOG, NO! COME HERE! RIGHT THIS--
HOT DOG--!
SCREEEE

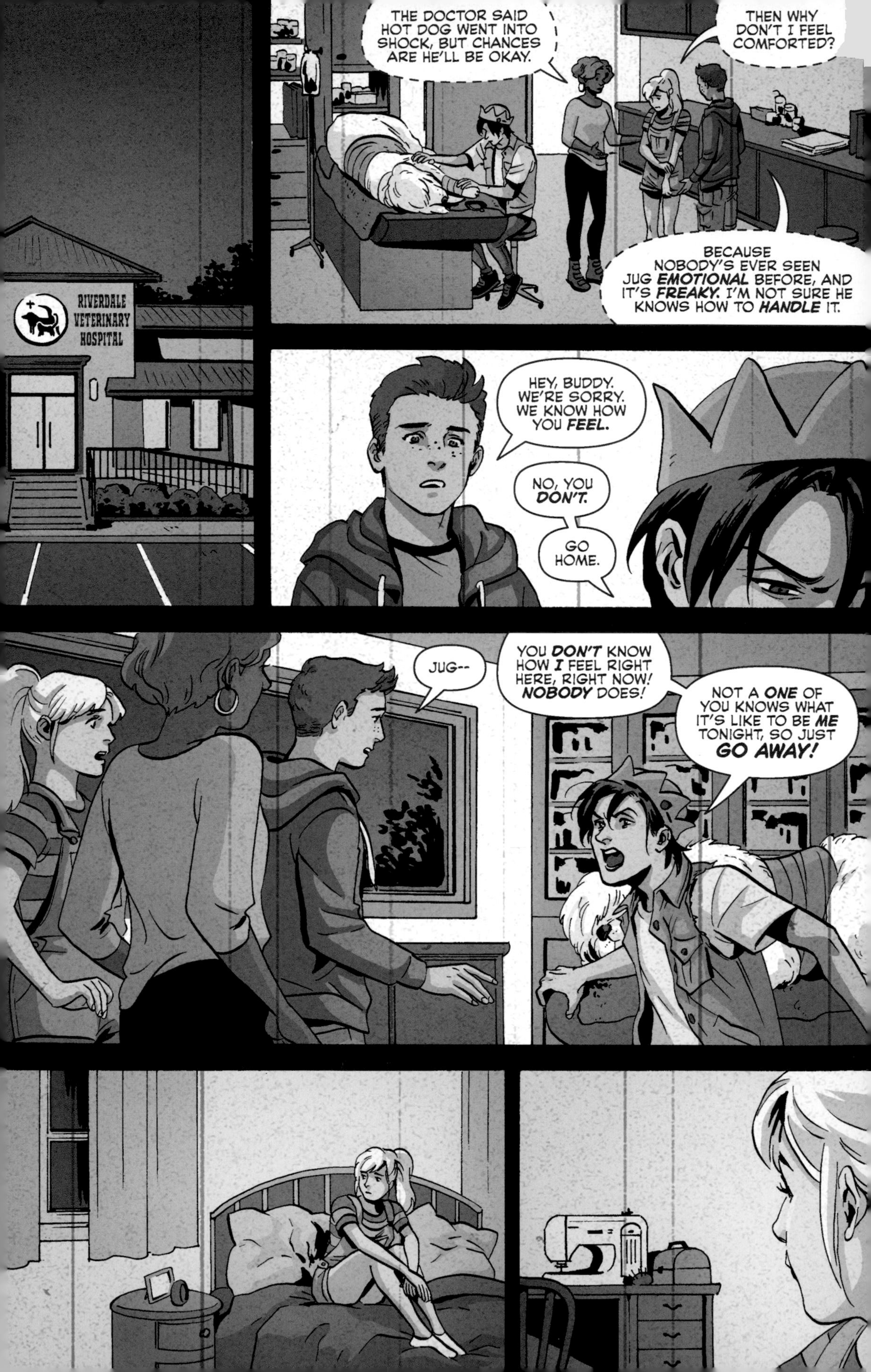
RIVERDALE VETERINARY HOSPITAL
THE DOCTOR SAID HOT DOG WENT INTO SHOCK, BUT CHANCES ARE HE'LL BE OKAY.
THEN WHY DON'T I FEEL COMFORTED?
BECAUSE NOBODY'S EVER SEEN JUG EMOTIONAL BEFORE, AND IT'S FREAKY. I'M NOT SURE HE KNOWS HOW TO HANDLE IT.
HEY, BUDDY. WE'RE SORRY. WE KNOW HOW YOU FEEL.
NO, YOU DON'T.
GO HOME.
JUG--
YOU DON'T KNOW HOW I FEEL RIGHT HERE, RIGHT NOW! NOBODY DOES!
NOT A ONE OF YOU KNOWS WHAT IT'S LIKE TO BE ME TONIGHT, SO JUST GO AWAY!

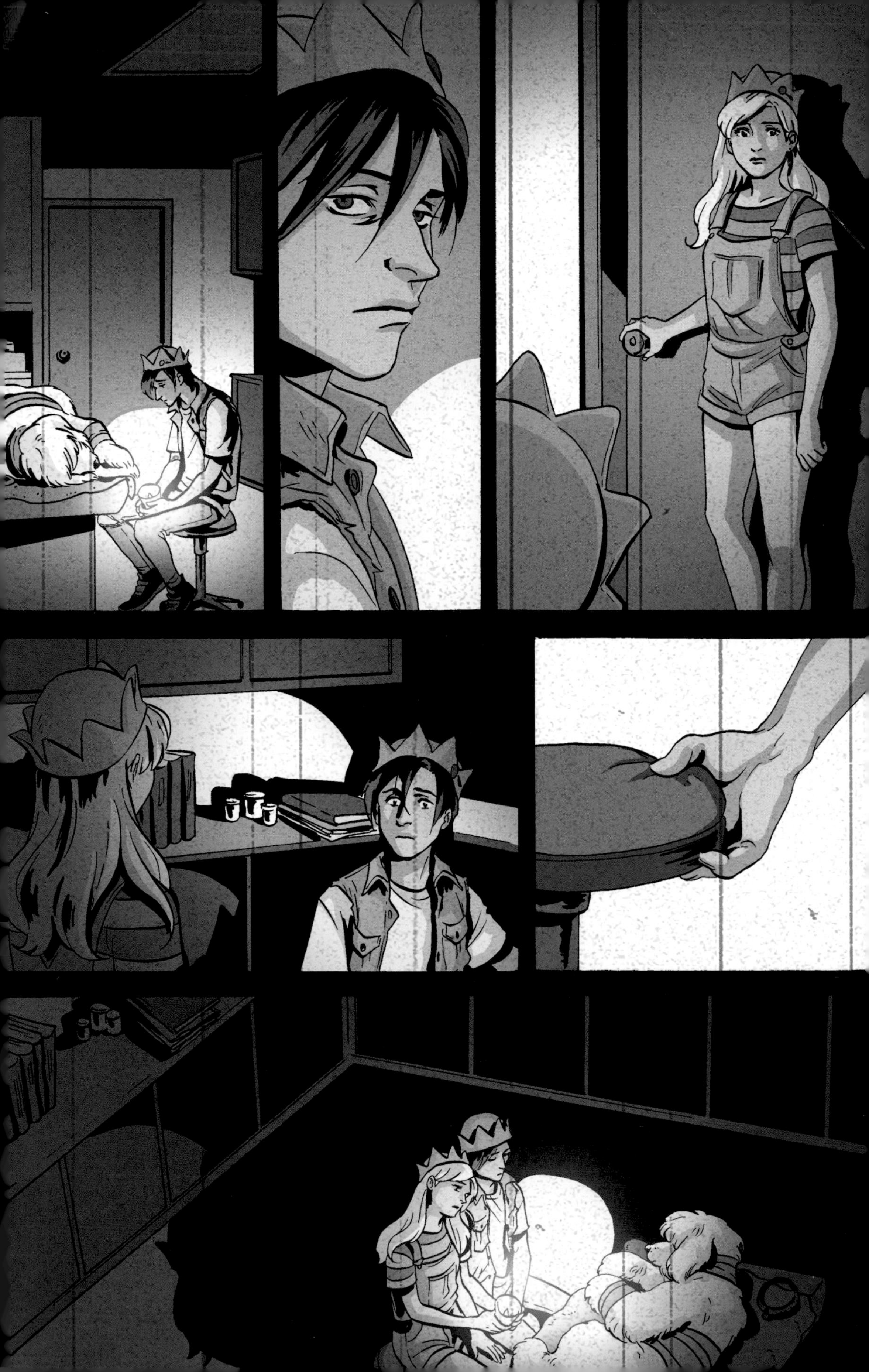

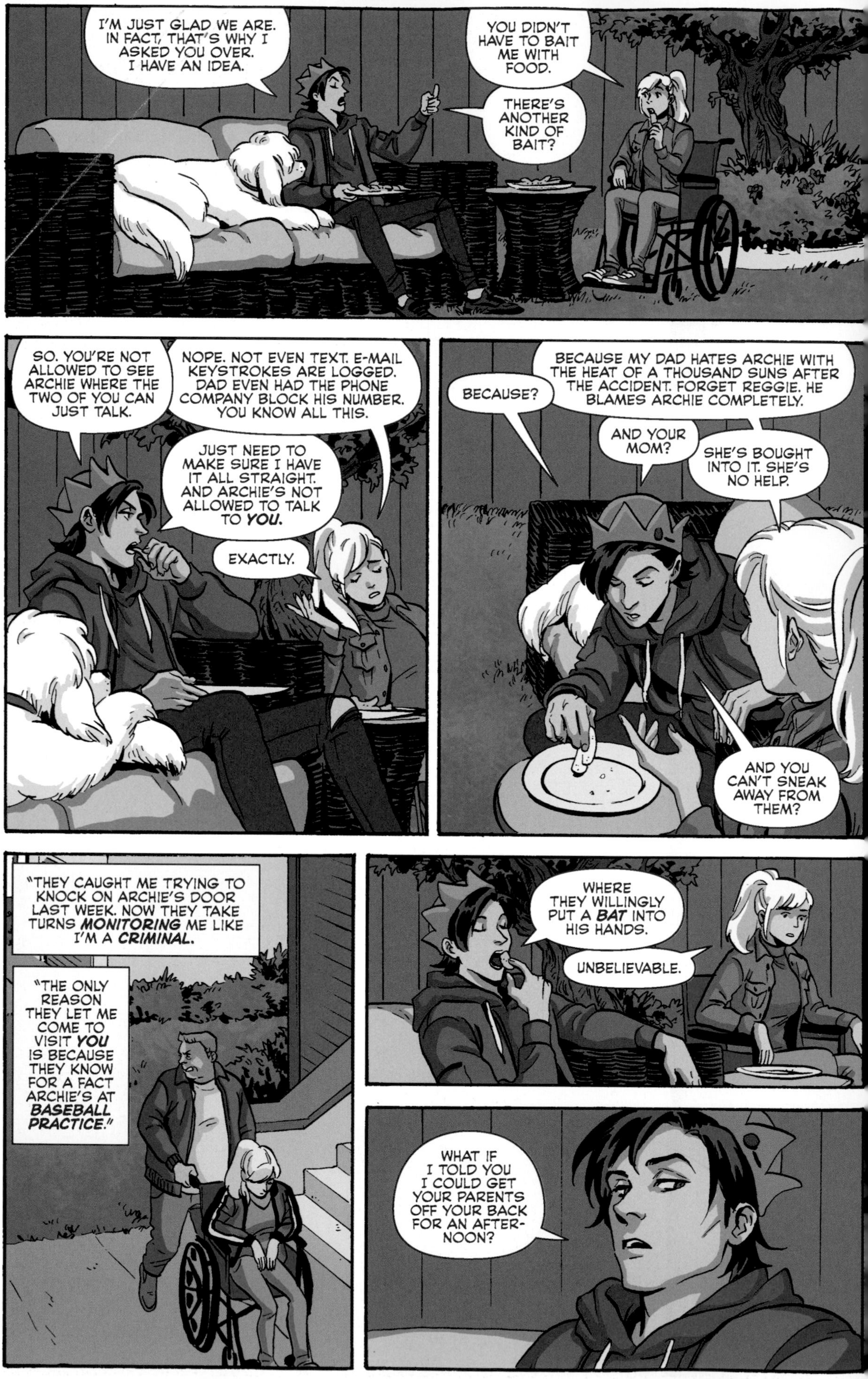
I'M JUST GLAD WE ARE. IN FACT, THAT'S WHY I ASKED YOU OVER. I HAVE AN IDEA.
YOU DIDN'T HAVE TO BAIT ME WITH FOOD.
THERE'S ANOTHER KIND OF BAIT?
SO. YOU'RE NOT ALLOWED TO SEE ARCHIE WHERE THE TWO OF YOU CAN JUST TALK.
NOPE. NOT EVEN TEXT. E-MAIL KEYSTROKES ARE LOGGED. DAD EVEN HAD THE PHONE COMPANY BLOCK HIS NUMBER. YOU KNOW ALL THIS.
JUST NEED TO MAKE SURE I HAVE IT ALL STRAIGHT. AND ARCHIE'S NOT ALLOWED TO TALK TO ***YOU.***
EXACTLY.
BECAUSE?
BECAUSE MY DAD HATES ARCHIE WITH THE HEAT OF A THOUSAND SUNS AFTER THE ACCIDENT. FORGET REGGIE. HE BLAMES ARCHIE COMPLETELY.
AND YOUR MOM?
SHE'S BOUGHT INTO IT. SHE'S NO HELP.
AND YOU CAN'T SNEAK AWAY FROM THEM?
"THEY CAUGHT ME TRYING TO KNOCK ON ARCHIE'S DOOR LAST WEEK. NOW THEY TAKE TURNS ***MONITORING*** ME LIKE I'M A ***CRIMINAL.***
"THE ONLY REASON THEY LET ME COME TO VISIT ***YOU*** IS BECAUSE THEY KNOW FOR A FACT ARCHIE'S AT ***BASEBALL PRACTICE.***"
WHERE THEY WILLINGLY PUT A ***BAT*** INTO HIS HANDS.
UNBELIEVABLE.
WHAT IF I TOLD YOU I COULD GET YOUR PARENTS OFF YOUR BACK FOR AN AFTER-NOON?

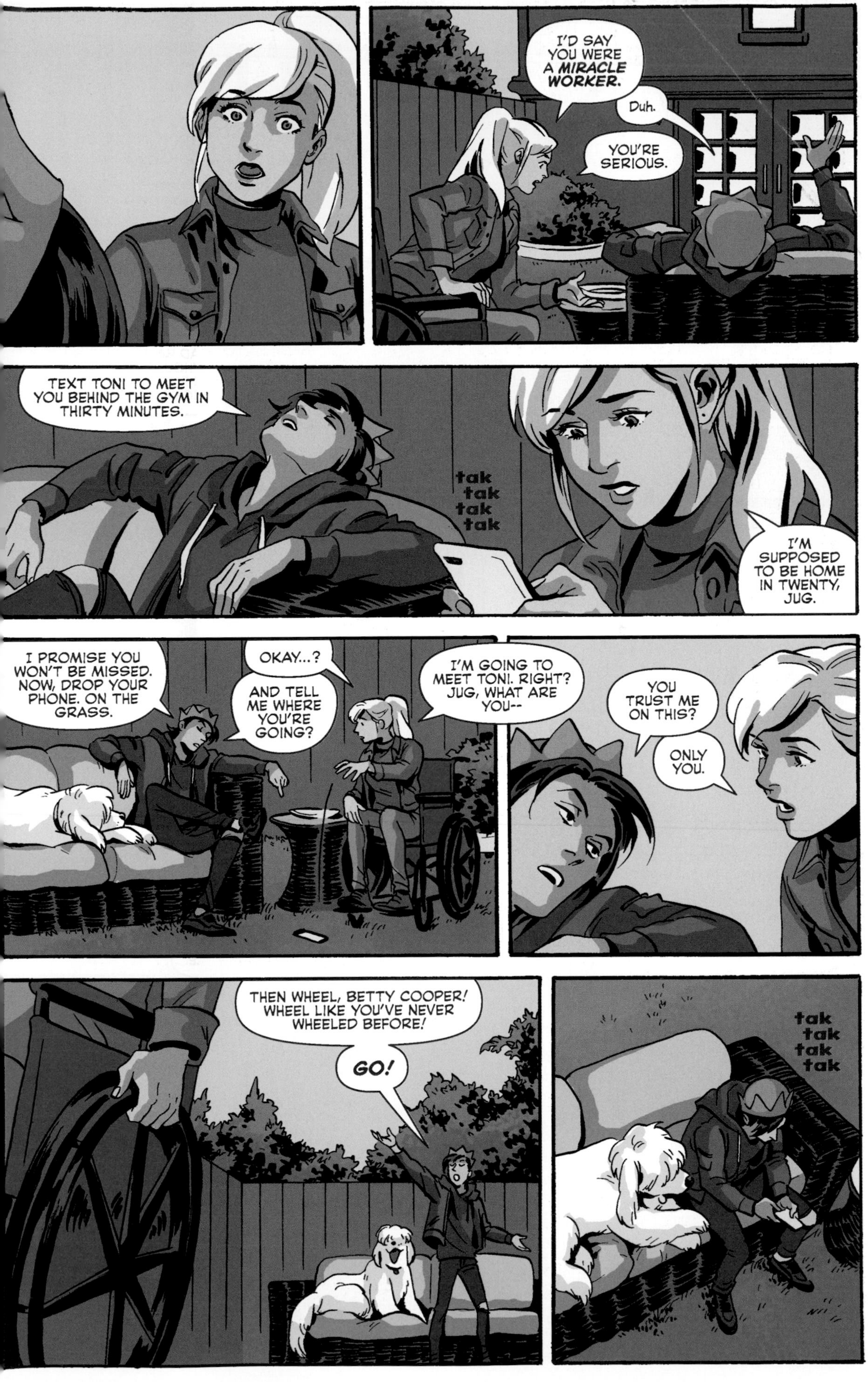
I'D SAY YOU WERE A MIRACLE WORKER.
Duh.
YOU'RE SERIOUS.
TEXT TONI TO MEET YOU BEHIND THE GYM IN THIRTY MINUTES.
tak tak tak tak
I'M SUPPOSED TO BE HOME IN TWENTY, JUG.
I PROMISE YOU WON'T BE MISSED. NOW, DROP YOUR PHONE. ON THE GRASS.
OKAY...?
AND TELL ME WHERE YOU'RE GOING?
I'M GOING TO MEET TONI. RIGHT? JUG, WHAT ARE YOU--
YOU TRUST ME ON THIS?
ONLY YOU.
THEN WHEEL, BETTY COOPER! WHEEL LIKE YOU'VE NEVER WHEELED BEFORE!
GO!
tak tak tak tak

CHAPTER THREE: MISTER TRUST FUND

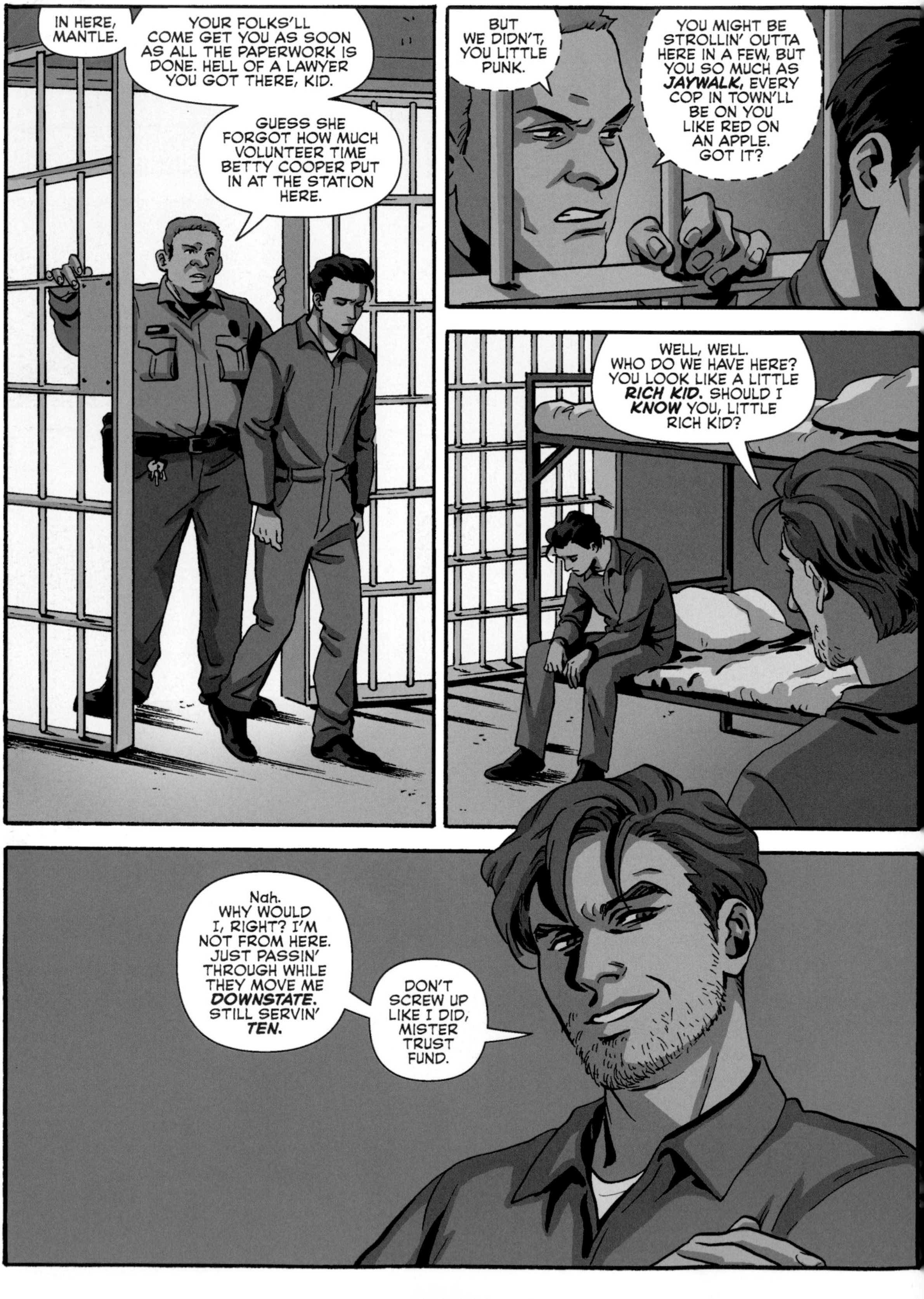
IN HERE, MANTLE.
YOUR FOLKS'LL COME GET YOU AS SOON AS ALL THE PAPERWORK IS DONE. HELL OF A LAWYER YOU GOT THERE, KID.
GUESS SHE FORGOT HOW MUCH VOLUNTEER TIME BETTY COOPER PUT IN AT THE STATION HERE.
BUT WE DIDN'T, YOU LITTLE PUNK.
YOU MIGHT BE STROLLIN' OUTTA HERE IN A FEW, BUT YOU SO MUCH AS JAYWALK, EVERY COP IN TOWN'LL BE ON YOU LIKE RED ON AN APPLE. GOT IT?
WELL, WELL. WHO DO WE HAVE HERE? YOU LOOK LIKE A LITTLE RICH KID. SHOULD I KNOW YOU, LITTLE RICH KID?
Nah. WHY WOULD I, RIGHT? I'M NOT FROM HERE. JUST PASSIN' THROUGH WHILE THEY MOVE ME DOWNSTATE. STILL SERVIN' TEN.
DON'T SCREW UP LIKE I DID, MISTER TRUST FUND.

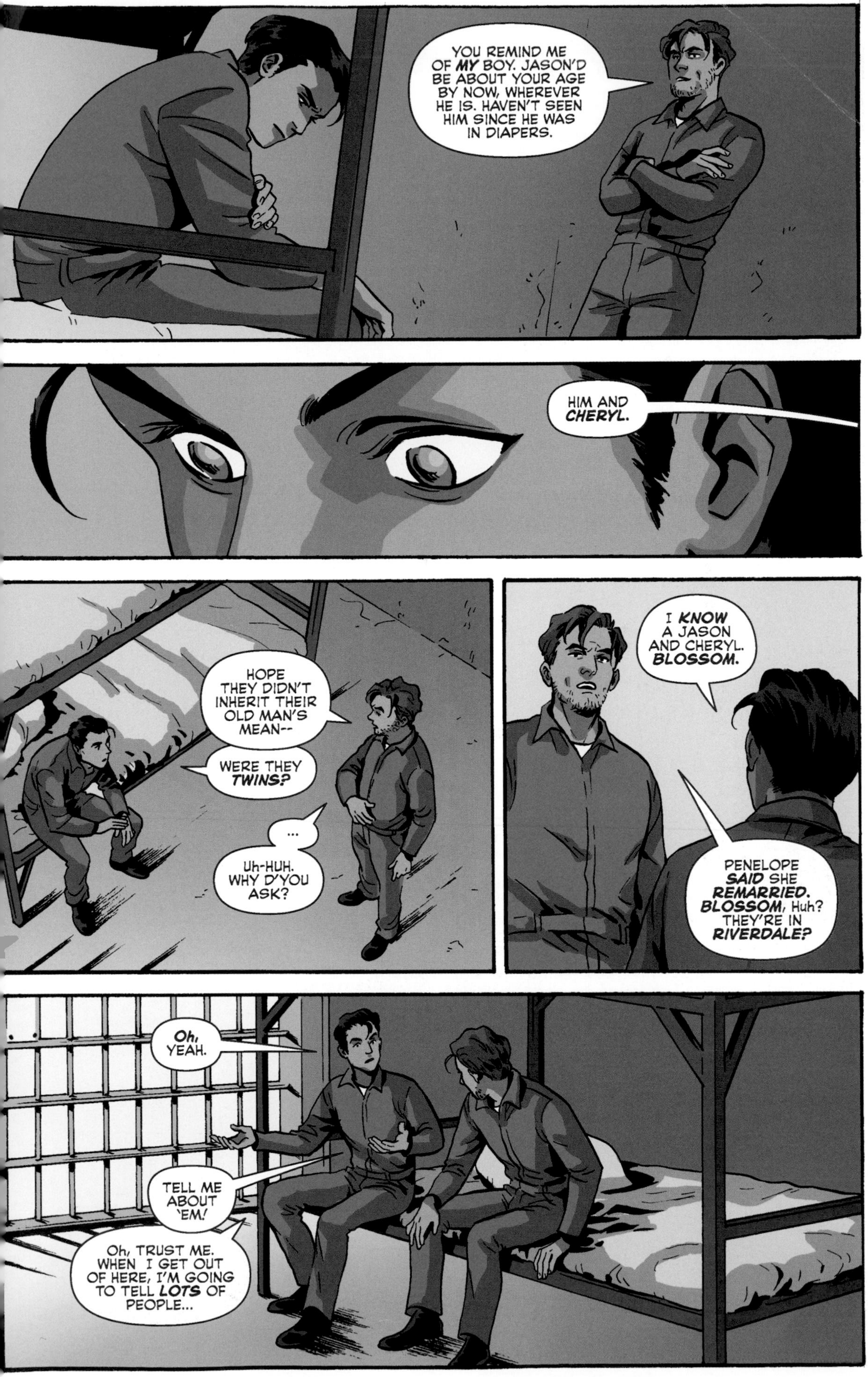
YOU REMIND ME OF MY BOY. JASON'D BE ABOUT YOUR AGE BY NOW, WHEREVER HE IS. HAVEN'T SEEN HIM SINCE HE WAS IN DIAPERS.
HIM AND CHERYL.
HOPE THEY DIDN'T INHERIT THEIR OLD MAN'S MEAN--
WERE THEY TWINS?
...
Uh-HUH. WHY D'YOU ASK?
I KNOW A JASON AND CHERYL. BLOSSOM.
PENELOPE SAID SHE REMARRIED. BLOSSOM, Huh? THEY'RE IN RIVERDALE?
Oh, YEAH.
TELL ME ABOUT 'EM!
Oh, TRUST ME. WHEN I GET OUT OF HERE, I'M GOING TO TELL LOTS OF PEOPLE...

CHAPTER FOUR: WE NEED TO TALK

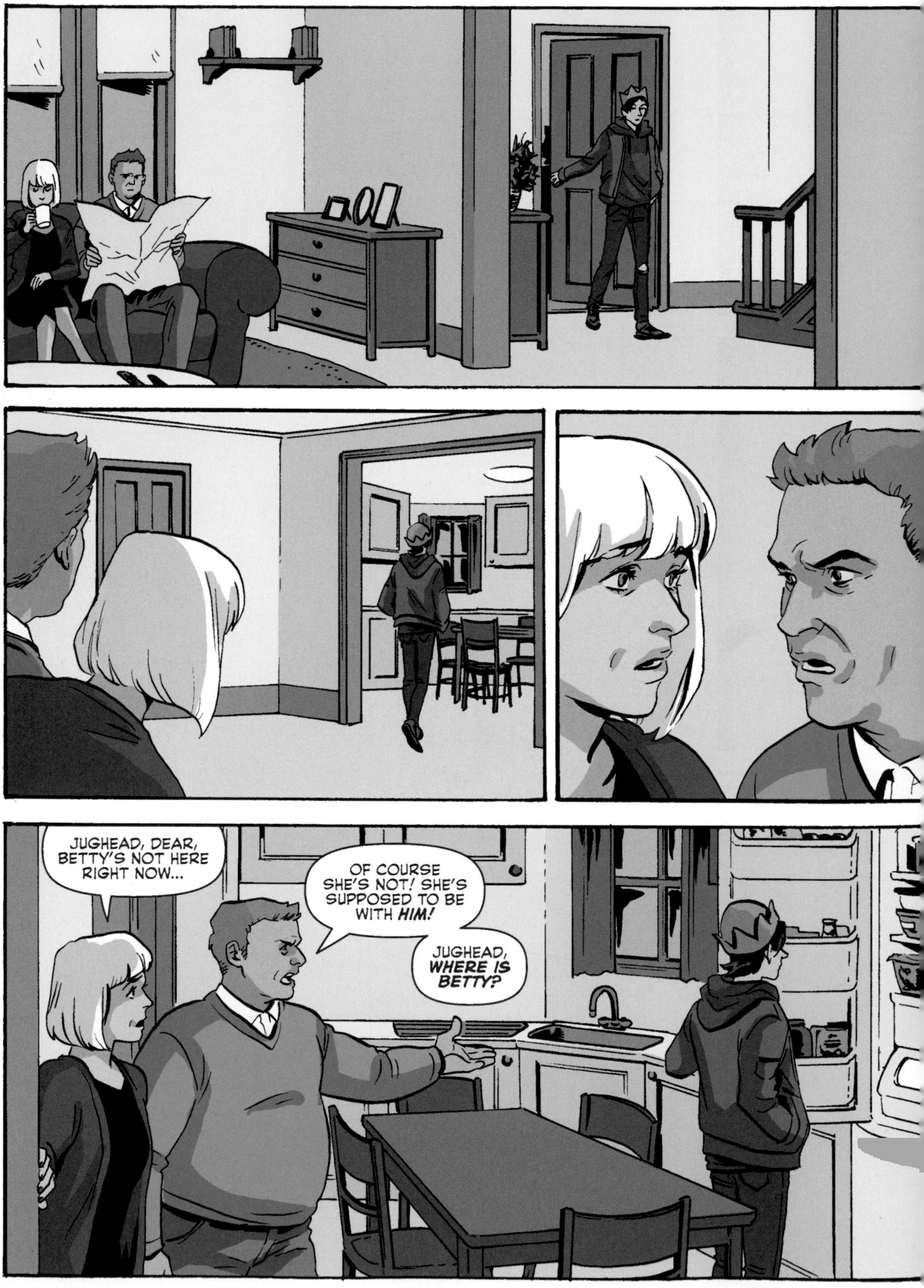
JUGHEAD, DEAR, BETTY'S NOT HERE RIGHT NOW...
OF COURSE SHE'S NOT! SHE'S SUPPOSED TO BE WITH *HIM!*
JUGHEAD, ***WHERE IS BETTY?***

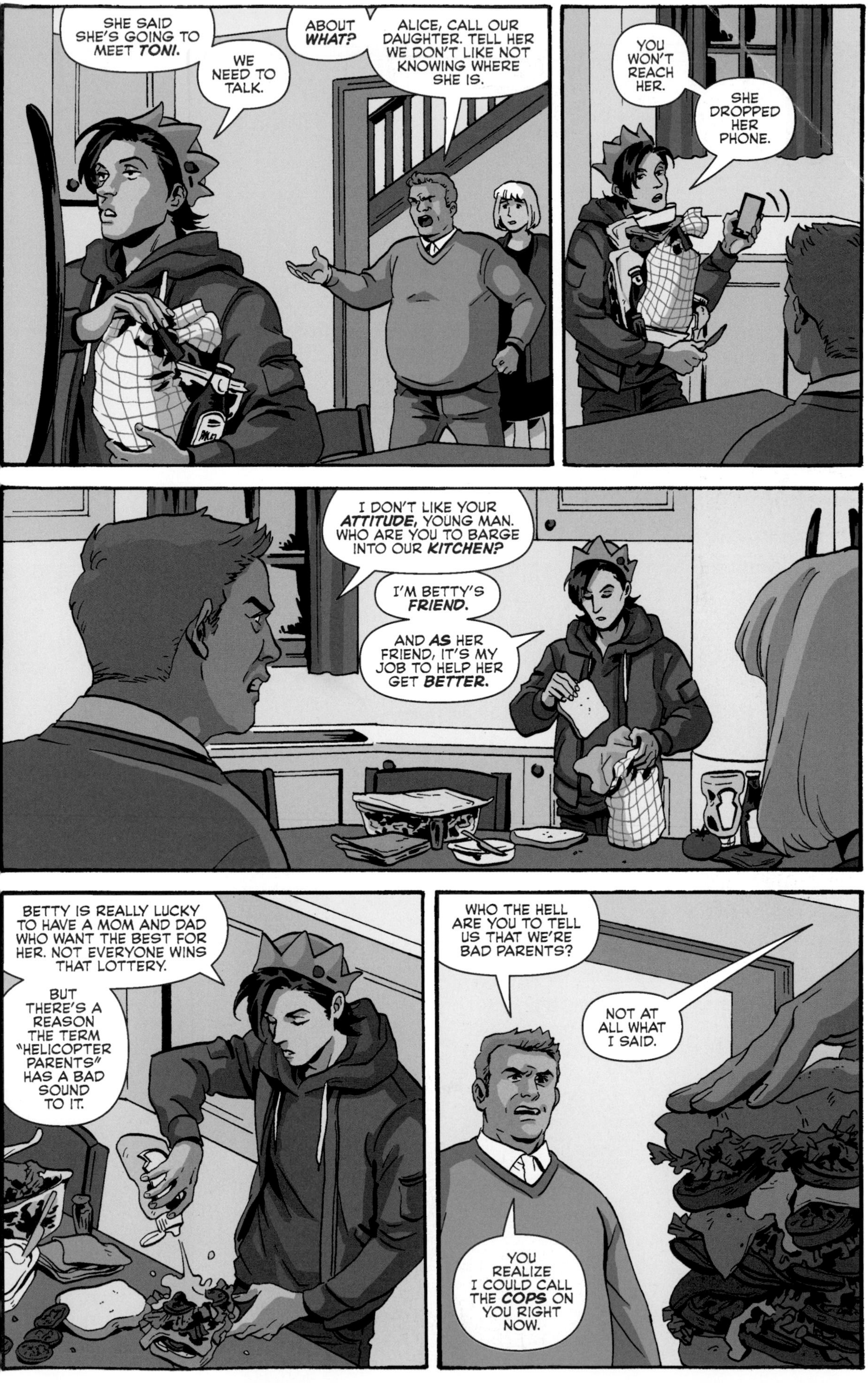
SHE SAID SHE'S GOING TO MEET ***TONI***.
WE NEED TO TALK.
ABOUT ***WHAT?***
ALICE, CALL OUR DAUGHTER. TELL HER WE DON'T LIKE NOT KNOWING WHERE SHE IS.
YOU WON'T REACH HER.
SHE DROPPED HER PHONE.
I DON'T LIKE YOUR ***ATTITUDE***, YOUNG MAN. WHO ARE YOU TO BARGE INTO OUR ***KITCHEN?***
I'M BETTY'S ***FRIEND***.
AND ***AS*** HER FRIEND, IT'S MY JOB TO HELP HER GET ***BETTER***.
BETTY IS REALLY LUCKY TO HAVE A MOM AND DAD WHO WANT THE BEST FOR HER. NOT EVERYONE WINS THAT LOTTERY.
BUT THERE'S A REASON THE TERM "HELICOPTER PARENTS" HAS A BAD SOUND TO IT.
WHO THE HELL ARE YOU TO TELL US THAT WE'RE BAD PARENTS?
NOT AT ALL WHAT I SAID.
YOU REALIZE I COULD CALL THE ***COPS*** ON YOU RIGHT NOW.

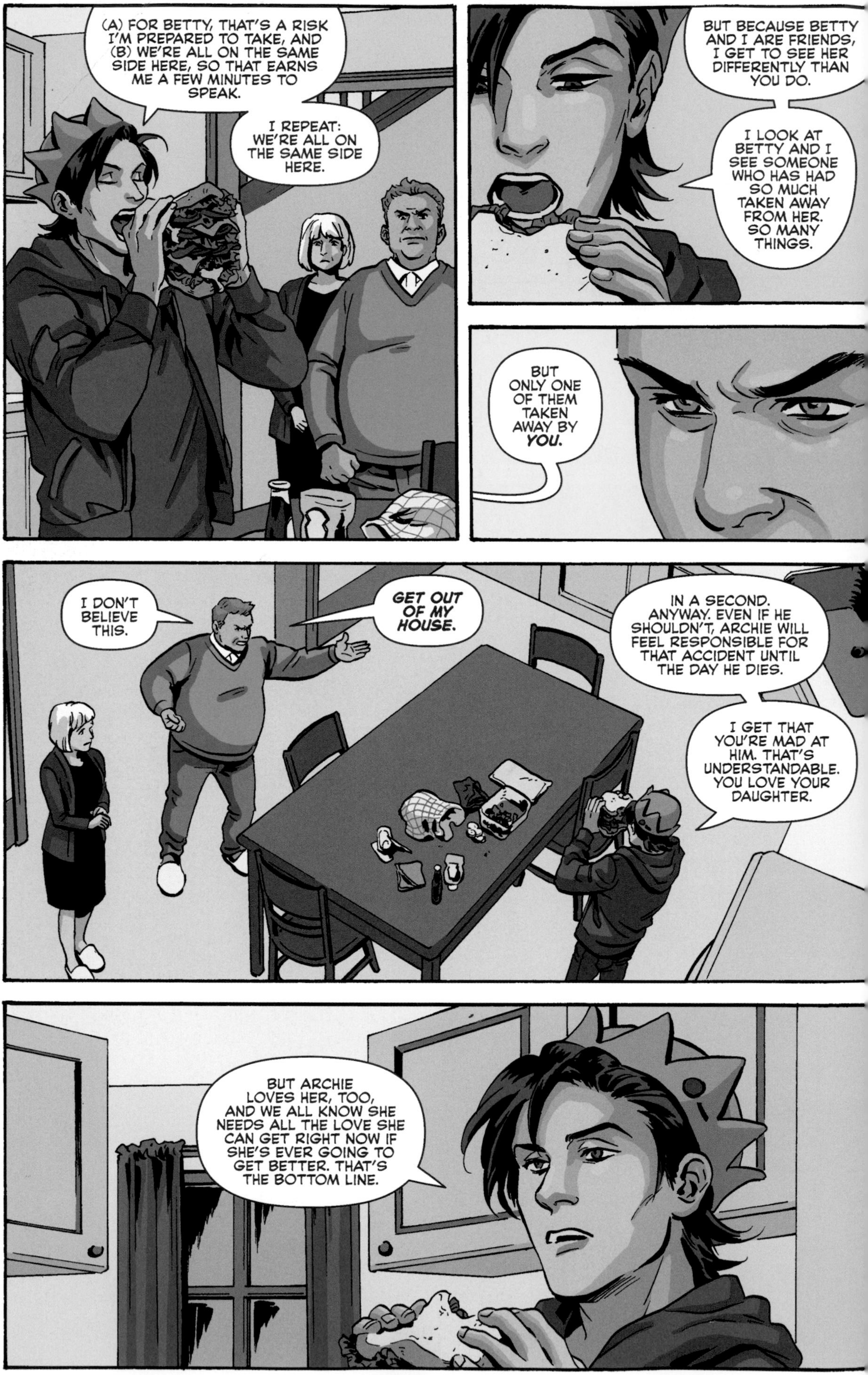
(A) FOR BETTY, THAT'S A RISK I'M PREPARED TO TAKE, AND (B) WE'RE ALL ON THE SAME SIDE HERE, SO THAT EARNS ME A FEW MINUTES TO SPEAK.
I REPEAT: WE'RE ALL ON THE SAME SIDE HERE.
BUT BECAUSE BETTY AND I ARE FRIENDS, I GET TO SEE HER DIFFERENTLY THAN YOU DO.
I LOOK AT BETTY AND I SEE SOMEONE WHO HAS HAD SO MUCH TAKEN AWAY FROM HER. SO MANY THINGS.
BUT ONLY ONE OF THEM TAKEN AWAY BY *YOU.*
I DON'T BELIEVE THIS.
GET OUT OF MY HOUSE.
IN A SECOND. ANYWAY. EVEN IF HE SHOULDN'T, ARCHIE WILL FEEL RESPONSIBLE FOR THAT ACCIDENT UNTIL THE DAY HE DIES.
I GET THAT YOU'RE MAD AT HIM. THAT'S UNDERSTANDABLE. YOU LOVE YOUR DAUGHTER.
BUT ARCHIE LOVES HER, TOO, AND WE ALL KNOW SHE NEEDS ALL THE LOVE SHE CAN GET RIGHT NOW IF SHE'S EVER GOING TO GET BETTER. THAT'S THE BOTTOM LINE.

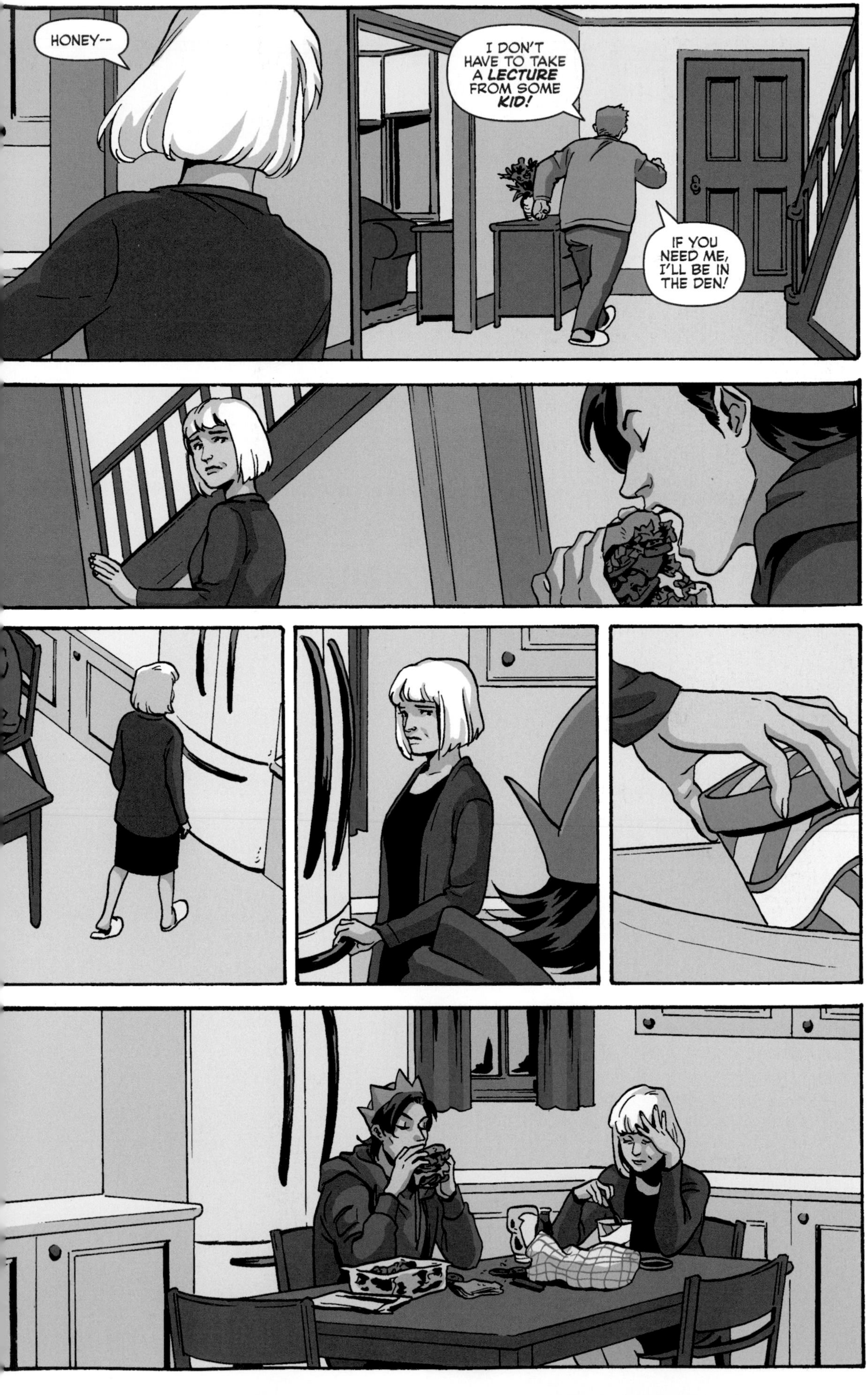
HONEY--
I DON'T HAVE TO TAKE A **LECTURE** FROM SOME **KID!**
IF YOU NEED ME, I'LL BE IN THE DEN!

CHAPTER FIVE: ALL THAT MATTERS

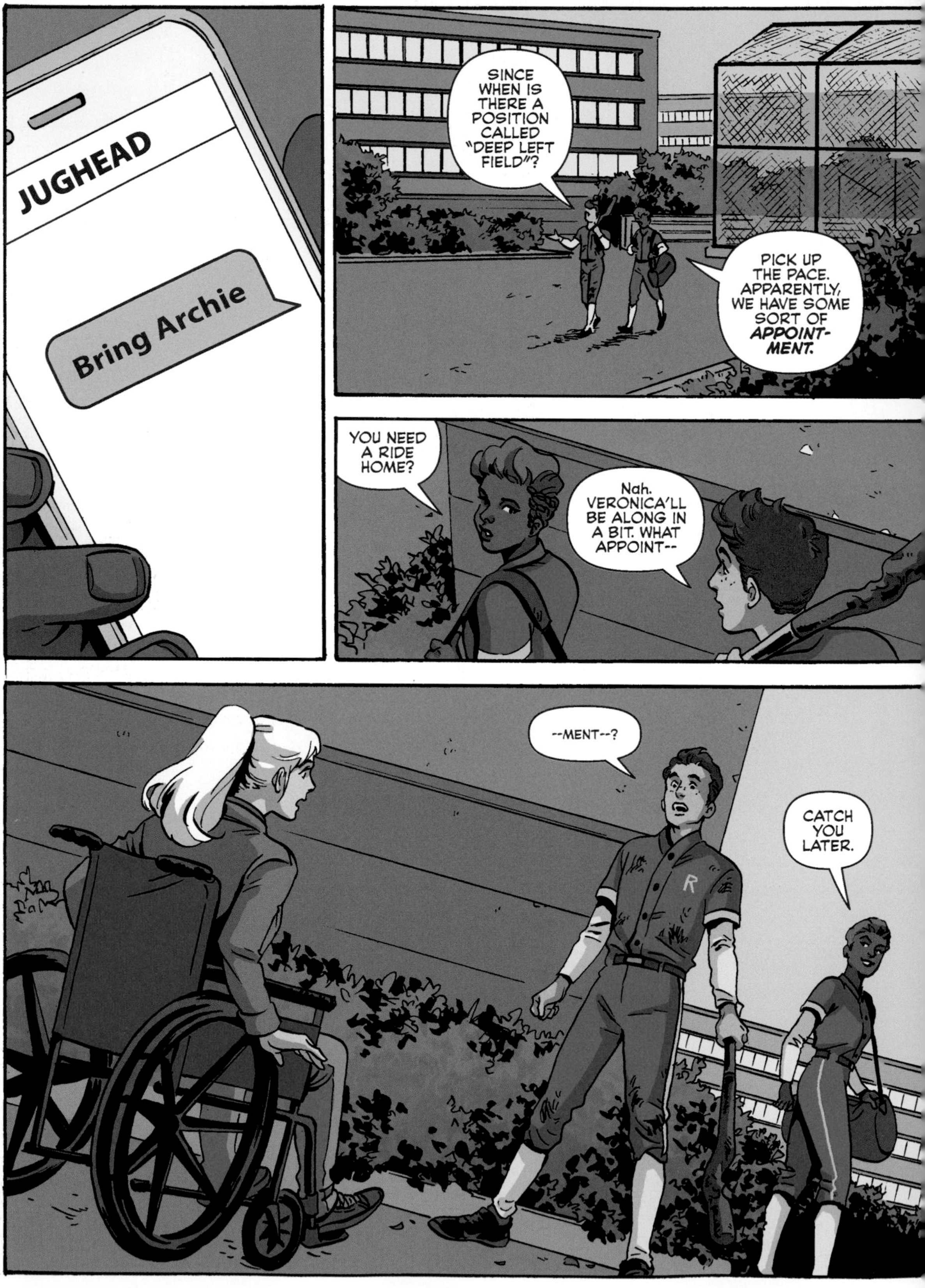
JUGHEAD
Bring Archie
SINCE WHEN IS THERE A POSITION CALLED "DEEP LEFT FIELD"?
PICK UP THE PACE. APPARENTLY, WE HAVE SOME SORT OF *APPOINTMENT.*
YOU NEED A RIDE HOME?
Nah. VERONICA'LL BE ALONG IN A BIT. WHAT APPOINT--
--MENT--?
CATCH YOU LATER.
R

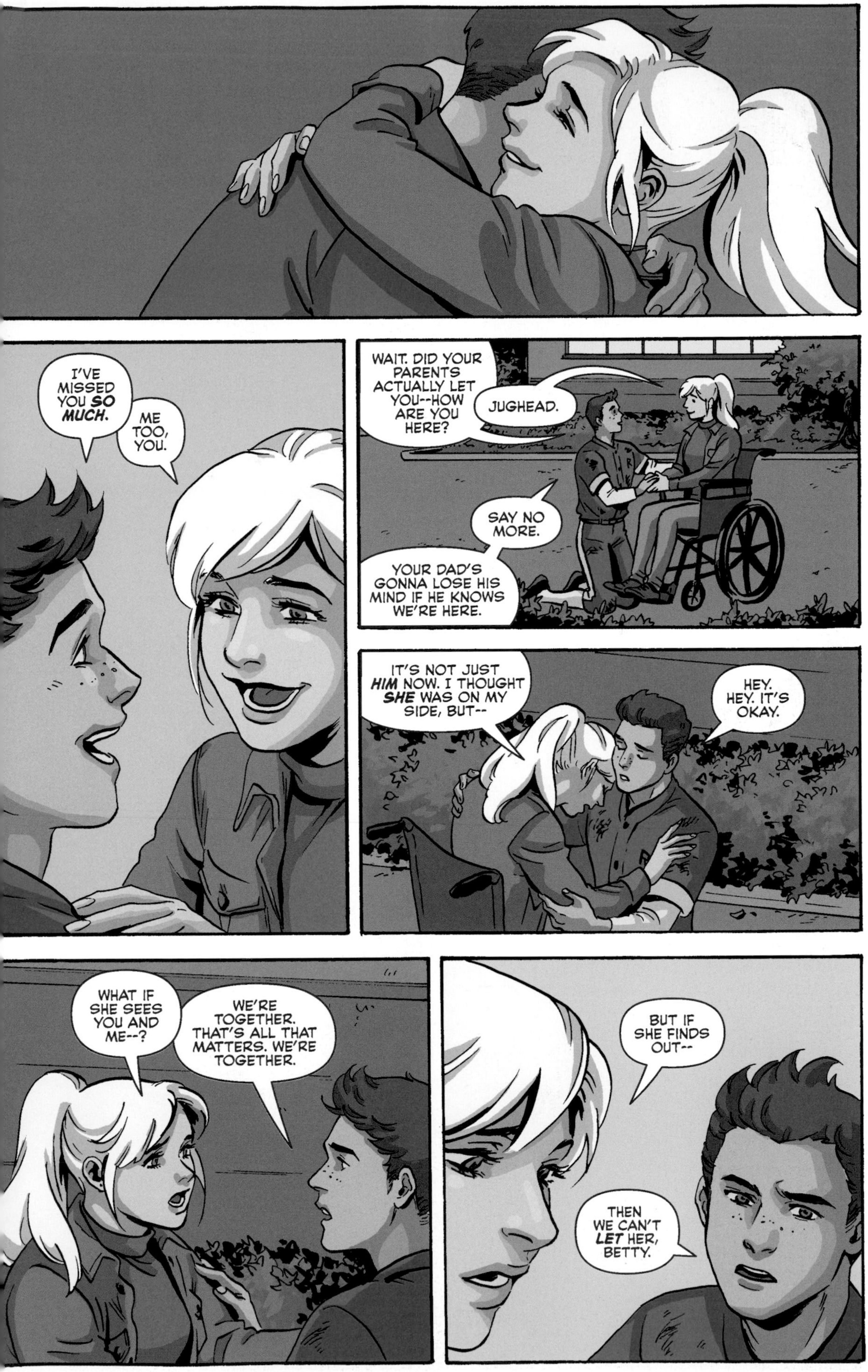
I'VE MISSED YOU SO MUCH.
ME TOO, YOU.
WAIT. DID YOUR PARENTS ACTUALLY LET YOU--HOW ARE YOU HERE?
JUGHEAD.
SAY NO MORE.
YOUR DAD'S GONNA LOSE HIS MIND IF HE KNOWS WE'RE HERE.
IT'S NOT JUST HIM NOW. I THOUGHT SHE WAS ON MY SIDE, BUT--
HEY. HEY. IT'S OKAY.
WHAT IF SHE SEES YOU AND ME--?
WE'RE TOGETHER. THAT'S ALL THAT MATTERS. WE'RE TOGETHER.
BUT IF SHE FINDS OUT--
THEN WE CAN'T LET HER, BETTY.

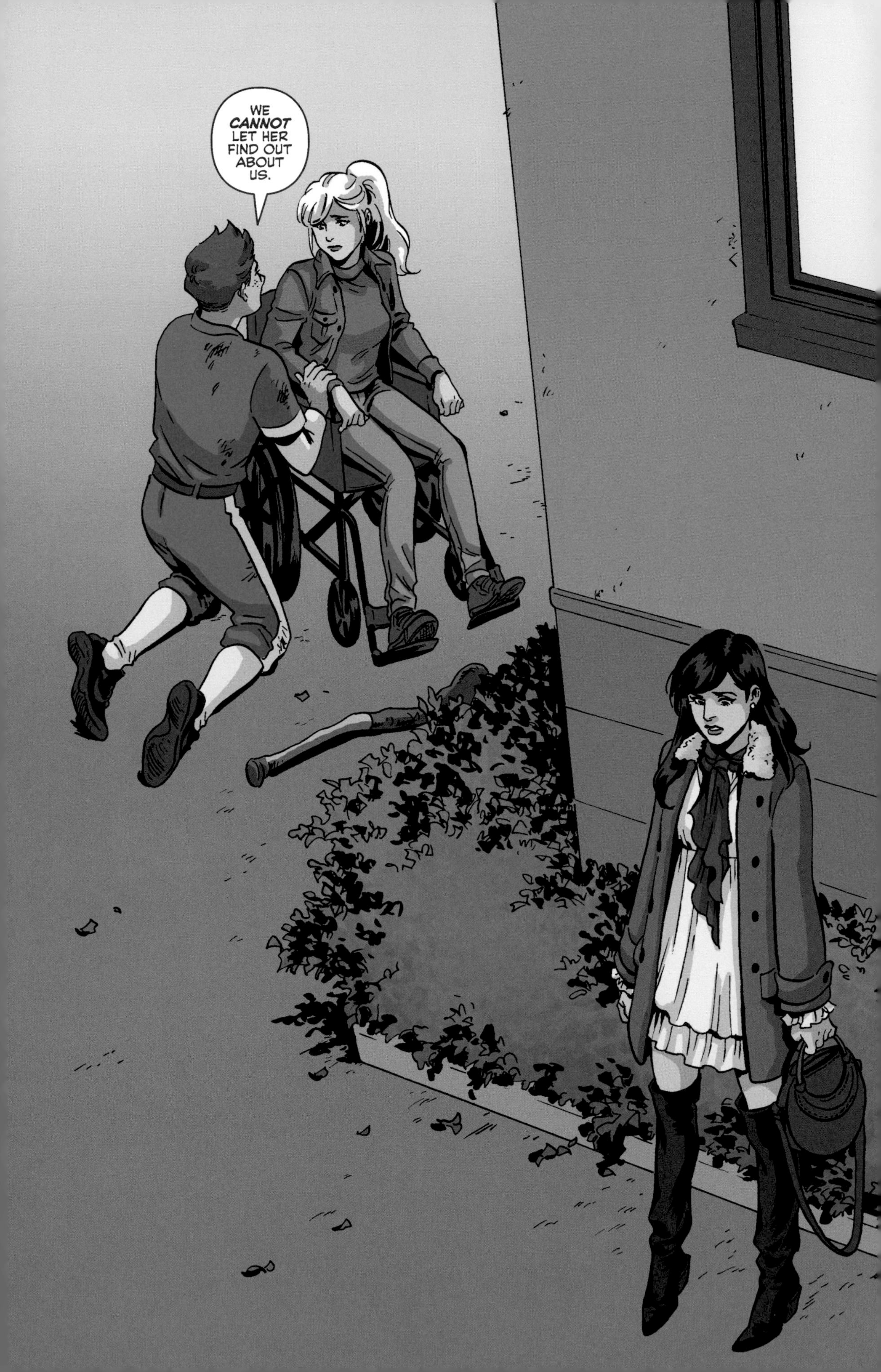
WE CANNOT LET HER FIND OUT ABOUT US.

TO BE CONTINUED...

ISSUE TWENTY-SIX

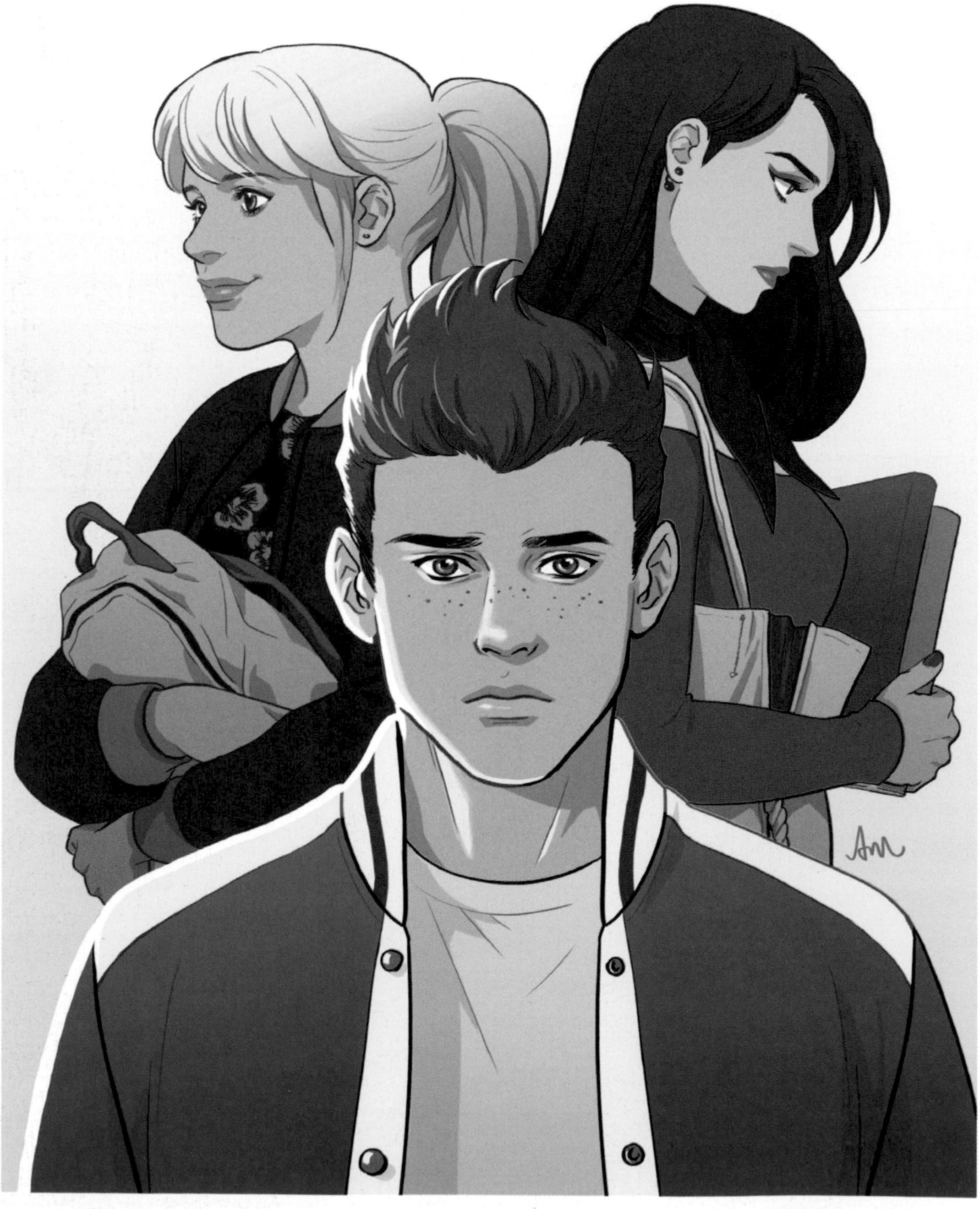

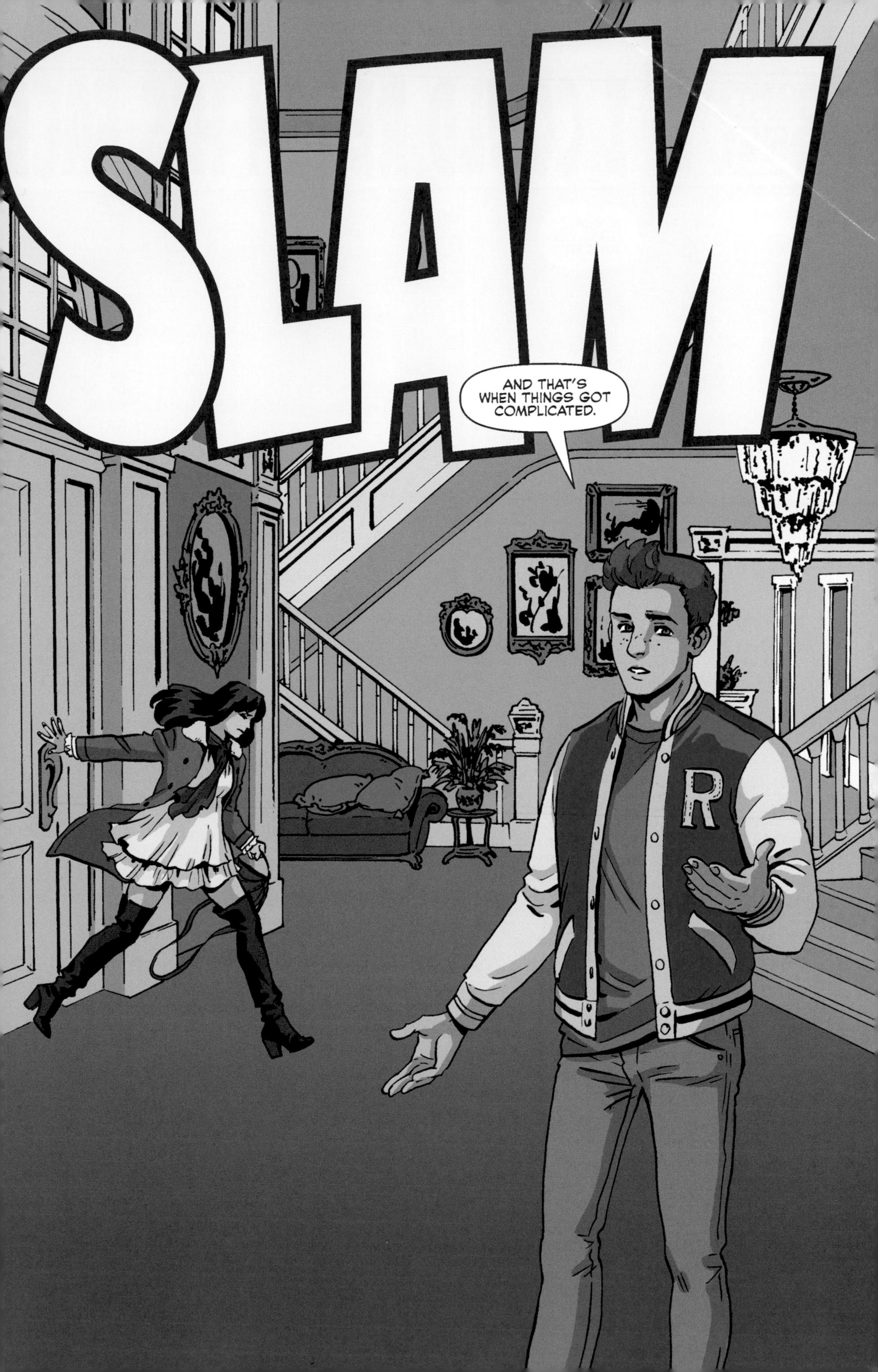
SLAM
AND THAT'S WHEN THINGS GOT COMPLICATED.

CHAPTER ONE: IF I COULD REACH HIS FACE

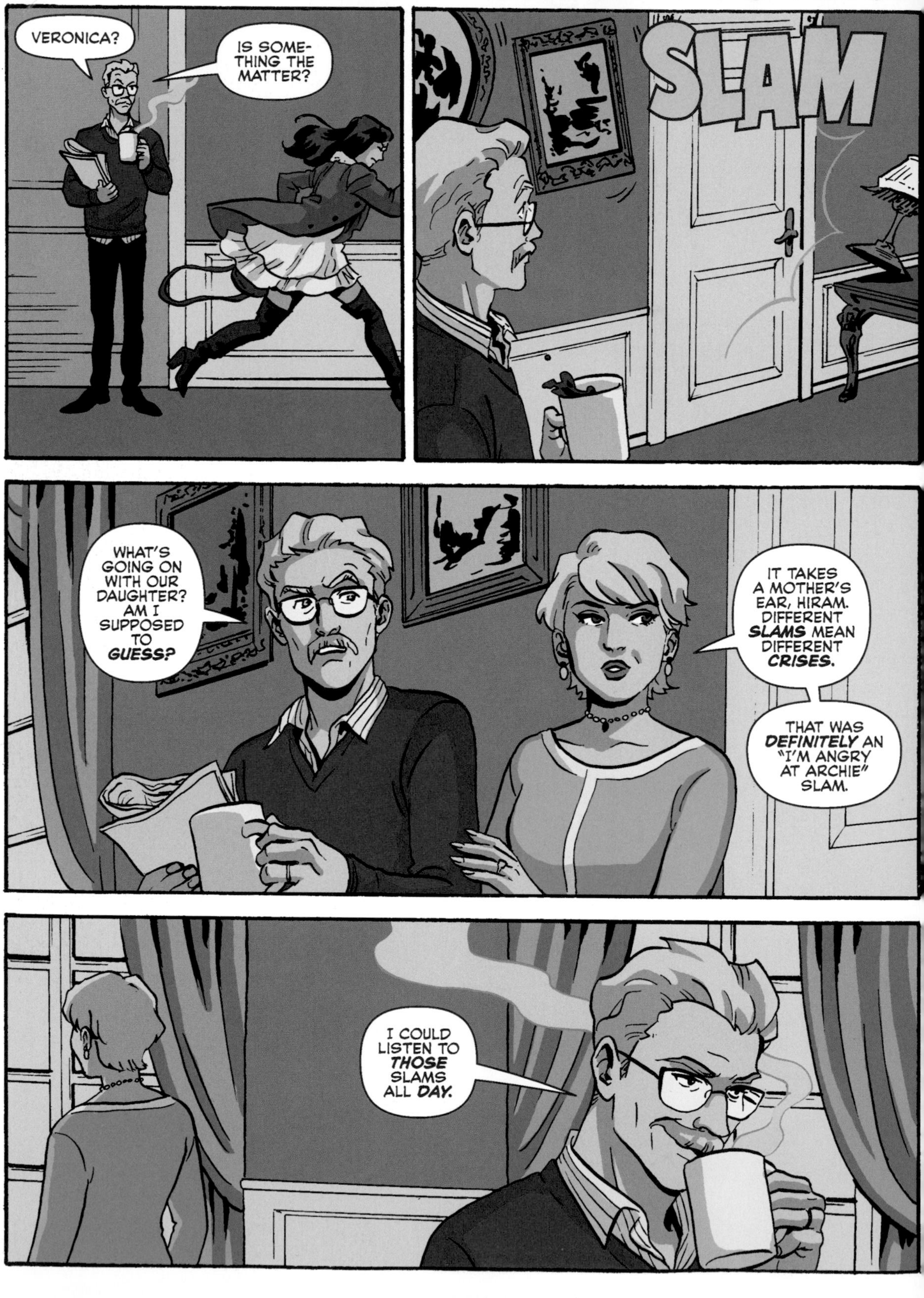
VERONICA?
IS SOMETHING THE MATTER?
SLAM
WHAT'S GOING ON WITH OUR DAUGHTER? AM I SUPPOSED TO *GUESS?*
IT TAKES A MOTHER'S EAR, HIRAM. DIFFERENT *SLAMS* MEAN DIFFERENT *CRISES.*
THAT WAS *DEFINITELY* AN "I'M ANGRY AT ARCHIE" SLAM.
I COULD LISTEN TO *THOSE* SLAMS ALL *DAY.*

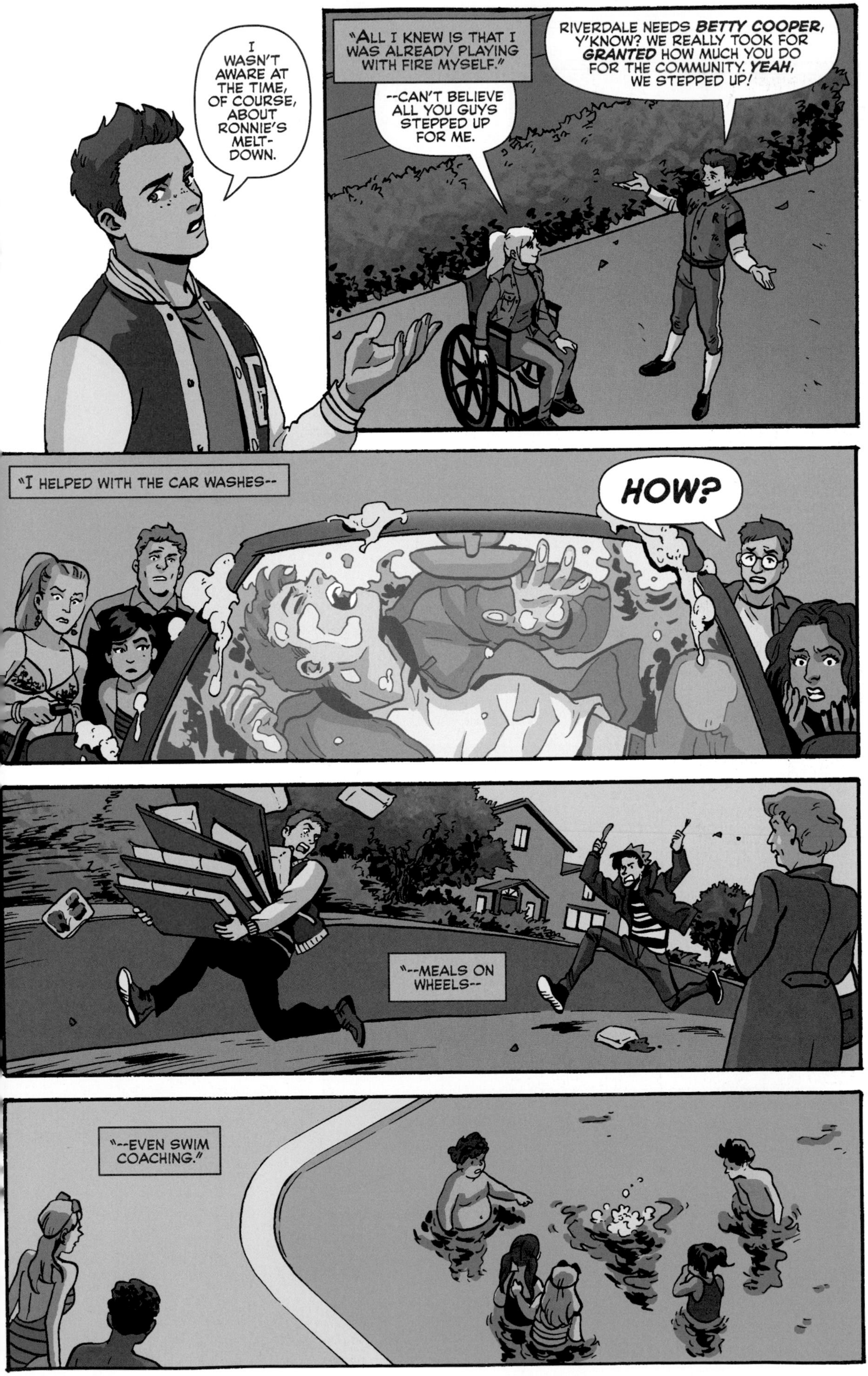
I WASN'T AWARE AT THE TIME, OF COURSE, ABOUT RONNIE'S MELT-DOWN.
"ALL I KNEW IS THAT I WAS ALREADY PLAYING WITH FIRE MYSELF."
--CAN'T BELIEVE ALL YOU GUYS STEPPED UP FOR ME.
RIVERDALE NEEDS BETTY COOPER, Y'KNOW? WE REALLY TOOK FOR GRANTED HOW MUCH YOU DO FOR THE COMMUNITY. YEAH, WE STEPPED UP!
"I HELPED WITH THE CAR WASHES--
HOW?
"--MEALS ON WHEELS--
"--EVEN SWIM COACHING."

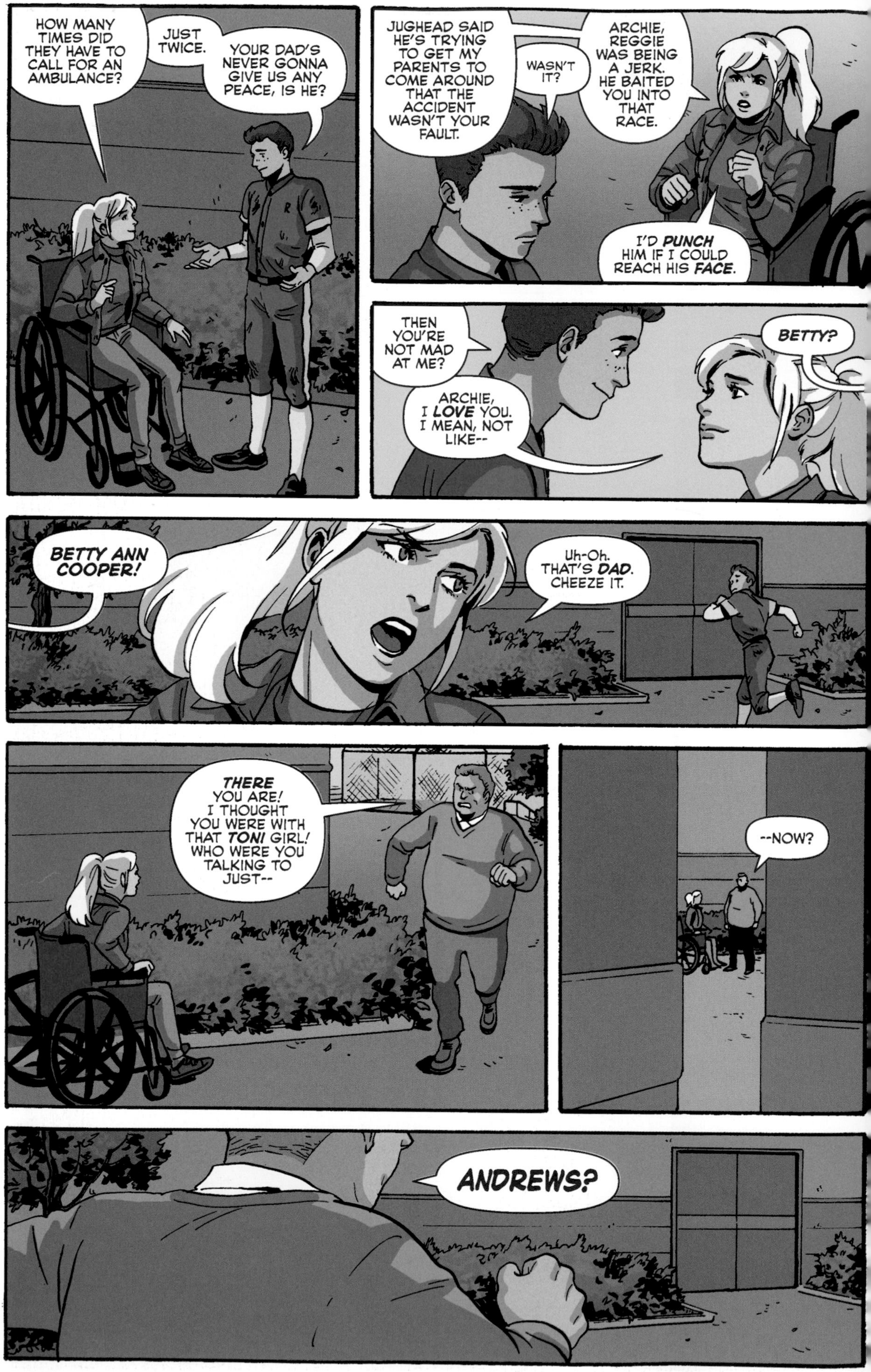
HOW MANY TIMES DID THEY HAVE TO CALL FOR AN AMBULANCE?
JUST TWICE.
YOUR DAD'S NEVER GONNA GIVE US ANY PEACE, IS HE?
JUGHEAD SAID HE'S TRYING TO GET MY PARENTS TO COME AROUND THAT THE ACCIDENT WASN'T YOUR FAULT.
WASN'T IT?
ARCHIE, REGGIE WAS BEING A JERK. HE BAITED YOU INTO THAT RACE.
I'D PUNCH HIM IF I COULD REACH HIS FACE.
THEN YOU'RE NOT MAD AT ME?
ARCHIE, I LOVE YOU. I MEAN, NOT LIKE--
BETTY?
BETTY ANN COOPER!
Uh-Oh. THAT'S DAD. CHEEZE IT.
THERE YOU ARE! I THOUGHT YOU WERE WITH THAT TONI GIRL! WHO WERE YOU TALKING TO JUST--
--NOW?
ANDREWS?

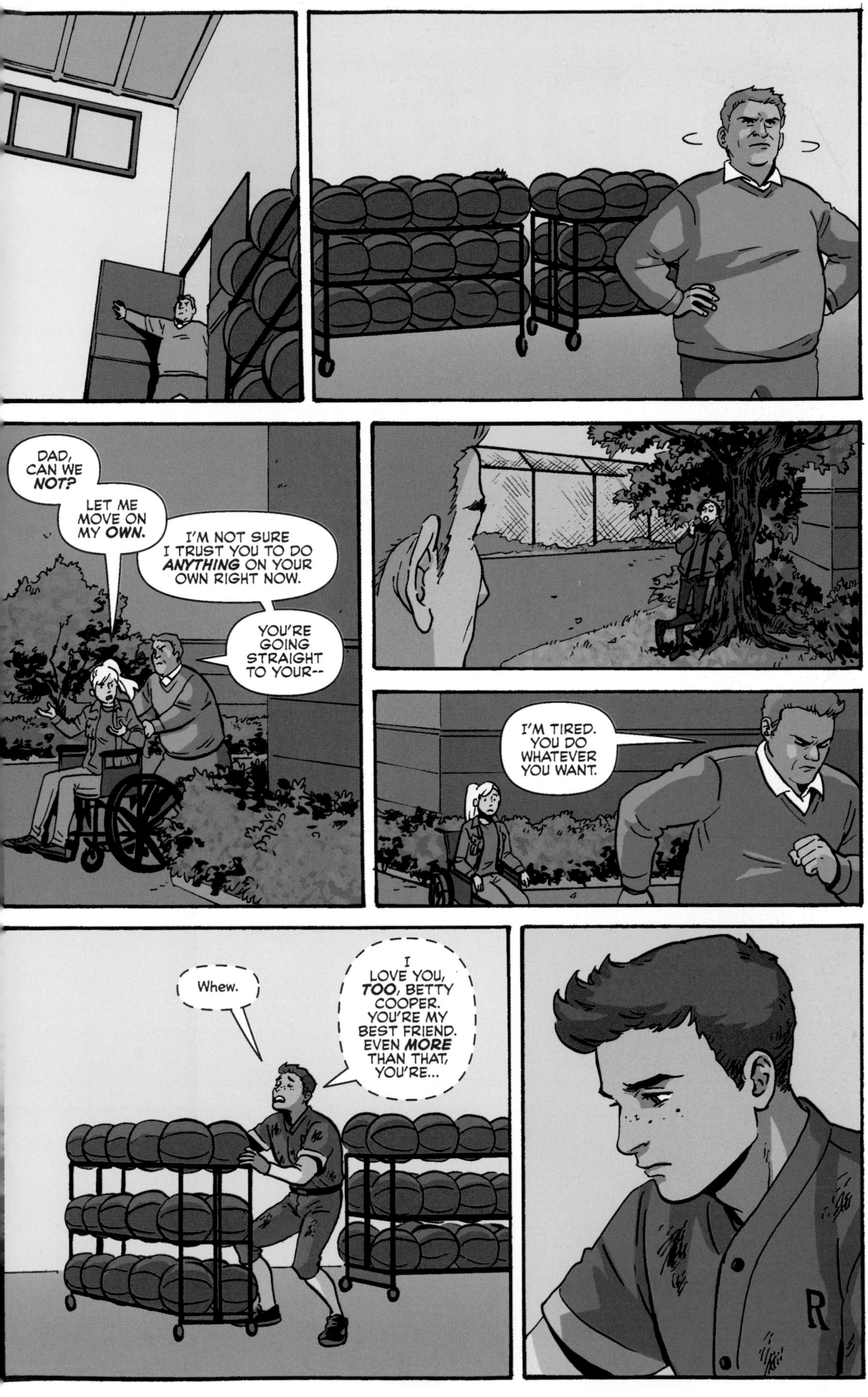
DAD, CAN WE NOT?
LET ME MOVE ON MY OWN.
I'M NOT SURE I TRUST YOU TO DO ANYTHING ON YOUR OWN RIGHT NOW.
YOU'RE GOING STRAIGHT TO YOUR--
I'M TIRED. YOU DO WHATEVER YOU WANT.
Whew.
I LOVE YOU, TOO, BETTY COOPER. YOU'RE MY BEST FRIEND. EVEN MORE THAN THAT, YOU'RE...
R

CHAPTER TWO: The Dilton Zone

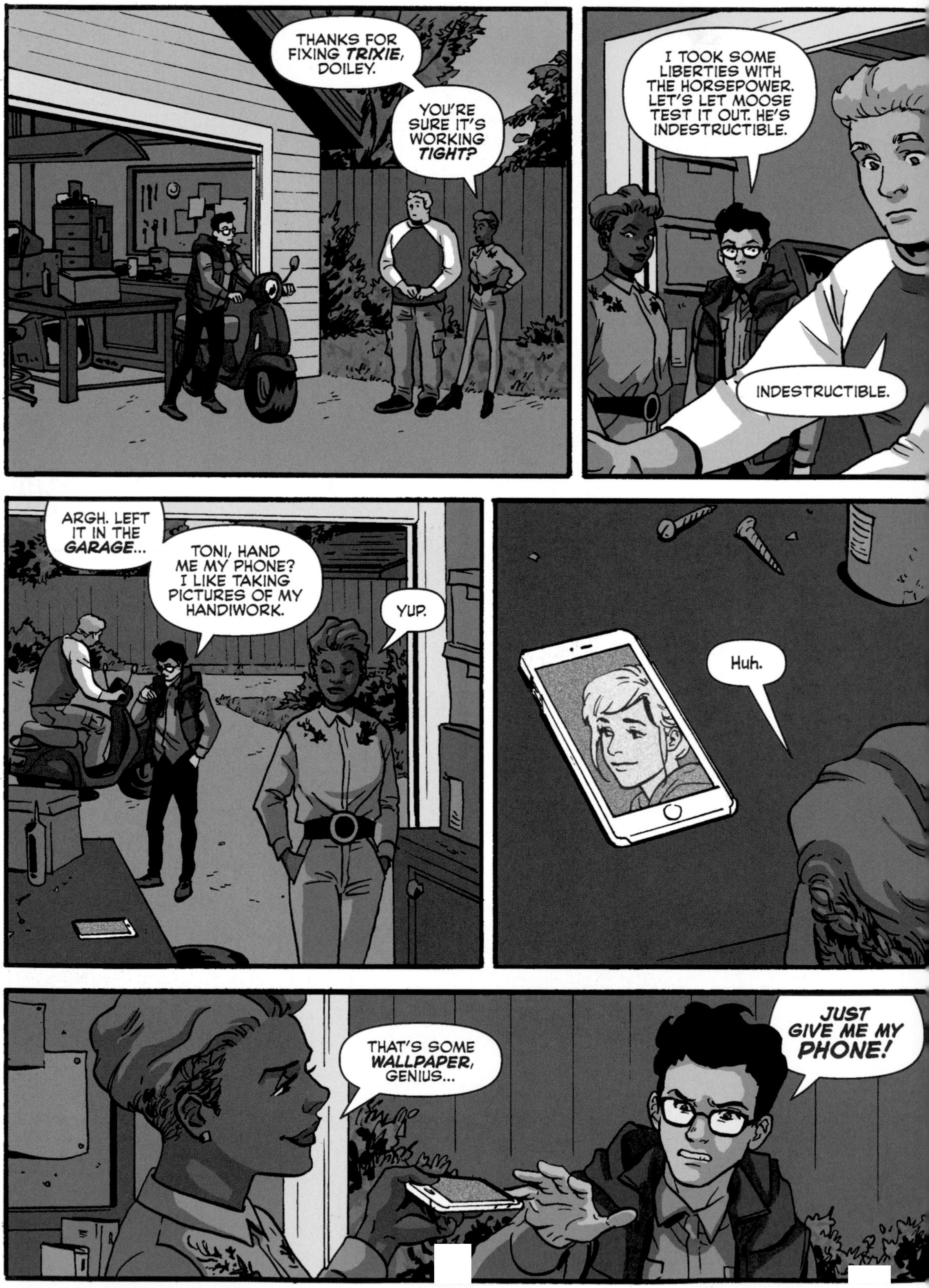
THANKS FOR FIXING *TRIXIE*, DOILEY.
YOU'RE SURE IT'S WORKING *TIGHT?*
I TOOK SOME LIBERTIES WITH THE HORSEPOWER. LET'S LET MOOSE TEST IT OUT. HE'S INDESTRUCTIBLE.
INDESTRUCTIBLE.
ARGH. LEFT IT IN THE *GARAGE*...
TONI, HAND ME MY PHONE? I LIKE TAKING PICTURES OF MY HANDIWORK.
YUP.
Huh.
THAT'S SOME *WALLPAPER*, GENIUS...
JUST GIVE ME MY PHONE!

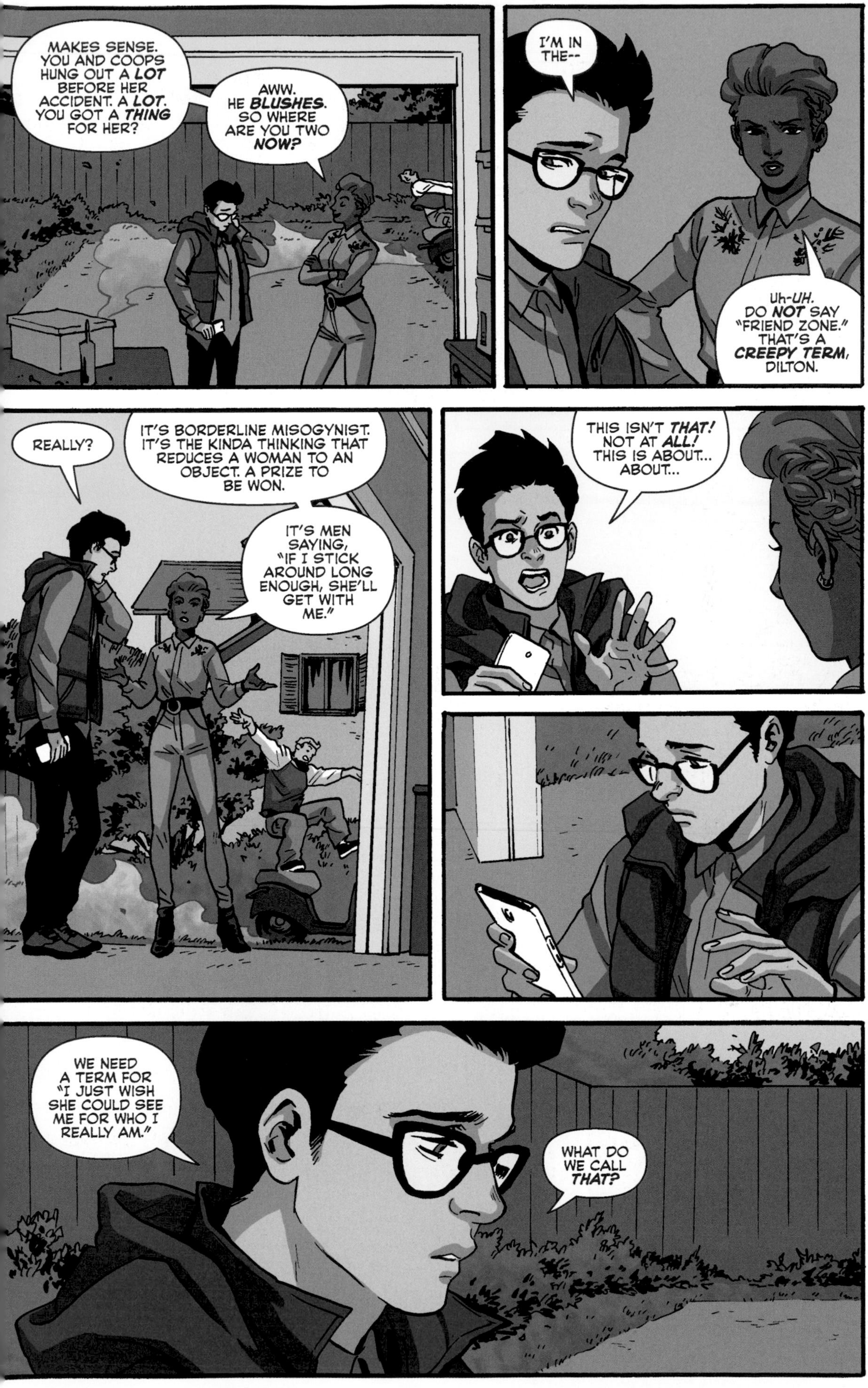
MAKES SENSE. YOU AND COOPS HUNG OUT A LOT BEFORE HER ACCIDENT. A LOT. YOU GOT A THING FOR HER?
AWW. HE BLUSHES. SO WHERE ARE YOU TWO NOW?
I'M IN THE--
Uh-UH. DO NOT SAY "FRIEND ZONE." THAT'S A CREEPY TERM, DILTON.
REALLY?
IT'S BORDERLINE MISOGYNIST. IT'S THE KINDA THINKING THAT REDUCES A WOMAN TO AN OBJECT. A PRIZE TO BE WON.
IT'S MEN SAYING, "IF I STICK AROUND LONG ENOUGH, SHE'LL GET WITH ME."
THIS ISN'T THAT! NOT AT ALL! THIS IS ABOUT... ABOUT...
WE NEED A TERM FOR "I JUST WISH SHE COULD SEE ME FOR WHO I REALLY AM."
WHAT DO WE CALL THAT?

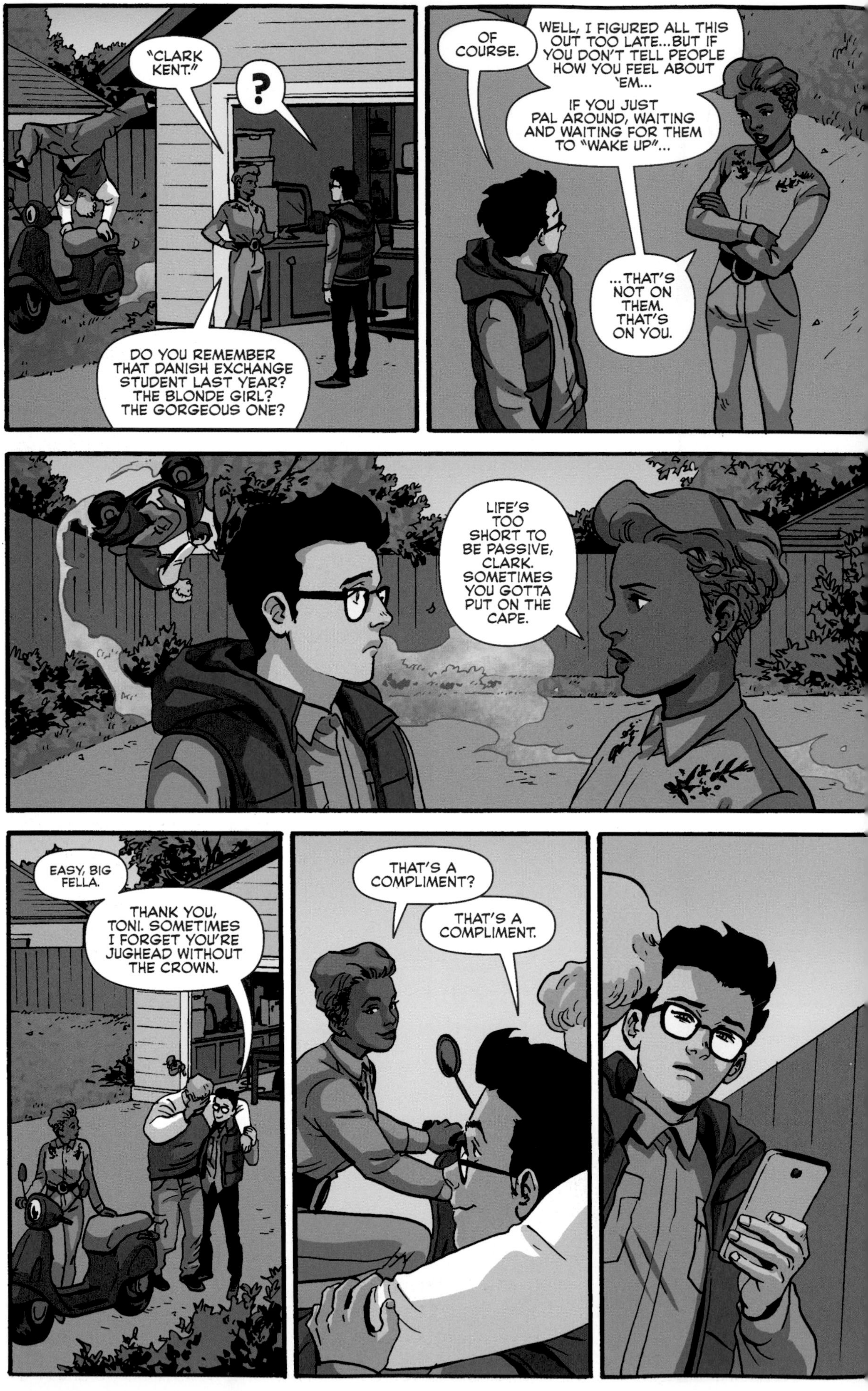
"CLARK KENT."
?
DO YOU REMEMBER THAT DANISH EXCHANGE STUDENT LAST YEAR? THE BLONDE GIRL? THE GORGEOUS ONE?
OF COURSE.
WELL, I FIGURED ALL THIS OUT TOO LATE...BUT IF YOU DON'T TELL PEOPLE HOW YOU FEEL ABOUT 'EM...
IF YOU JUST PAL AROUND, WAITING AND WAITING FOR THEM TO "WAKE UP"...
...THAT'S NOT ON THEM. THAT'S ON YOU.
LIFE'S TOO SHORT TO BE PASSIVE, CLARK. SOMETIMES YOU GOTTA PUT ON THE CAPE.
EASY, BIG FELLA.
THANK YOU, TONI. SOMETIMES I FORGET YOU'RE JUGHEAD WITHOUT THE CROWN.
THAT'S A COMPLIMENT?
THAT'S A COMPLIMENT.

CHAPTER THREE: EVERY TIME

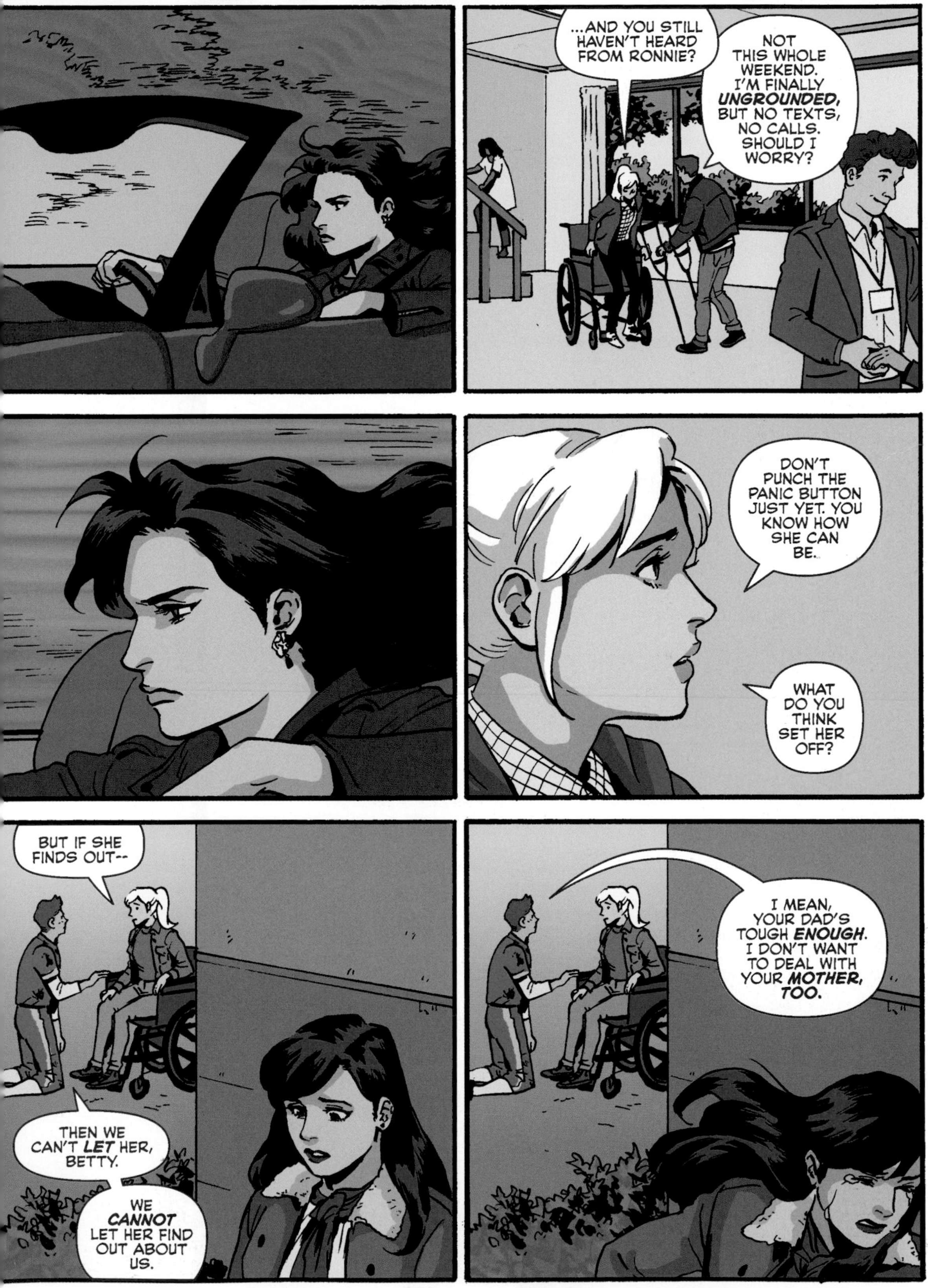
...AND YOU STILL HAVEN'T HEARD FROM RONNIE?
NOT THIS WHOLE WEEKEND. I'M FINALLY UNGROUNDED, BUT NO TEXTS, NO CALLS. SHOULD I WORRY?
DON'T PUNCH THE PANIC BUTTON JUST YET. YOU KNOW HOW SHE CAN BE.
WHAT DO YOU THINK SET HER OFF?
BUT IF SHE FINDS OUT--
THEN WE CAN'T LET HER, BETTY.
WE CANNOT LET HER FIND OUT ABOUT US.
I MEAN, YOUR DAD'S TOUGH ENOUGH. I DON'T WANT TO DEAL WITH YOUR MOTHER, TOO.

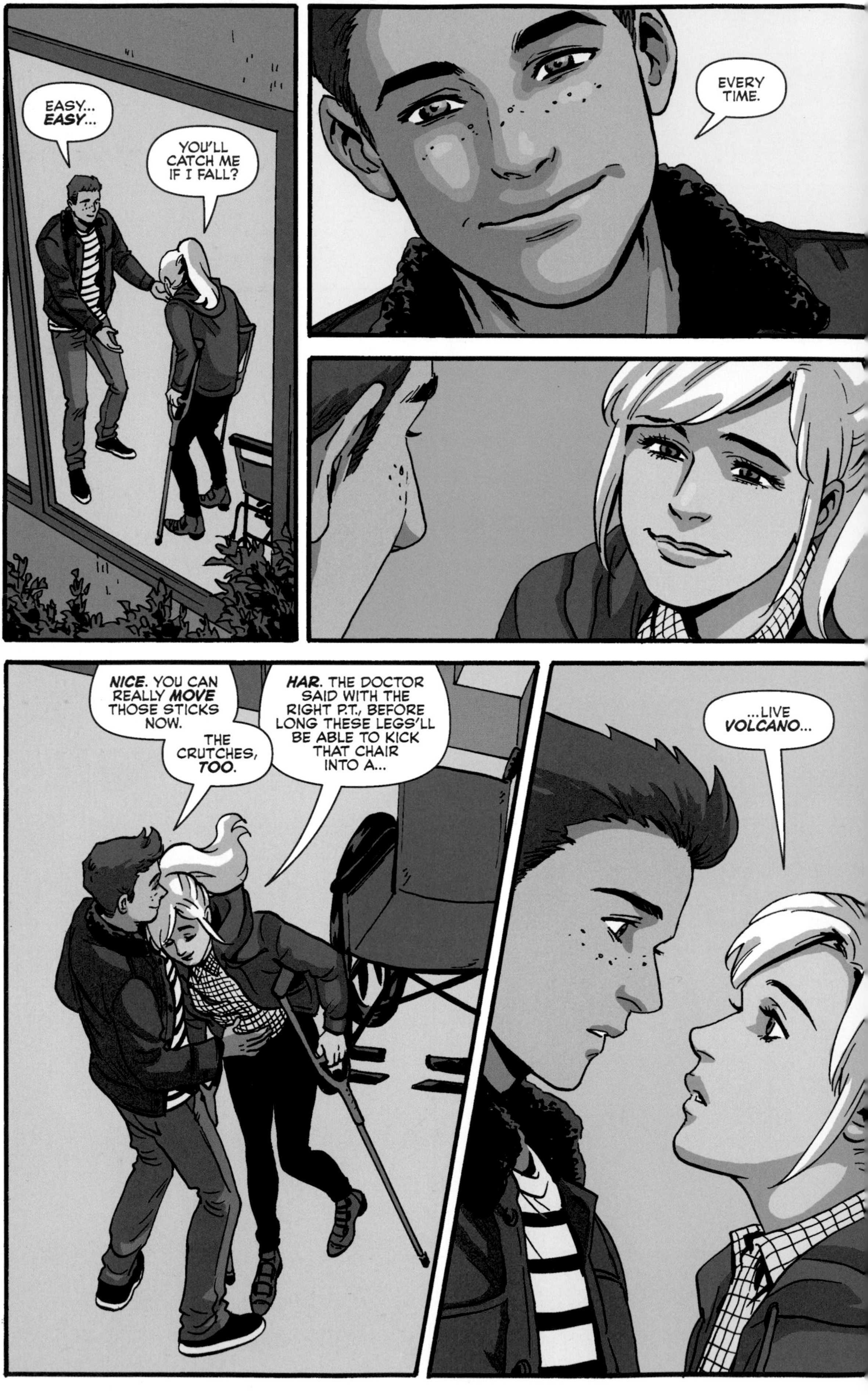

EASY... EASY...
YOU'LL CATCH ME IF I FALL?
EVERY TIME.
NICE. YOU CAN REALLY MOVE THOSE STICKS NOW.
THE CRUTCHES, TOO.
HAR. THE DOCTOR SAID WITH THE RIGHT P.T., BEFORE LONG THESE LEGS'LL BE ABLE TO KICK THAT CHAIR INTO A...
...LIVE VOLCANO...

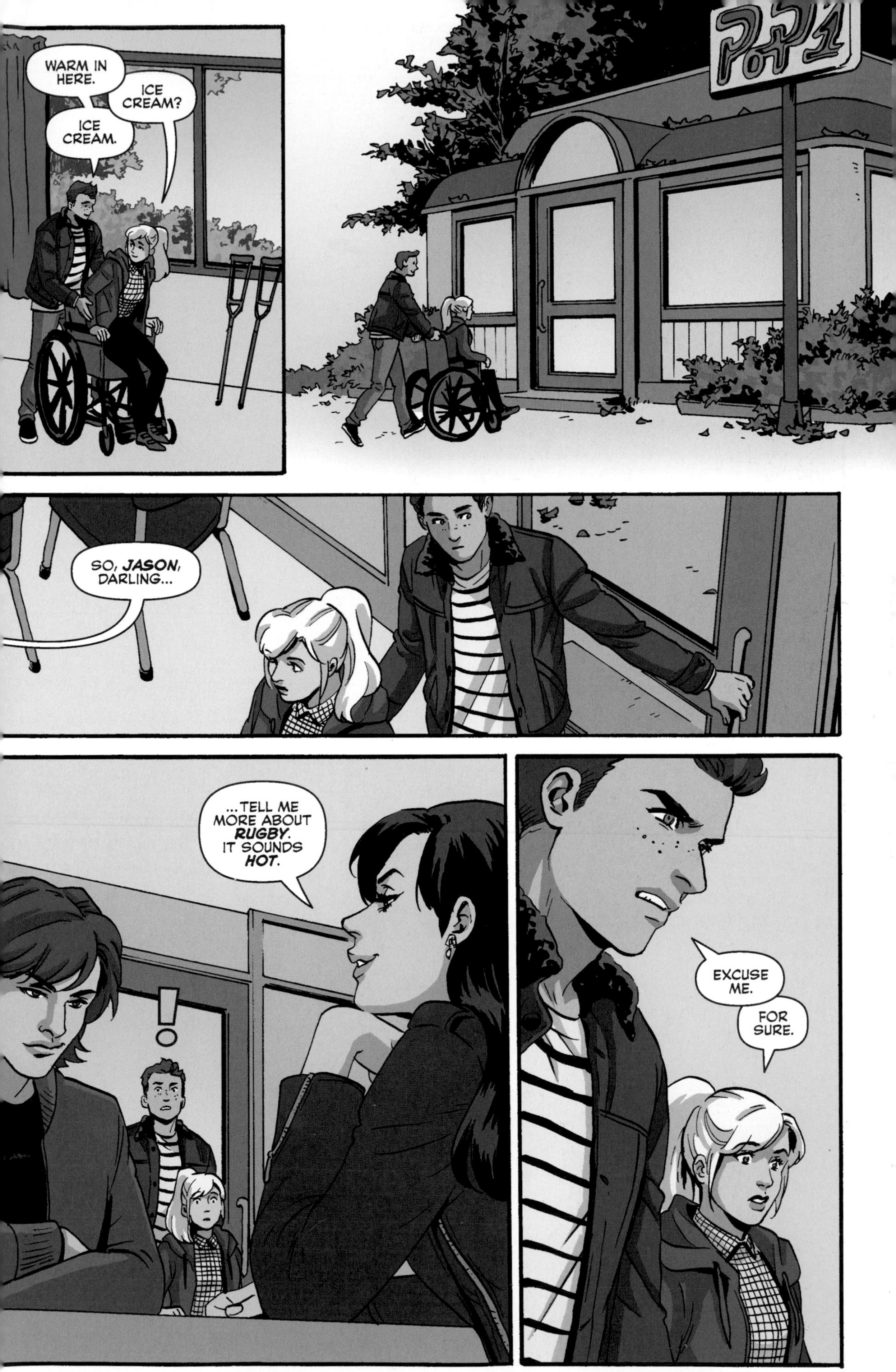
WARM IN HERE.
ICE CREAM?
ICE CREAM.
Pop's
SO, JASON, DARLING...
...TELL ME MORE ABOUT RUGBY. IT SOUNDS HOT.
!
EXCUSE ME.
FOR SURE.

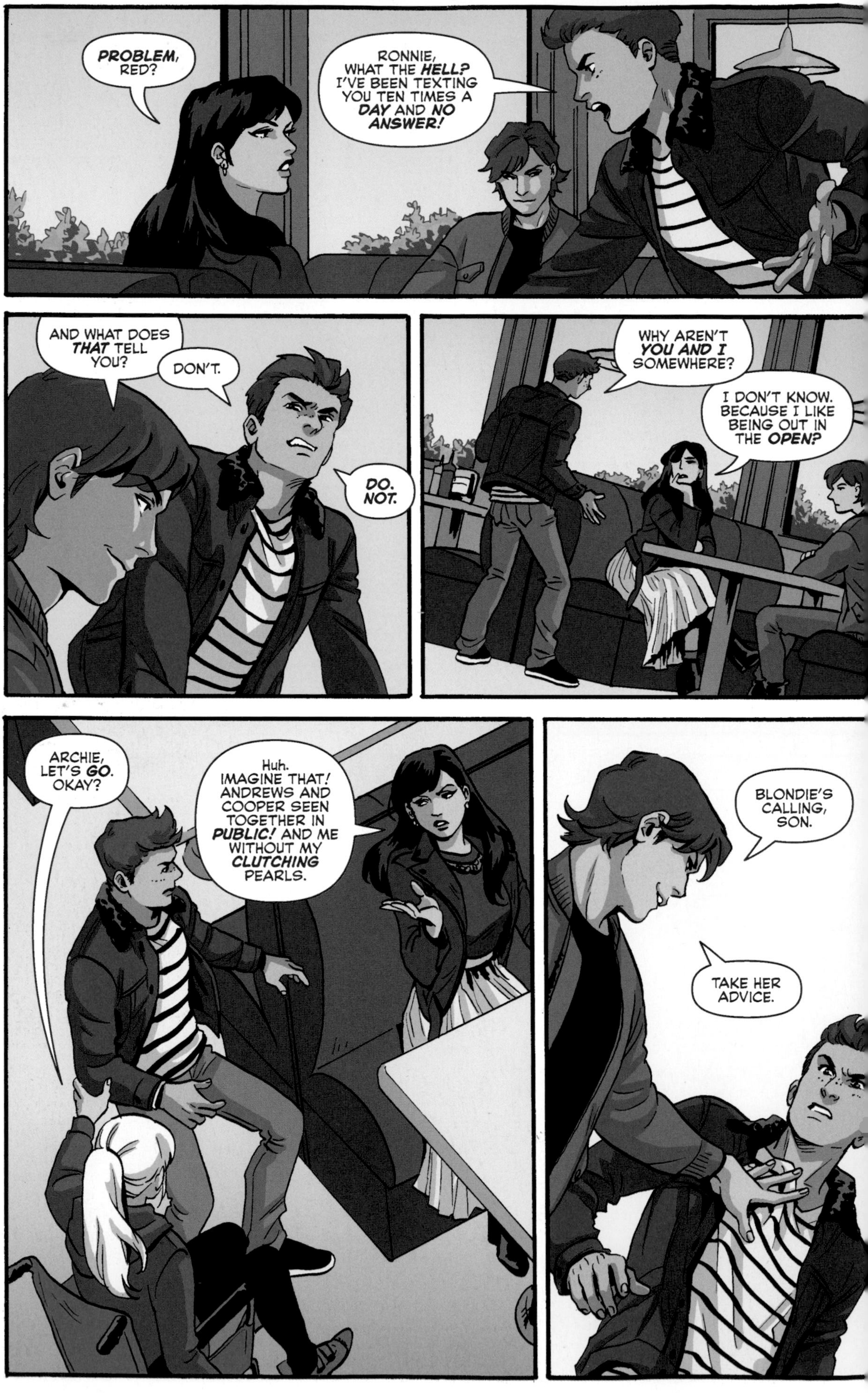
PROBLEM, RED?
RONNIE, WHAT THE HELL? I'VE BEEN TEXTING YOU TEN TIMES A DAY AND NO ANSWER!
AND WHAT DOES THAT TELL YOU?
DON'T.
DO. NOT.
WHY AREN'T YOU AND I SOMEWHERE?
I DON'T KNOW. BECAUSE I LIKE BEING OUT IN THE OPEN?
ARCHIE, LET'S GO. OKAY?
Huh. IMAGINE THAT! ANDREWS AND COOPER SEEN TOGETHER IN PUBLIC! AND ME WITHOUT MY CLUTCHING PEARLS.
BLONDIE'S CALLING, SON.
TAKE HER ADVICE.

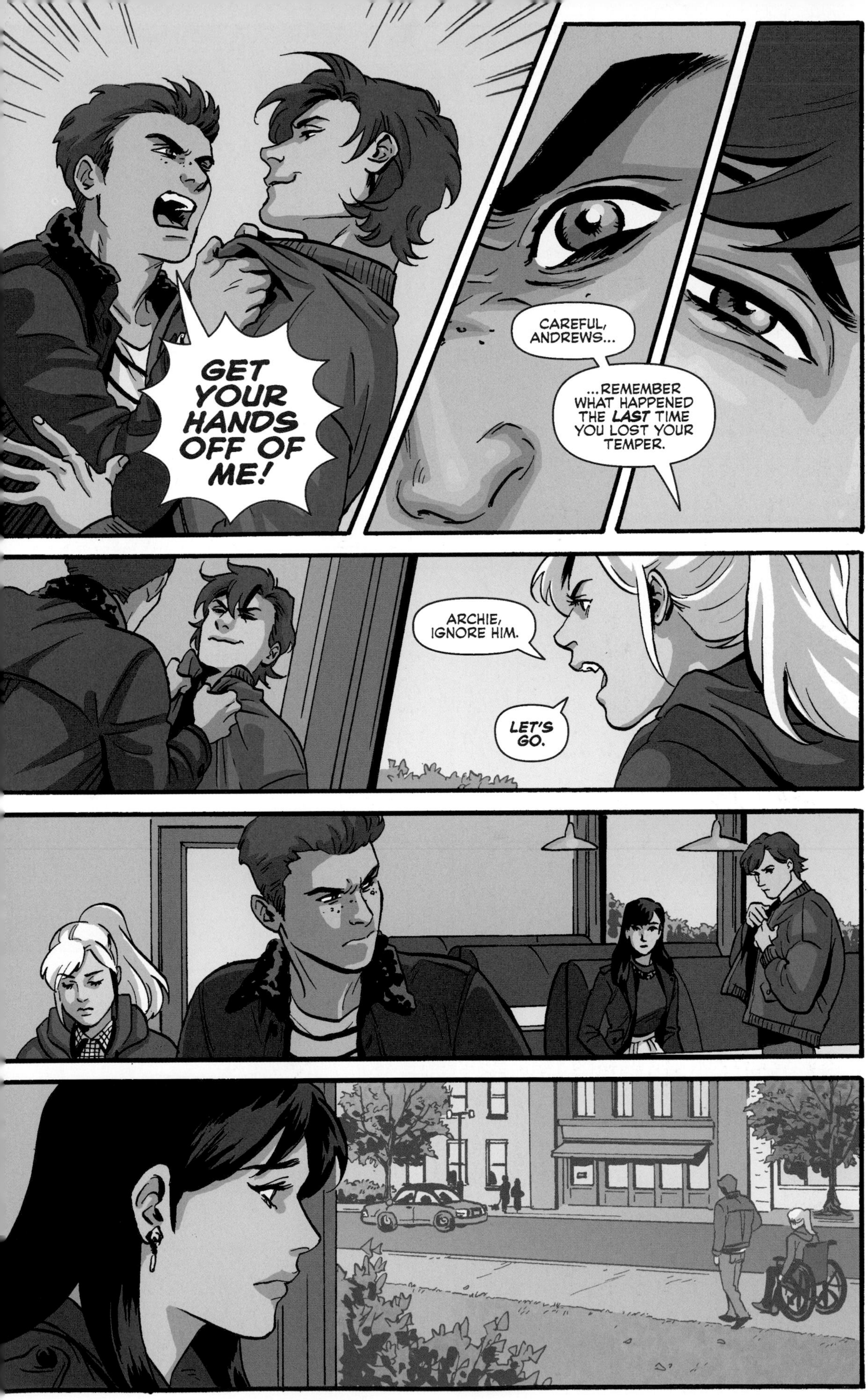
GET YOUR HANDS OFF OF ME!
CAREFUL, ANDREWS...
...REMEMBER WHAT HAPPENED THE LAST TIME YOU LOST YOUR TEMPER.
ARCHIE, IGNORE HIM.
LET'S GO.

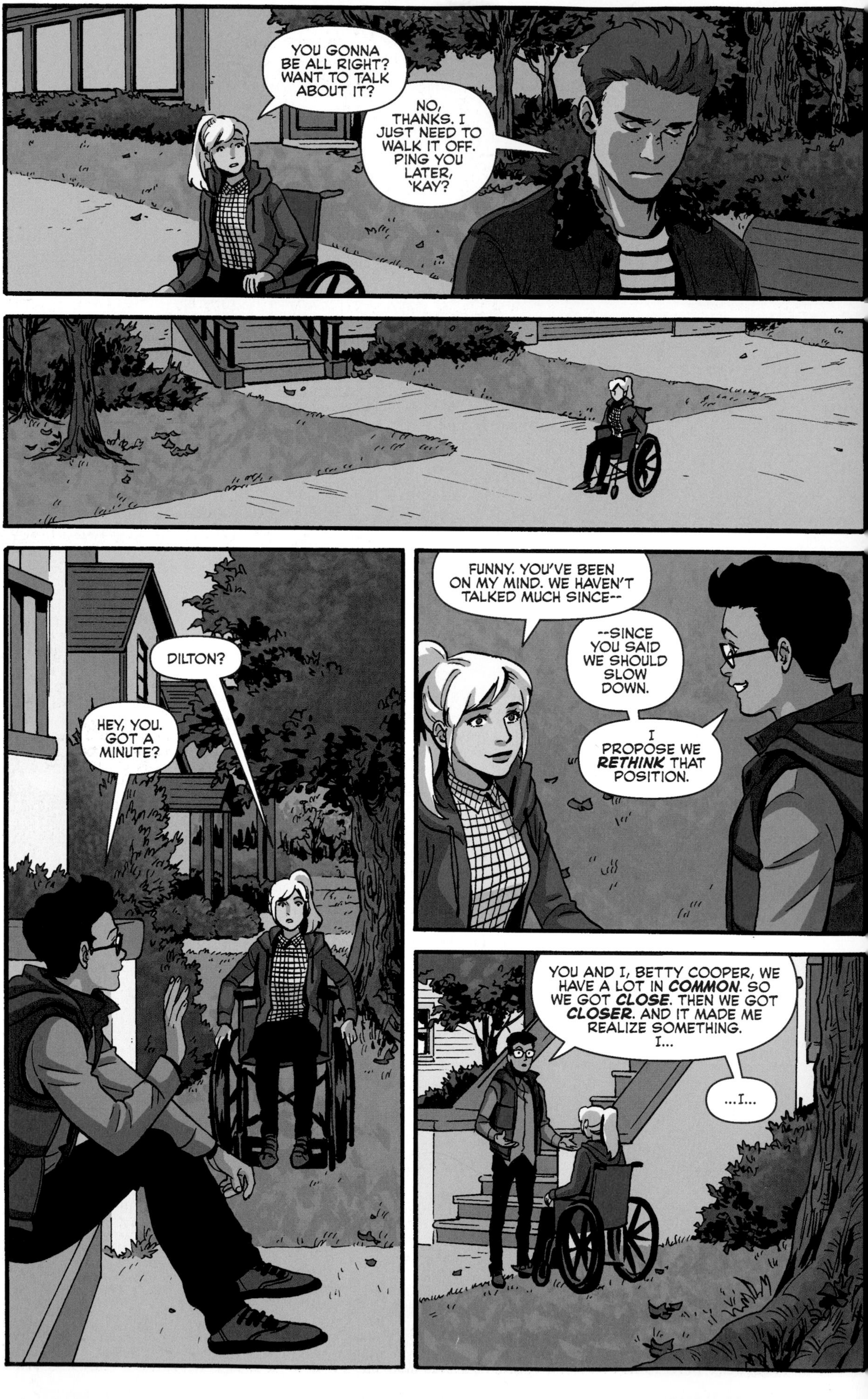
YOU GONNA BE ALL RIGHT? WANT TO TALK ABOUT IT?
NO, THANKS. I JUST NEED TO WALK IT OFF. PING YOU LATER, 'KAY?
DILTON?
HEY, YOU. GOT A MINUTE?
FUNNY. YOU'VE BEEN ON MY MIND. WE HAVEN'T TALKED MUCH SINCE--
--SINCE YOU SAID WE SHOULD SLOW DOWN.
I PROPOSE WE ***RETHINK*** THAT POSITION.
YOU AND I, BETTY COOPER, WE HAVE A LOT IN ***COMMON***. SO WE GOT ***CLOSE***. THEN WE GOT ***CLOSER***. AND IT MADE ME REALIZE SOMETHING. I...
...I...

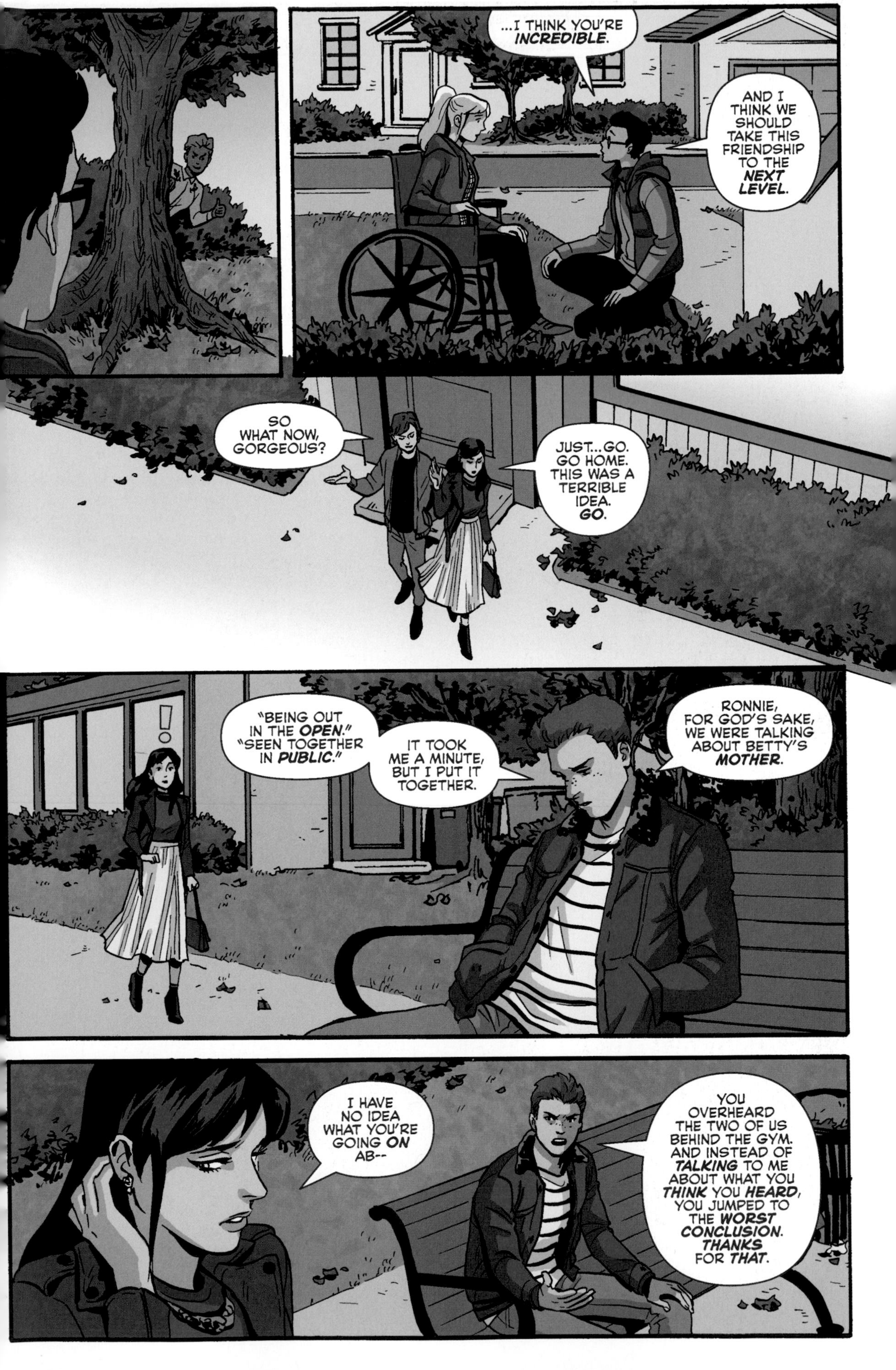
...I THINK YOU'RE INCREDIBLE.
AND I THINK WE SHOULD TAKE THIS FRIENDSHIP TO THE NEXT LEVEL.
SO WHAT NOW, GORGEOUS?
JUST...GO. GO HOME. THIS WAS A TERRIBLE IDEA. GO.
!
"BEING OUT IN THE OPEN." "SEEN TOGETHER IN PUBLIC."
IT TOOK ME A MINUTE, BUT I PUT IT TOGETHER.
RONNIE, FOR GOD'S SAKE, WE WERE TALKING ABOUT BETTY'S MOTHER.
I HAVE NO IDEA WHAT YOU'RE GOING ON AB--
YOU OVERHEARD THE TWO OF US BEHIND THE GYM. AND INSTEAD OF TALKING TO ME ABOUT WHAT YOU THINK YOU HEARD, YOU JUMPED TO THE WORST CONCLUSION. THANKS FOR THAT.

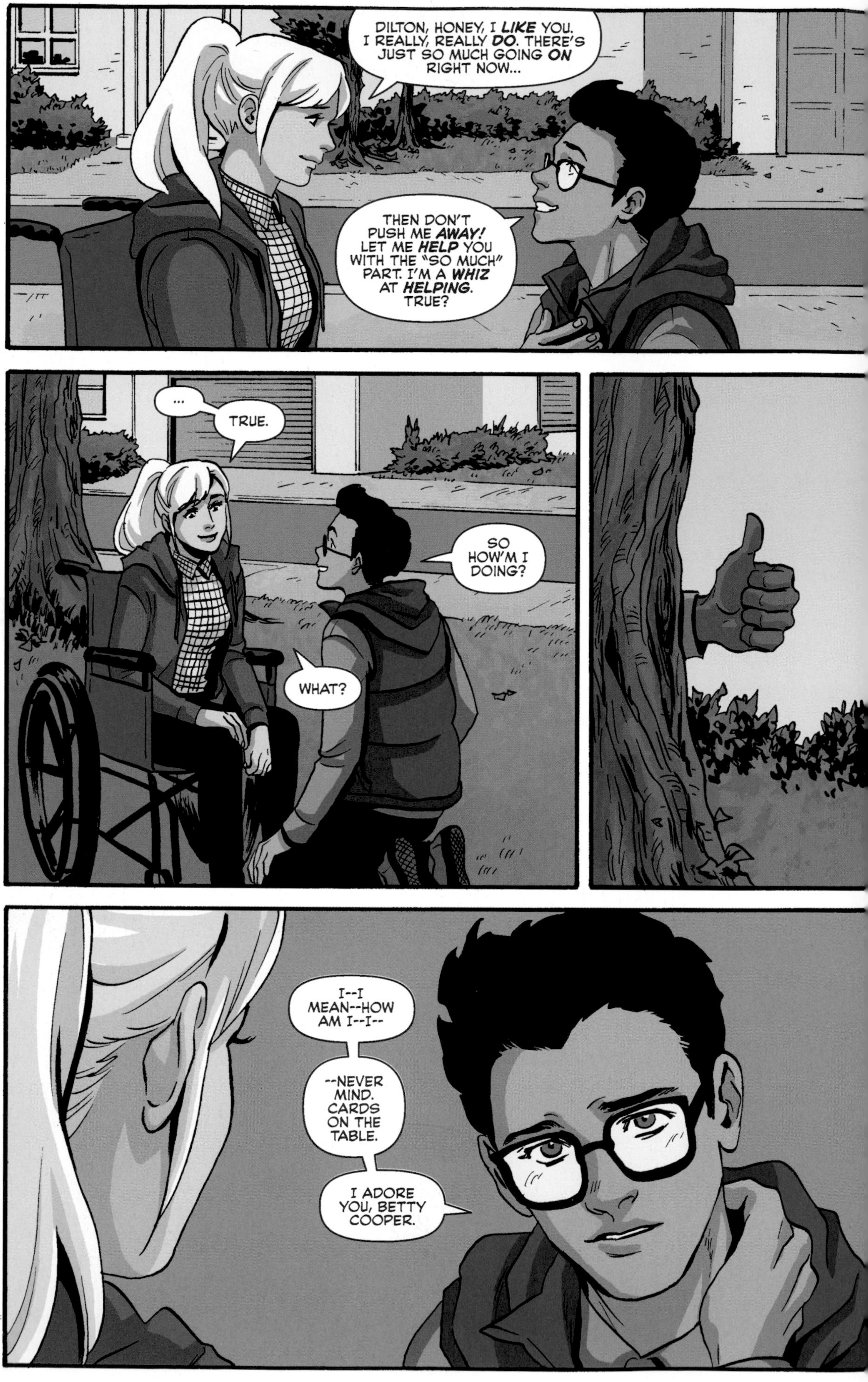
DILTON, HONEY, I LIKE YOU. I REALLY, REALLY DO. THERE'S JUST SO MUCH GOING ON RIGHT NOW...
THEN DON'T PUSH ME AWAY! LET ME HELP YOU WITH THE "SO MUCH" PART. I'M A WHIZ AT HELPING. TRUE?
...
TRUE.
SO HOW'M I DOING?
WHAT?
I--I MEAN--HOW AM I--I--
--NEVER MIND. CARDS ON THE TABLE.
I ADORE YOU, BETTY COOPER.

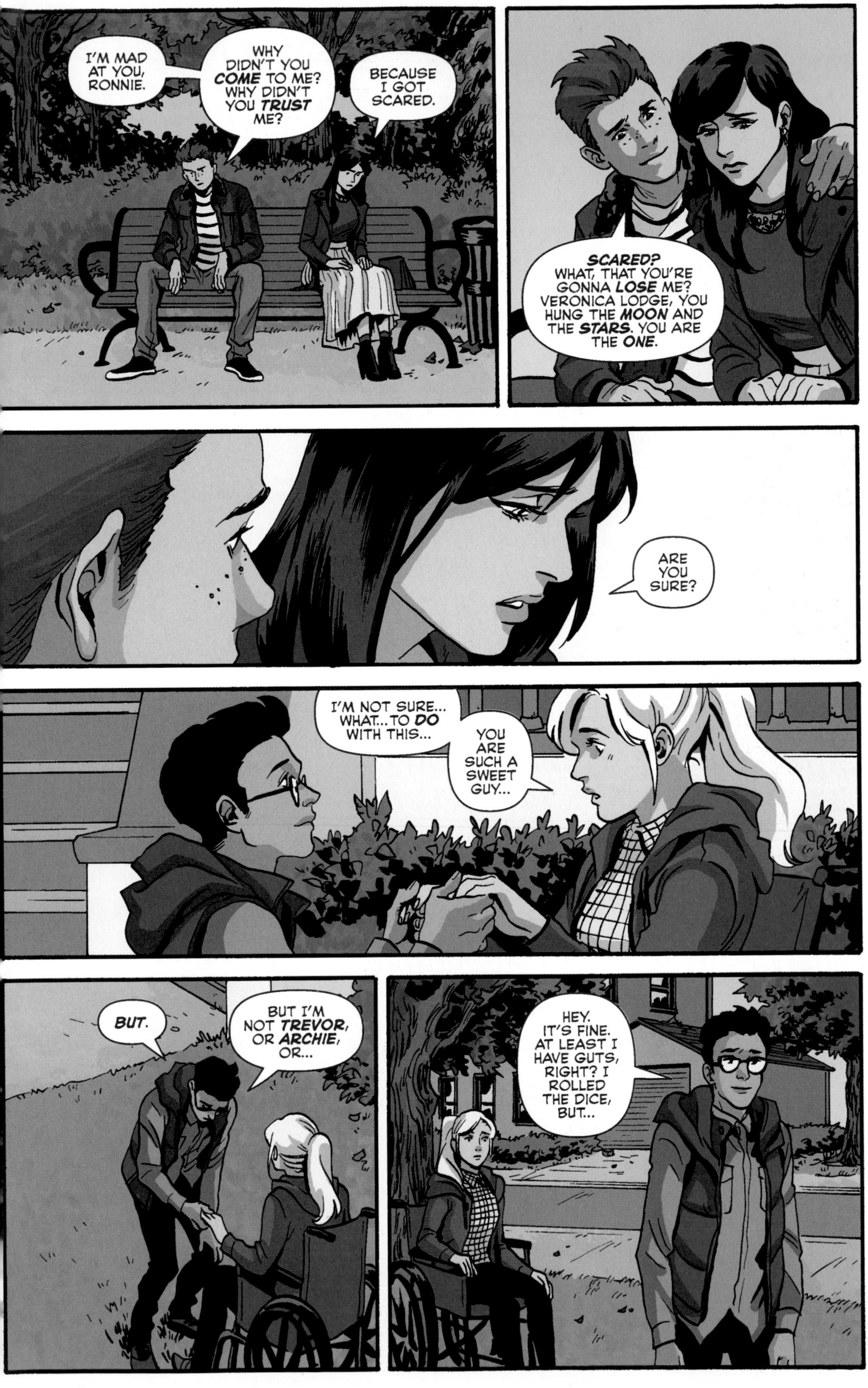
I'M MAD AT YOU, RONNIE.
WHY DIDN'T YOU COME TO ME? WHY DIDN'T YOU TRUST ME?
BECAUSE I GOT SCARED.
SCARED? WHAT, THAT YOU'RE GONNA LOSE ME? VERONICA LODGE, YOU HUNG THE MOON AND THE STARS. YOU ARE THE ONE.
ARE YOU SURE?
I'M NOT SURE... WHAT...TO DO WITH THIS...
YOU ARE SUCH A SWEET GUY...
BUT.
BUT I'M NOT TREVOR, OR ARCHIE, OR...
HEY. IT'S FINE. AT LEAST I HAVE GUTS, RIGHT? I ROLLED THE DICE, BUT...

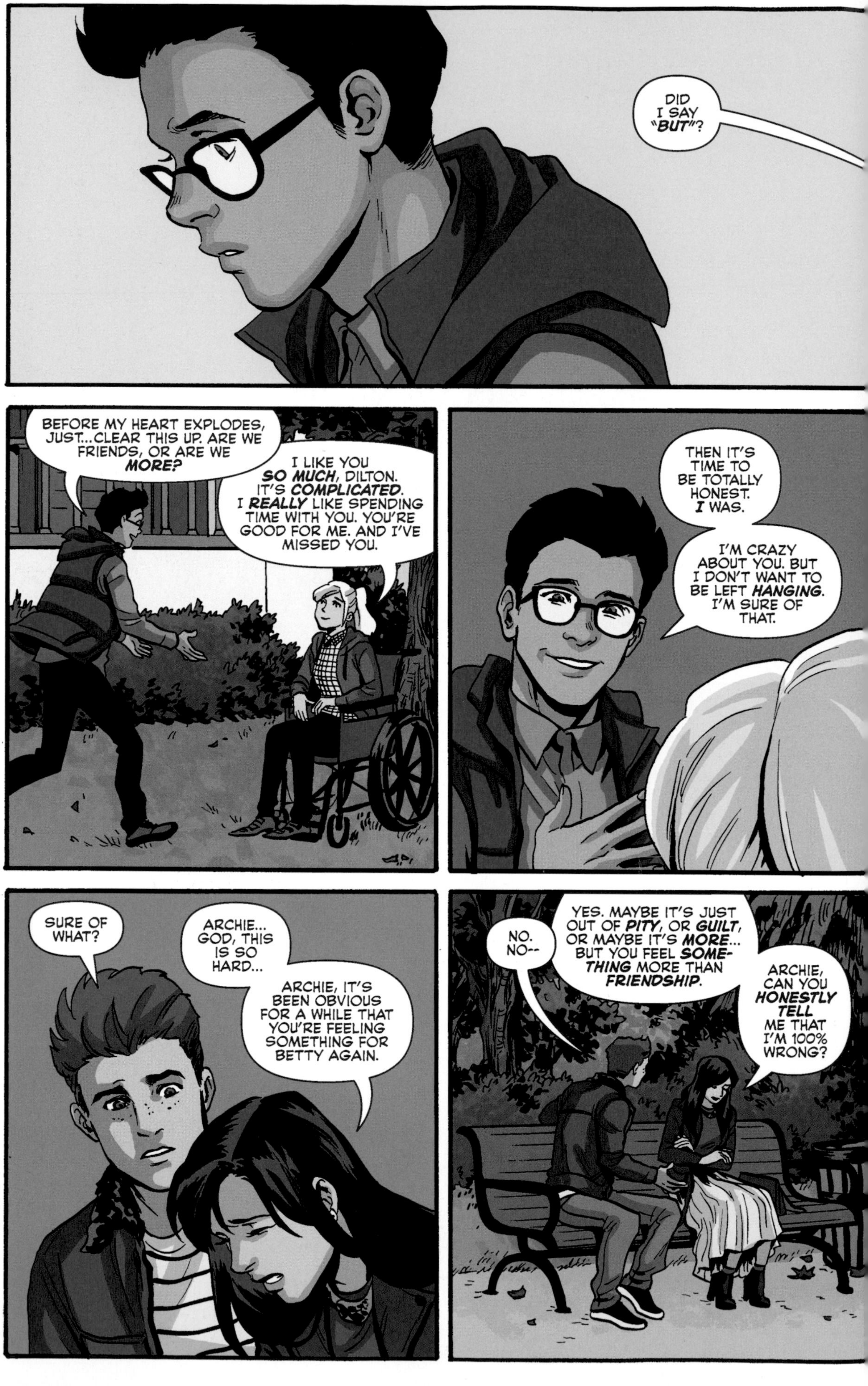
DID I SAY "BUT"?
BEFORE MY HEART EXPLODES, JUST...CLEAR THIS UP. ARE WE FRIENDS, OR ARE WE MORE?
I LIKE YOU SO MUCH, DILTON. IT'S COMPLICATED. I REALLY LIKE SPENDING TIME WITH YOU. YOU'RE GOOD FOR ME. AND I'VE MISSED YOU.
THEN IT'S TIME TO BE TOTALLY HONEST. I WAS.
I'M CRAZY ABOUT YOU. BUT I DON'T WANT TO BE LEFT HANGING. I'M SURE OF THAT.
SURE OF WHAT?
ARCHIE... GOD, THIS IS SO HARD...
ARCHIE, IT'S BEEN OBVIOUS FOR A WHILE THAT YOU'RE FEELING SOMETHING FOR BETTY AGAIN.
NO. NO--
YES. MAYBE IT'S JUST OUT OF PITY, OR GUILT, OR MAYBE IT'S MORE... BUT YOU FEEL SOMETHING MORE THAN FRIENDSHIP.
ARCHIE, CAN YOU HONESTLY TELL ME THAT I'M 100% WRONG?

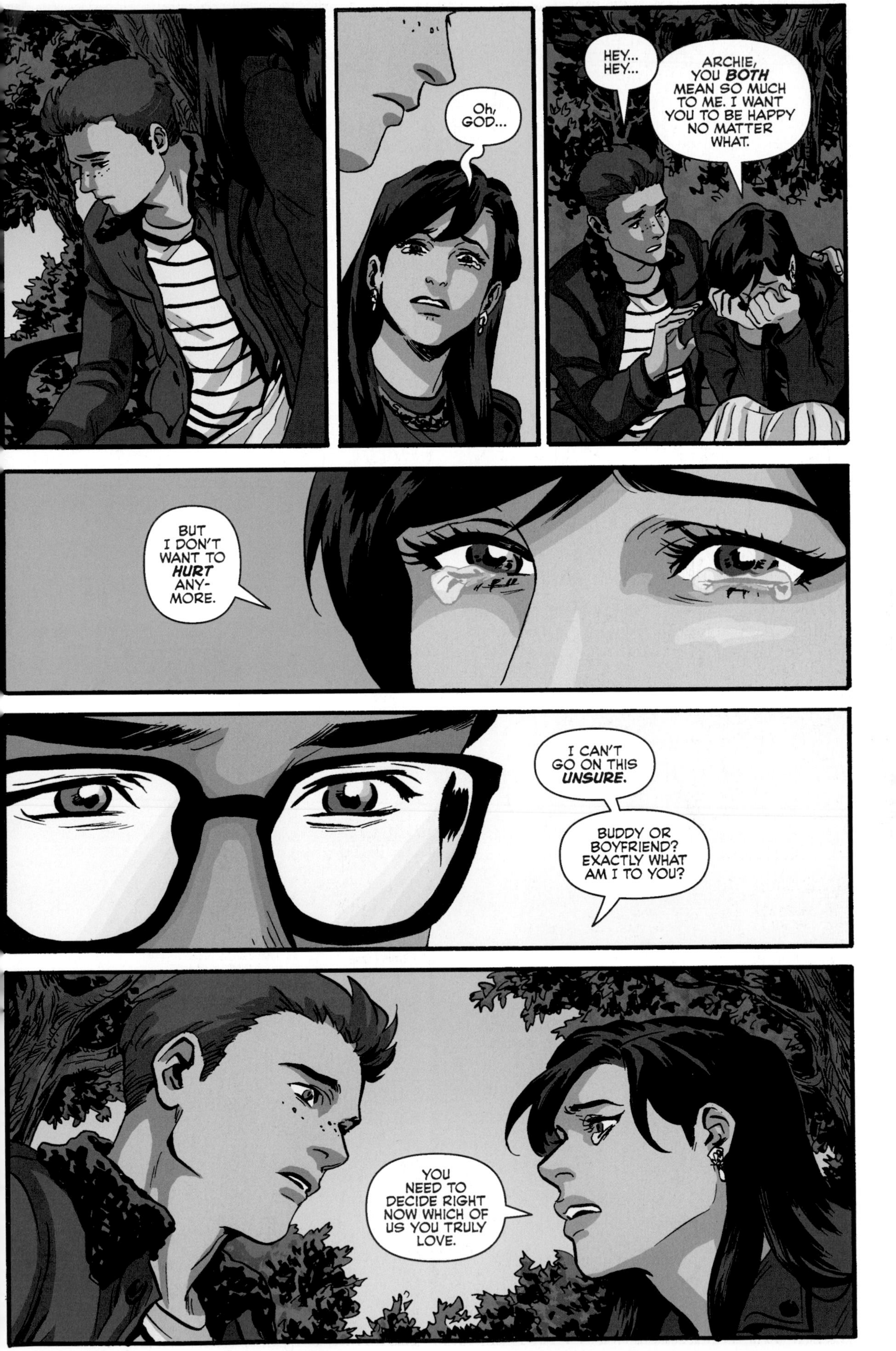
Oh, GOD...
HEY... HEY...
ARCHIE, YOU BOTH MEAN SO MUCH TO ME. I WANT YOU TO BE HAPPY NO MATTER WHAT.
BUT I DON'T WANT TO HURT ANY-MORE.
I CAN'T GO ON THIS UNSURE.
BUDDY OR BOYFRIEND? EXACTLY WHAT AM I TO YOU?
YOU NEED TO DECIDE RIGHT NOW WHICH OF US YOU TRULY LOVE.

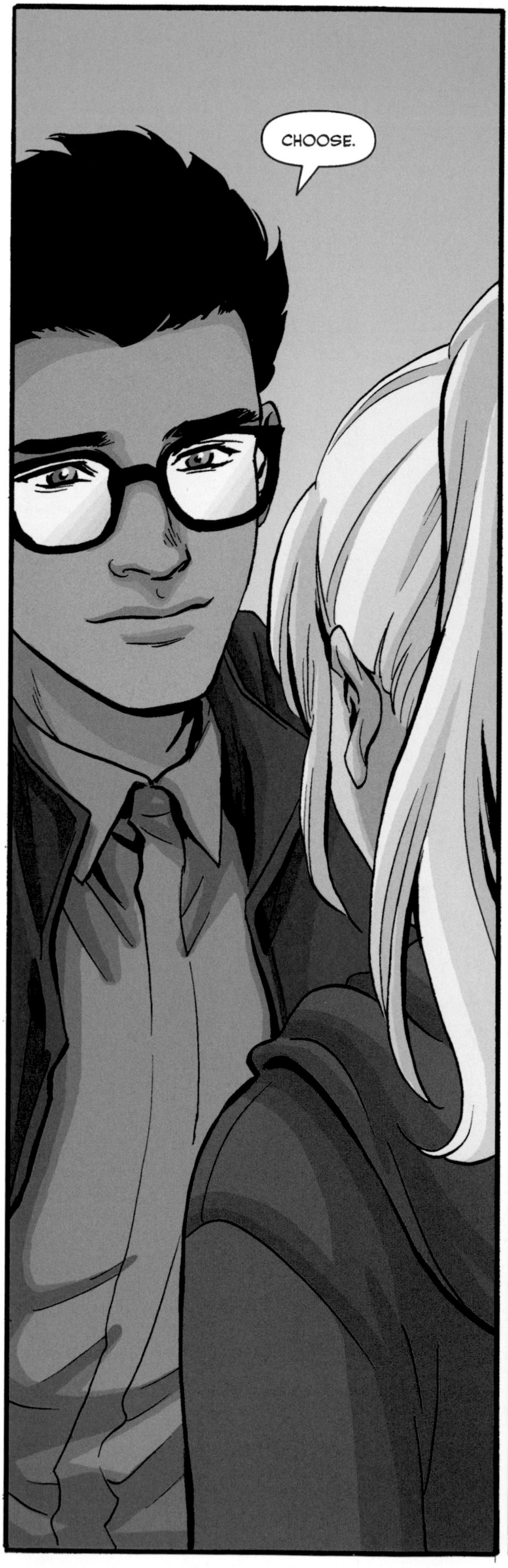
CHOOSE.
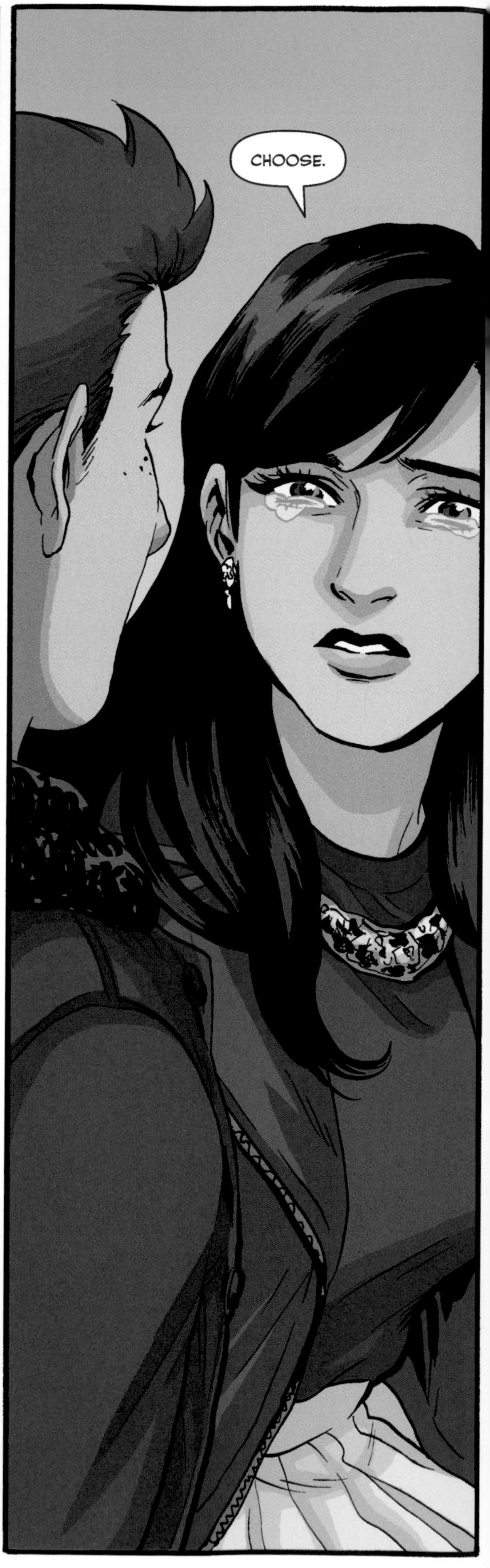
CHOOSE.

TO BE CONTINUED...

ISSUE TWENTY-SEVEN

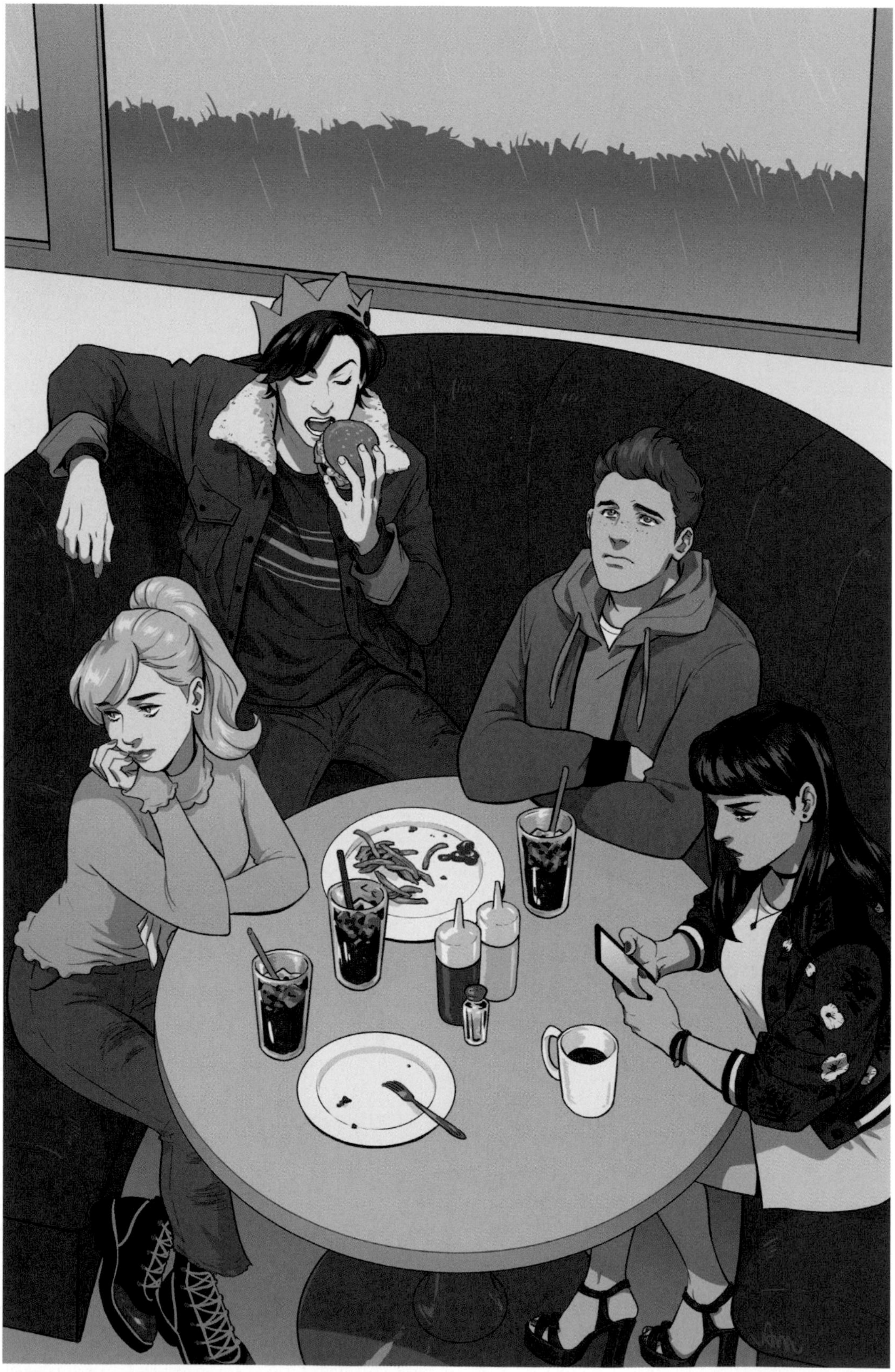

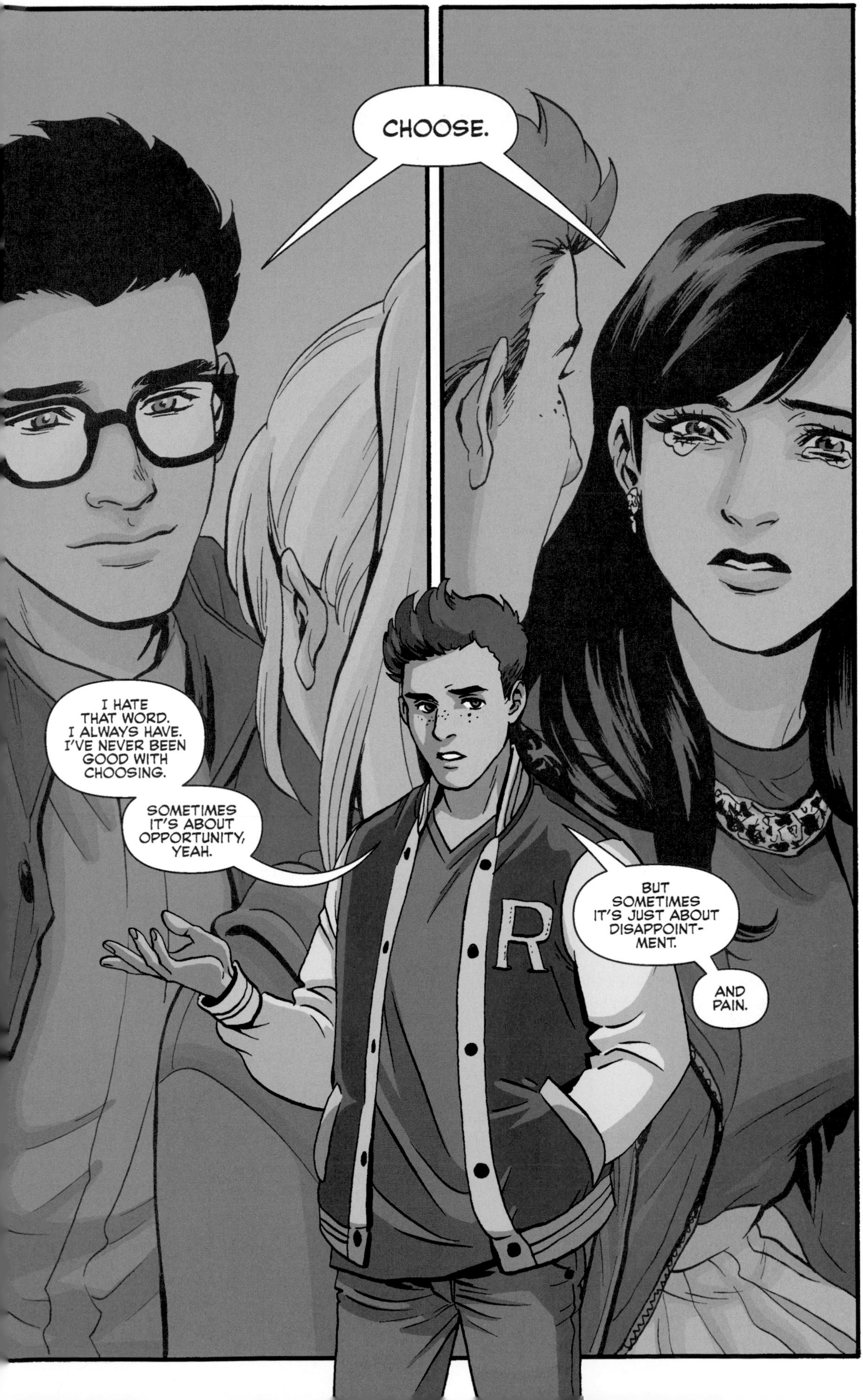
CHOOSE.
I HATE THAT WORD. I ALWAYS HAVE. I'VE NEVER BEEN GOOD WITH CHOOSING.
SOMETIMES IT'S ABOUT OPPORTUNITY, YEAH.
BUT SOMETIMES IT'S JUST ABOUT DISAPPOINT-MENT.
AND PAIN.

CHAPTER ONE: I BUILT A SPEED ◷ METER

VERONICA, HOP IN.

DADDY--

NOW. YOUR *PIANO TEACHER* GETS PAID WHETHER YOU'RE THERE OR *NOT*, AND I WON'T WASTE *MONEY. GET IN.*

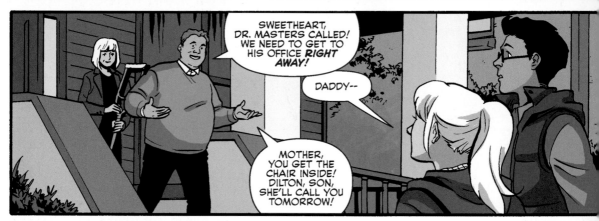

SWEETHEART, DR. MASTERS CALLED! WE NEED TO GET TO HIS OFFICE *RIGHT AWAY!*

DADDY--

MOTHER, YOU GET THE CHAIR INSIDE! DILTON, SON, SHE'LL CALL YOU TOMORROW!

RONNIE, WAIT! YOU *KNOW*, DON'T YOU? HOW I *FEEL?*

RONNIE?

WE'LL TALK TOMORROW, OKAY? COME BY AFTER SCHOOL IF I'M NOT THERE.

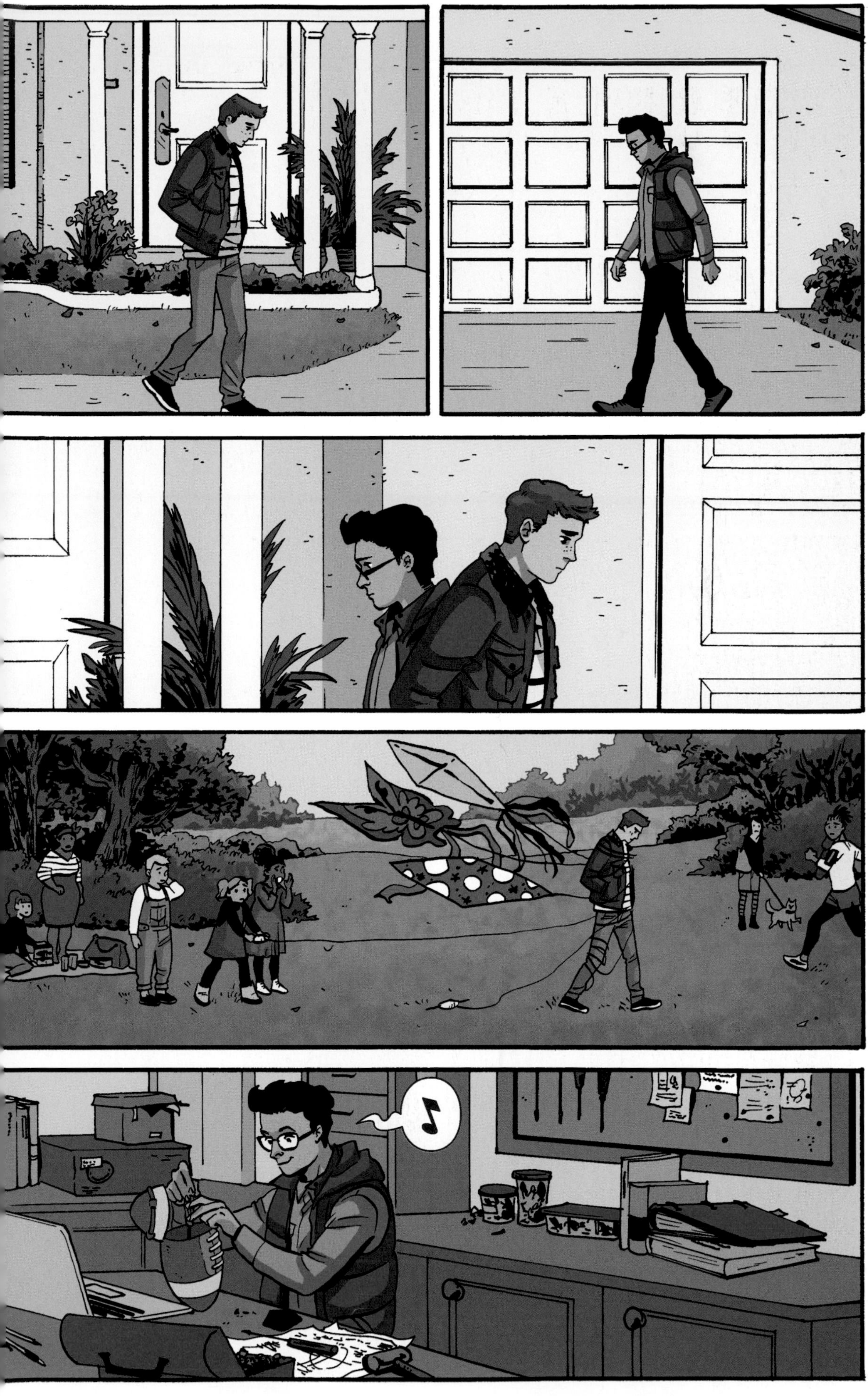

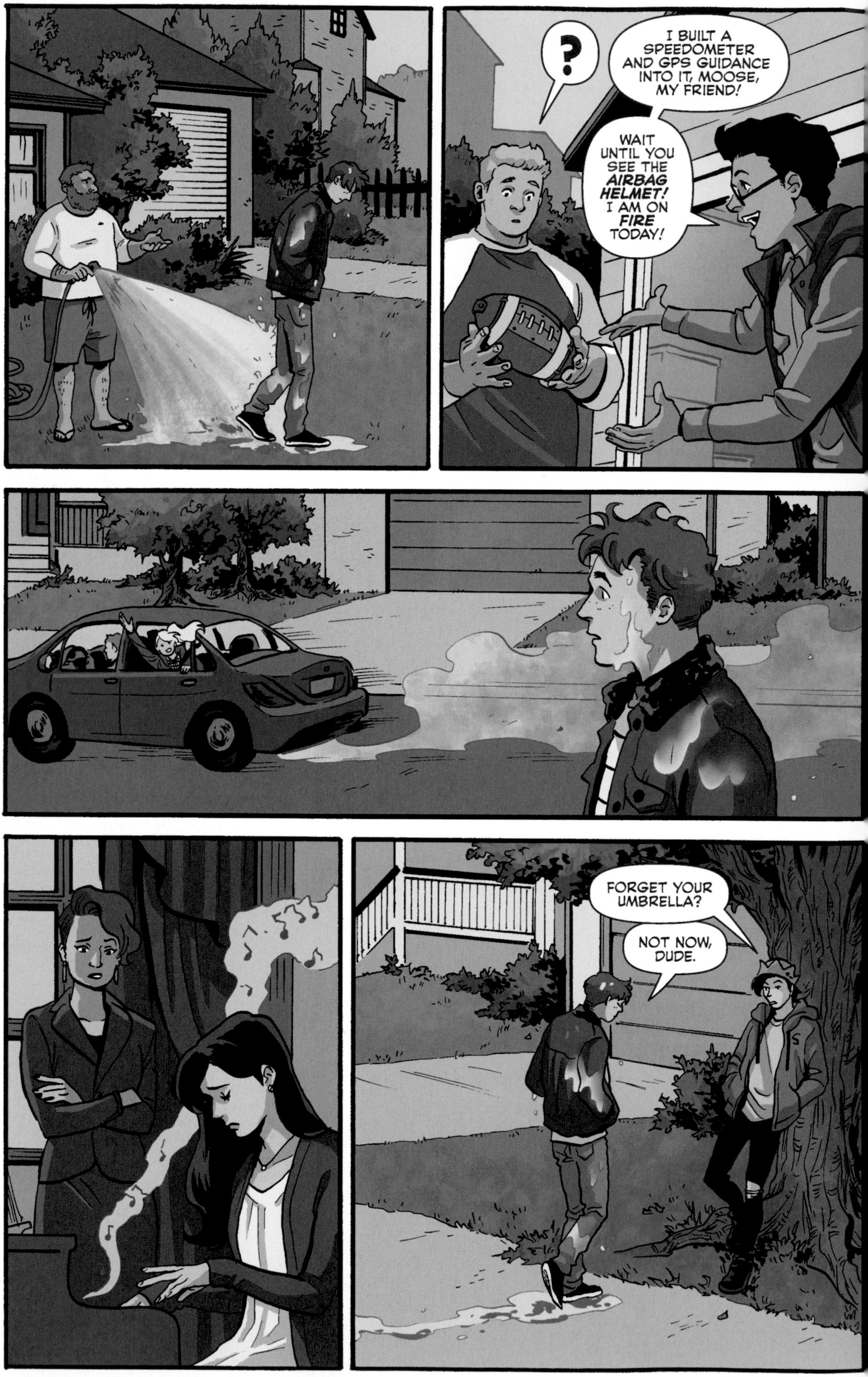
?
I BUILT A SPEEDOMETER AND GPS GUIDANCE INTO IT, MOOSE, MY FRIEND!
WAIT UNTIL YOU SEE THE AIRBAG HELMET! I AM ON FIRE TODAY!
FORGET YOUR UMBRELLA?
NOT NOW, DUDE.

CHAPTER TWO: DON'T GET COCKY

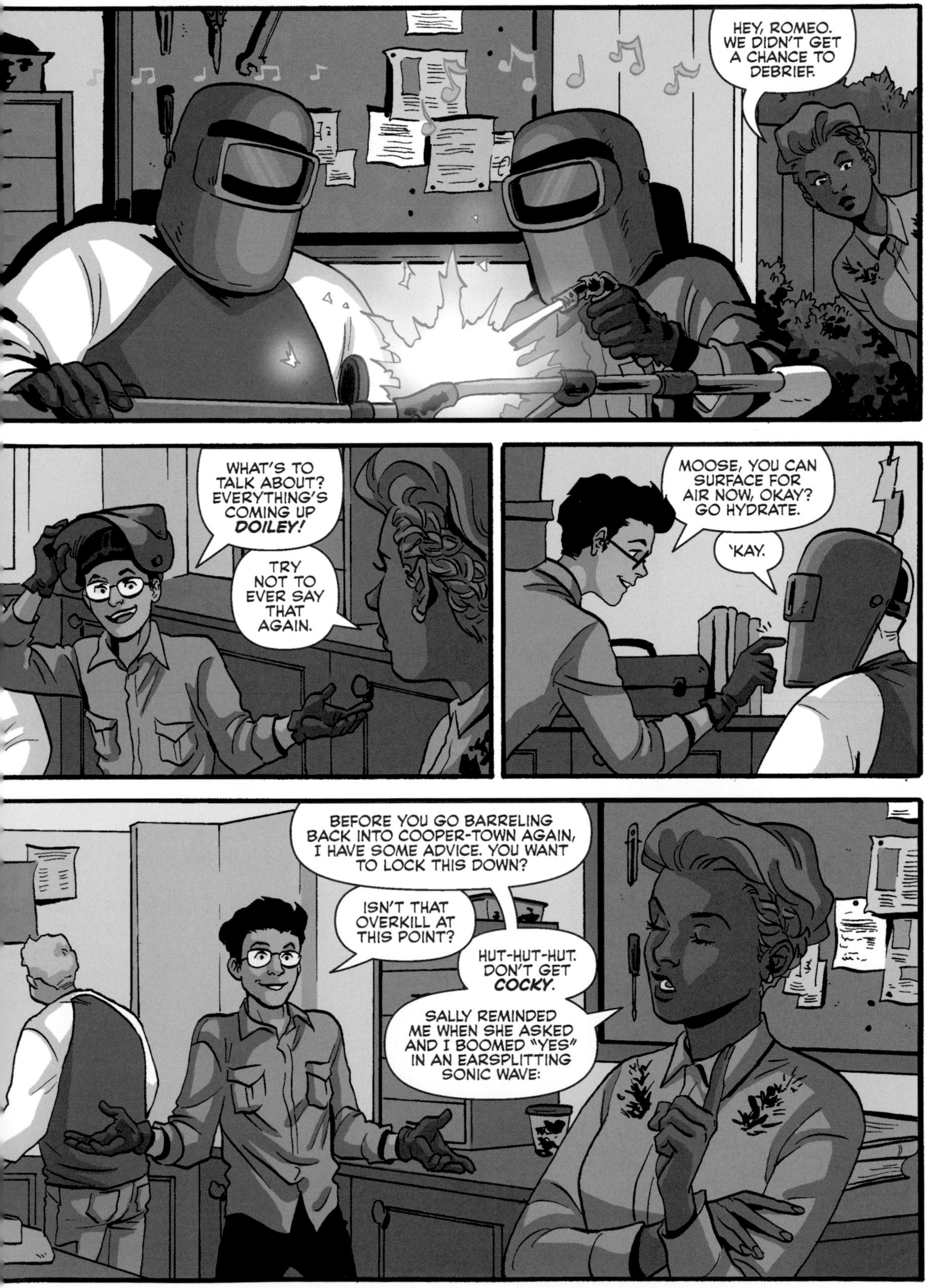
HEY, ROMEO. WE DIDN'T GET A CHANCE TO DEBRIEF.
WHAT'S TO TALK ABOUT? EVERYTHING'S COMING UP DOILEY!
TRY NOT TO EVER SAY THAT AGAIN.
MOOSE, YOU CAN SURFACE FOR AIR NOW, OKAY? GO HYDRATE.
'KAY.
BEFORE YOU GO BARRELING BACK INTO COOPER-TOWN AGAIN, I HAVE SOME ADVICE. YOU WANT TO LOCK THIS DOWN?
ISN'T THAT OVERKILL AT THIS POINT?
HUT-HUT-HUT. DON'T GET COCKY.
SALLY REMINDED ME WHEN SHE ASKED AND I BOOMED "YES" IN AN EARSPLITTING SONIC WAVE:

SPRING DANCE IS COMING.

ASK BETTY BEFORE SOMEONE ELSE BEATS YOU TO IT.

DILTON?

Oh. SORRY.

WATER.

I'LL RENT A TUX *NOW*. YOU ARE *INSPIRING*.

WE'RE ALL GENIUSES IN OUR OWN WAY, EDISON.

SHE'LL SAY YES, RIGHT? NOW I'M NERVOUS, BECAUSE SPRING DANCE IS A BIG DEAL AND--

ASK. HER.

BUT WHAT IF--

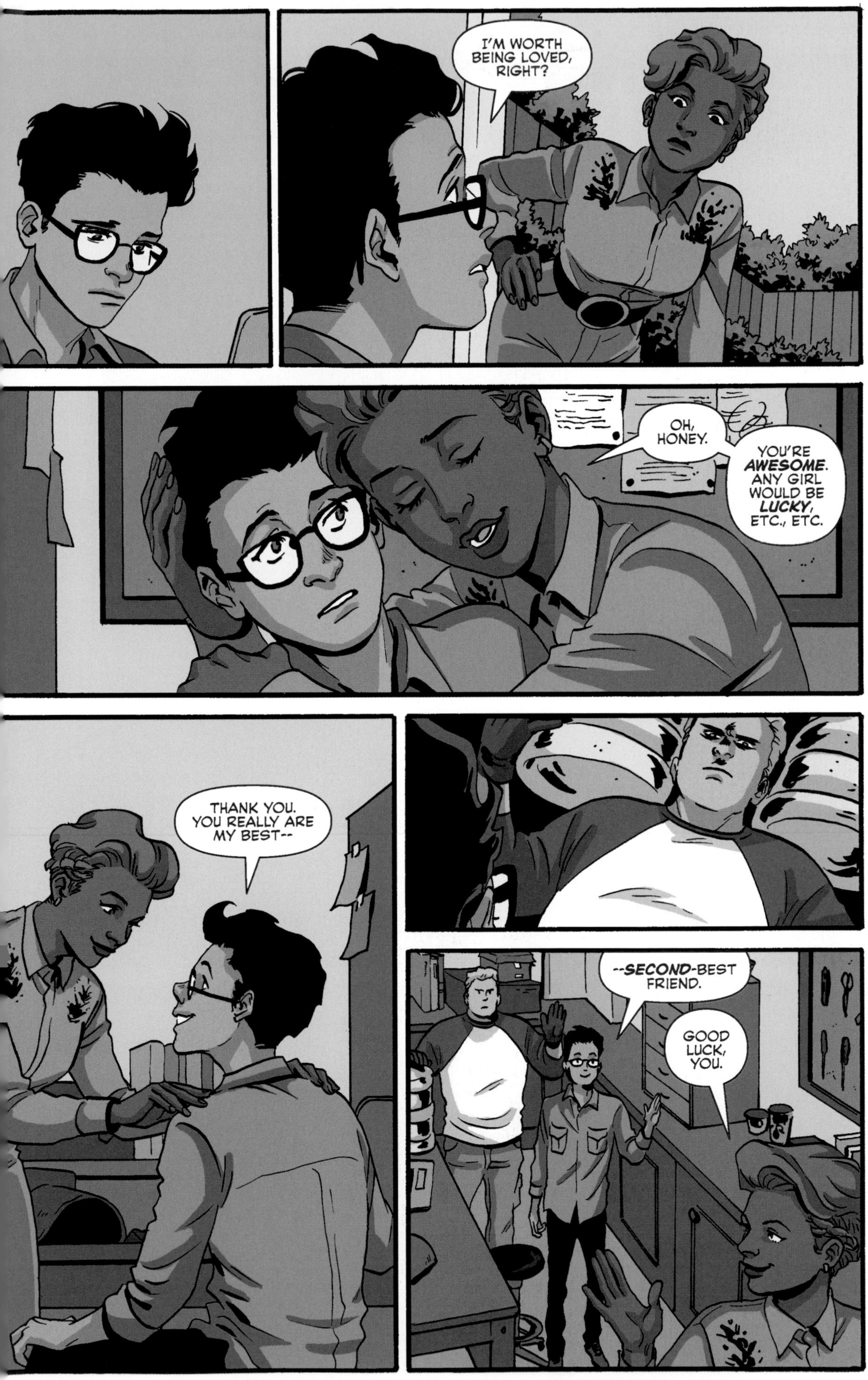
I'M WORTH BEING LOVED, RIGHT?
OH, HONEY.
YOU'RE AWESOME. ANY GIRL WOULD BE LUCKY, ETC., ETC.
THANK YOU. YOU REALLY ARE MY BEST--
--SECOND-BEST FRIEND.
GOOD LUCK, YOU.

CHAPTER THREE: LONG NIGHT'S JOURNEY INTO DAY

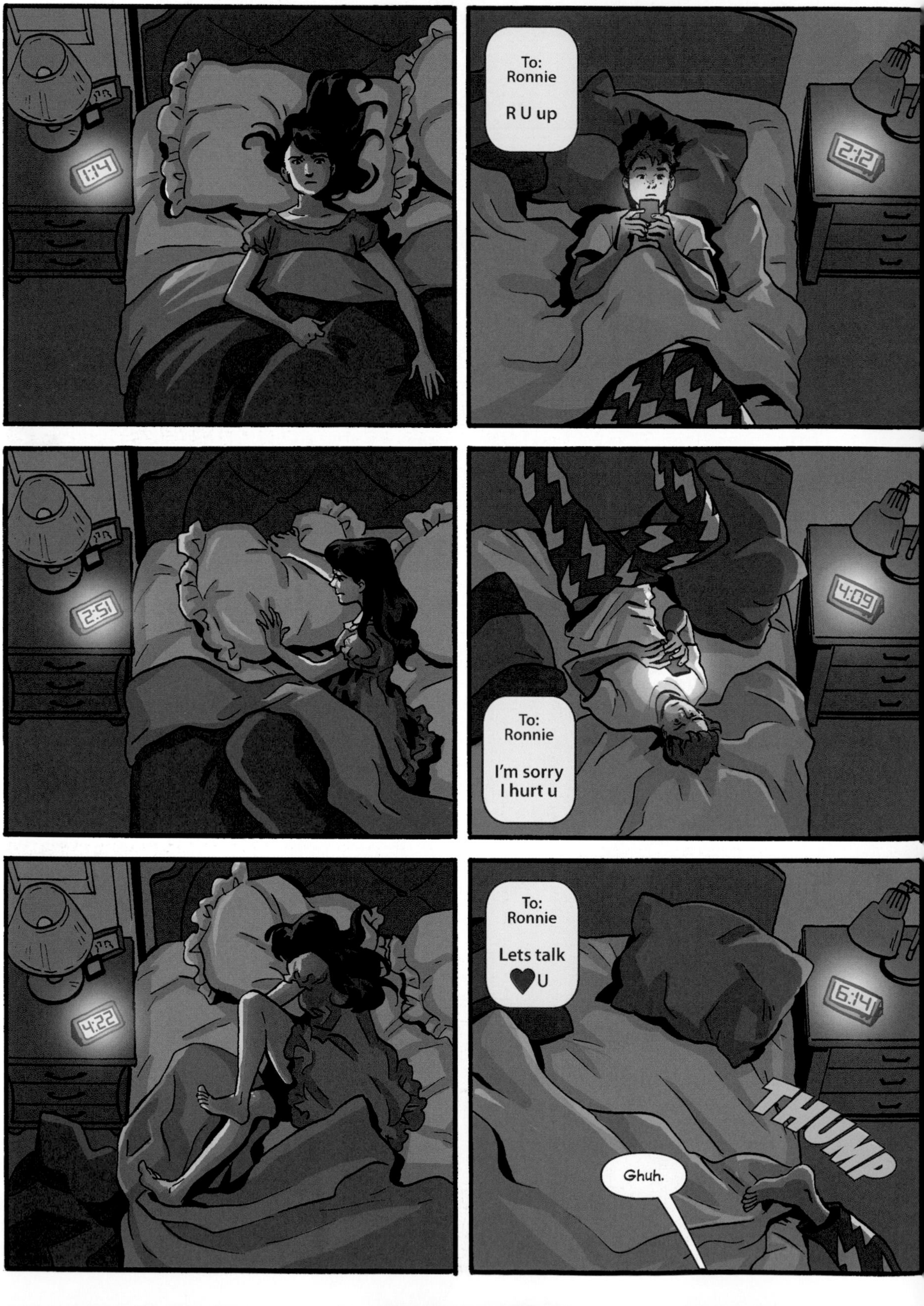
1:14
To: Ronnie
R U up
2:12
2:51
4:09
To: Ronnie
I'm sorry I hurt u
4:22
To: Ronnie
Lets talk
♥U
6:14
THUMP
Ghuh.

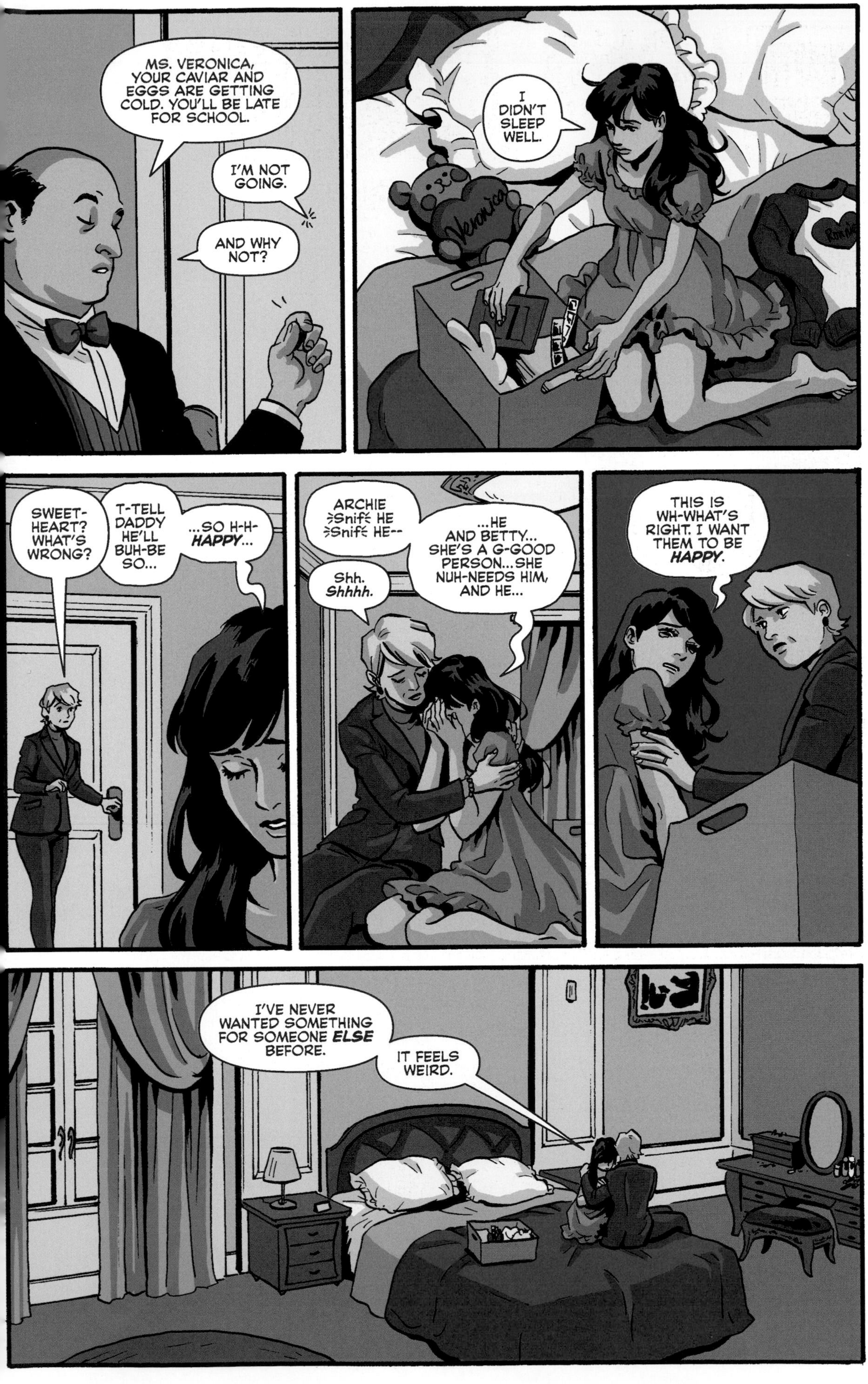
MS. VERONICA, YOUR CAVIAR AND EGGS ARE GETTING COLD. YOU'LL BE LATE FOR SCHOOL.
I'M NOT GOING.
AND WHY NOT?
I DIDN'T SLEEP WELL.
SWEET-HEART? WHAT'S WRONG?
T-TELL DADDY HE'LL BUH-BE SO...
...SO H-H-HAPPY...
ARCHIE *SNIF* HE *SNIF* HE--
Shh. Shhhh.
...HE AND BETTY... SHE'S A G-GOOD PERSON...SHE NUH-NEEDS HIM, AND HE...
THIS IS WH-WHAT'S RIGHT. I WANT THEM TO BE HAPPY.
I'VE NEVER WANTED SOMETHING FOR SOMEONE ELSE BEFORE.
IT FEELS WEIRD.

IS IT *LUNCH* YET?

DUDE, IT'S 3:30. SHAME, TOO. YOU'VE BEEN A LOT OF FUN TO *WATCH* TODAY.

HOW LONG HAVE I BEEN WEARING THESE?

ALL DAY.

WHY DIDN'T YOU SAY SOMETHING?

NEVER WAKE A SLEEP-WALKER.

JUG, RONNIE SAYS I STILL FEEL SOMETHING FOR *BETTY*. AND SHE'S...

...SHE'S NOT WRONG. AND I DON'T KNOW WHAT TO DO.

WET CEMENT

BETTY. RONNIE. BETTY. RONNIE. RONNIE WANTS ME TO *CHOOSE*. WHY DO I HATE CHOOSING SO MUCH?

BECAUSE YOU'LL GO A MILLION MILES OUT OF YOUR WAY NOT TO *HURT* ANYBODY.

REALLY?

THERE'S A *REASON* YOUR FRIENDS SPEND ALL THEIR TIME SAVING YOU FROM CERTAIN DEATH.

YOU *TRULY* WANT TO SETTLE THIS?

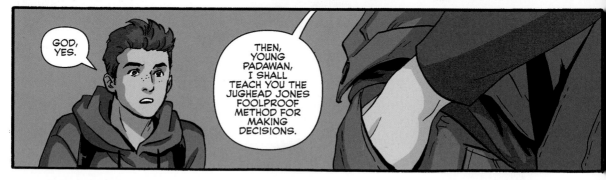

GOD, YES.

THEN, YOUNG PADAWAN, I SHALL TEACH YOU THE JUGHEAD JONES FOOLPROOF METHOD FOR MAKING DECISIONS.

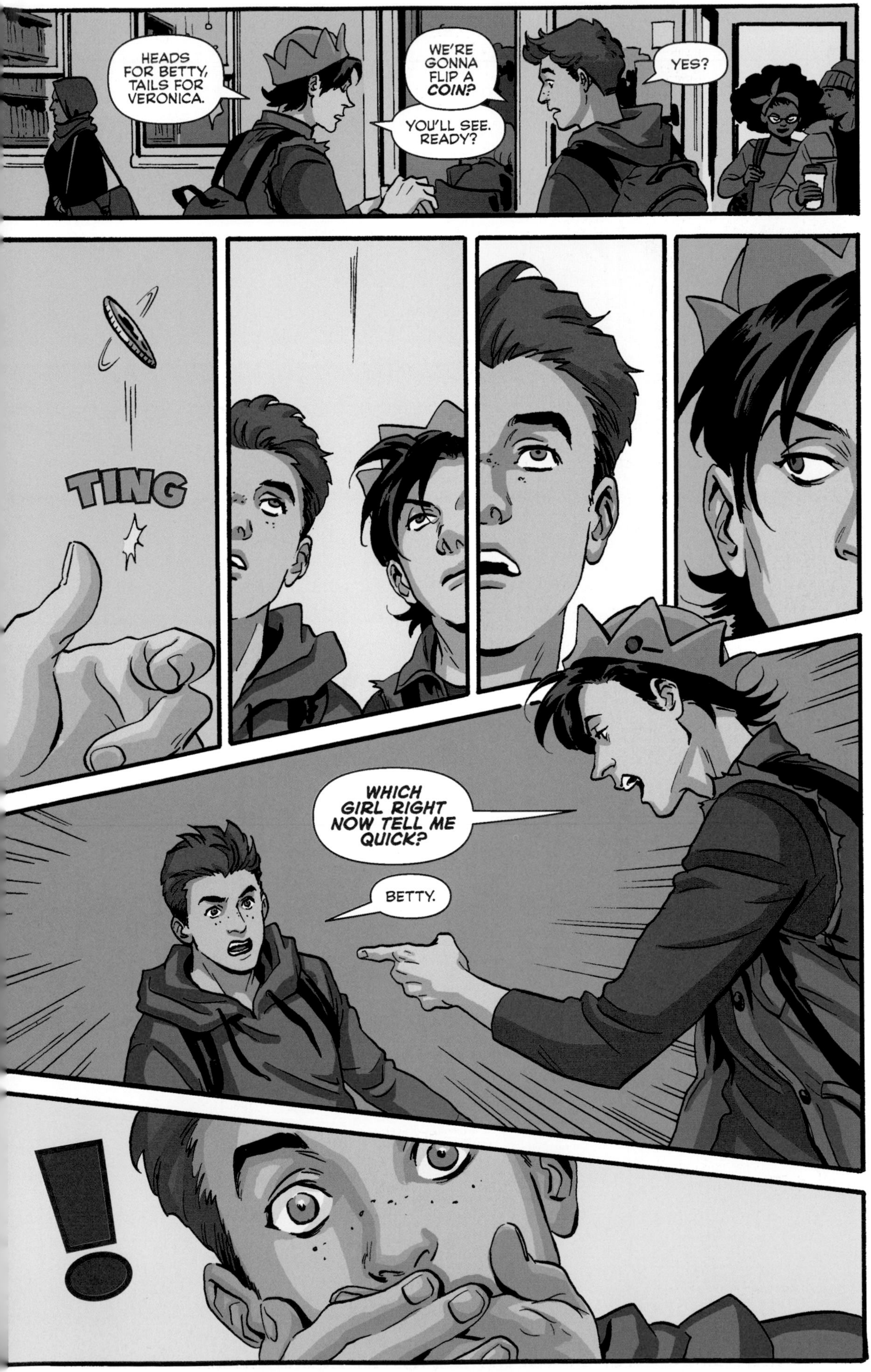
HEADS FOR BETTY, TAILS FOR VERONICA.
WE'RE GONNA FLIP A *COIN?*
YOU'LL SEE. READY?
YES?
TING
WHICH GIRL RIGHT NOW TELL ME QUICK?
BETTY.
!

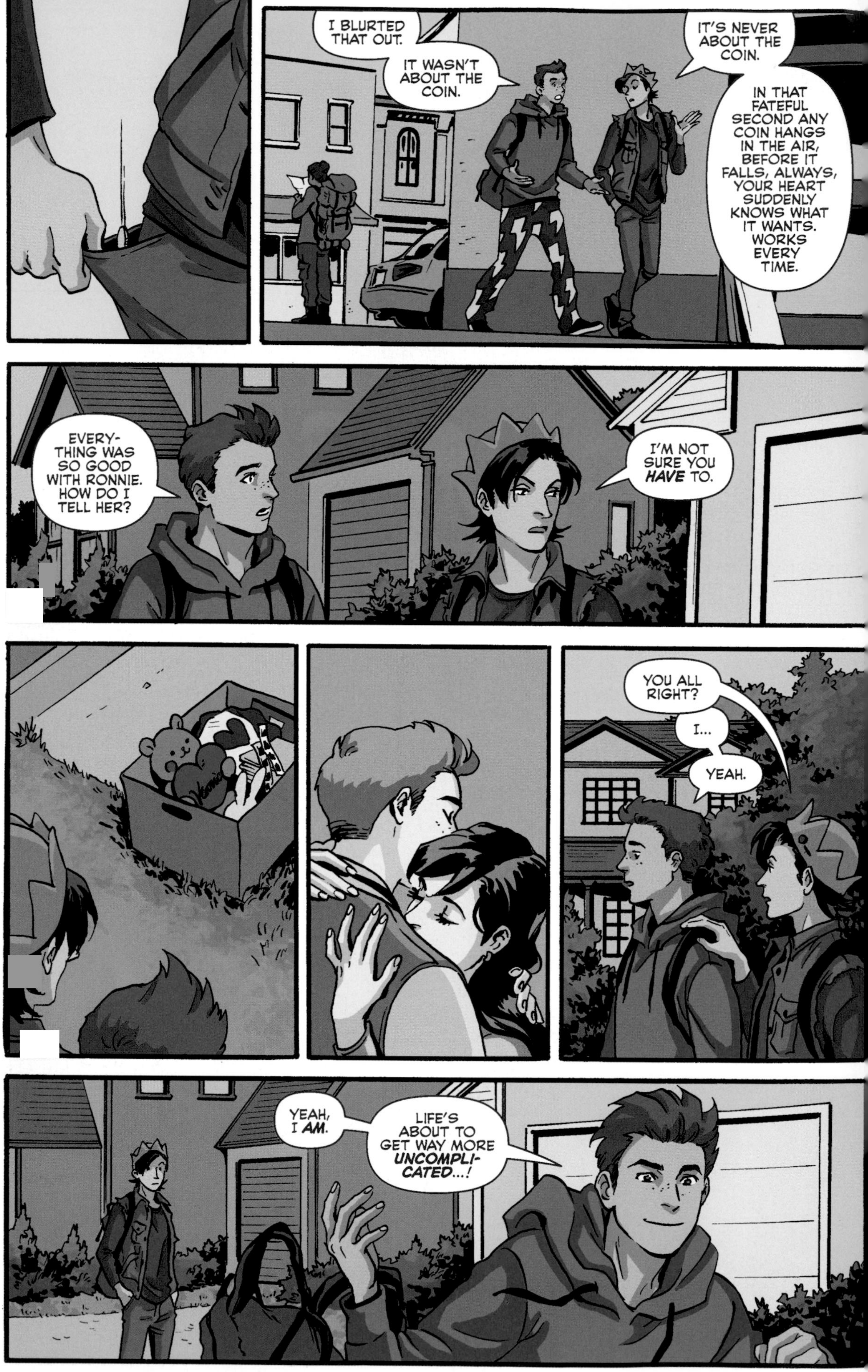
I BLURTED THAT OUT.
IT WASN'T ABOUT THE COIN.
IT'S NEVER ABOUT THE COIN.
IN THAT FATEFUL SECOND ANY COIN HANGS IN THE AIR, BEFORE IT FALLS, ALWAYS, YOUR HEART SUDDENLY KNOWS WHAT IT WANTS. WORKS EVERY TIME.
EVERY-THING WAS SO GOOD WITH RONNIE. HOW DO I TELL HER?
I'M NOT SURE YOU *HAVE* TO.
YOU ALL RIGHT?
I...
YEAH.
YEAH, I *AM*.
LIFE'S ABOUT TO GET WAY MORE *UNCOMPLI-CATED...!*

CHAPTER FOUR: CHOOSE

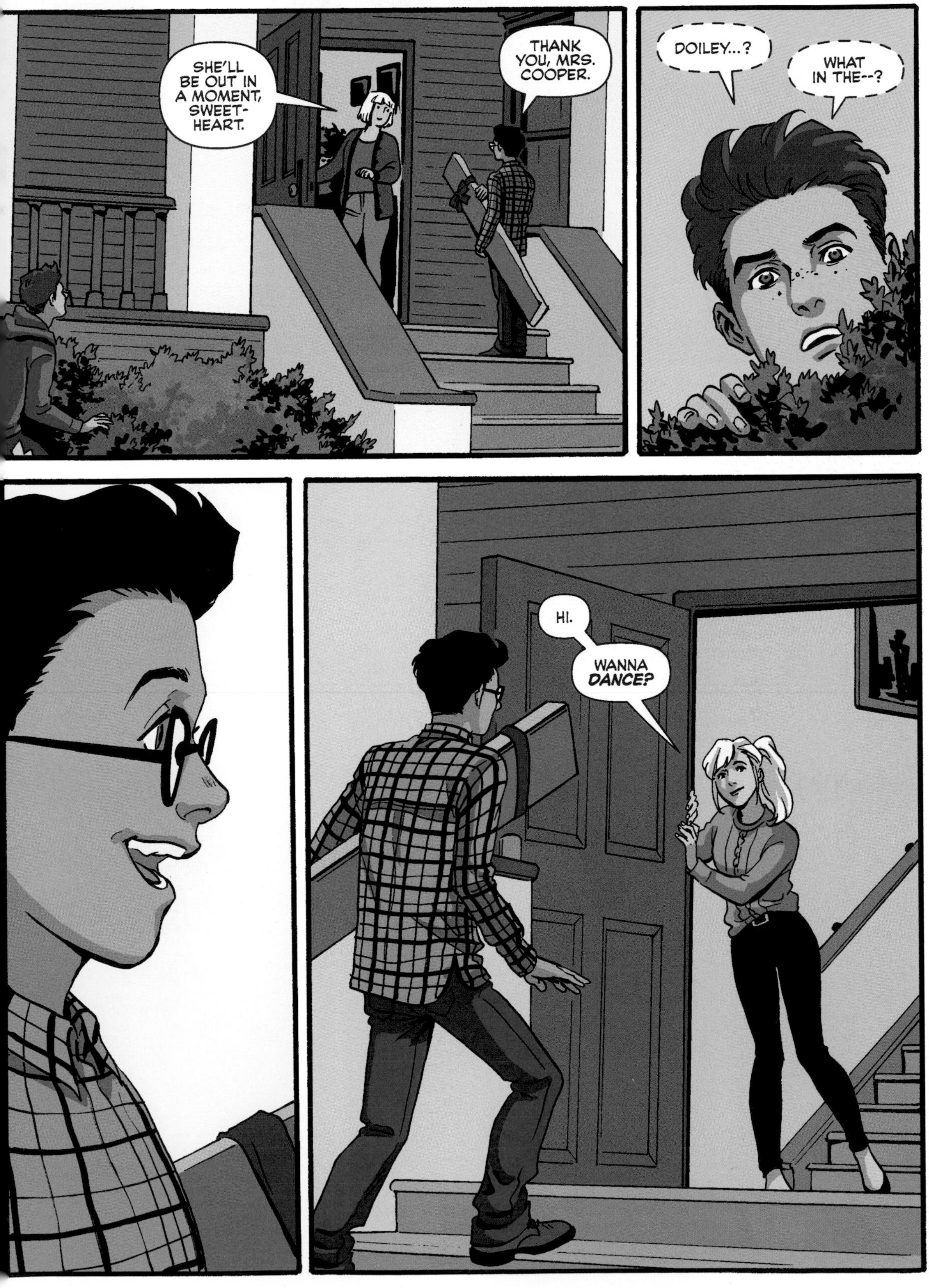
SHE'LL BE OUT IN A MOMENT, SWEET-HEART.
THANK YOU, MRS. COOPER.
DOILEY...?
WHAT IN THE--?
HI.
WANNA *DANCE?*

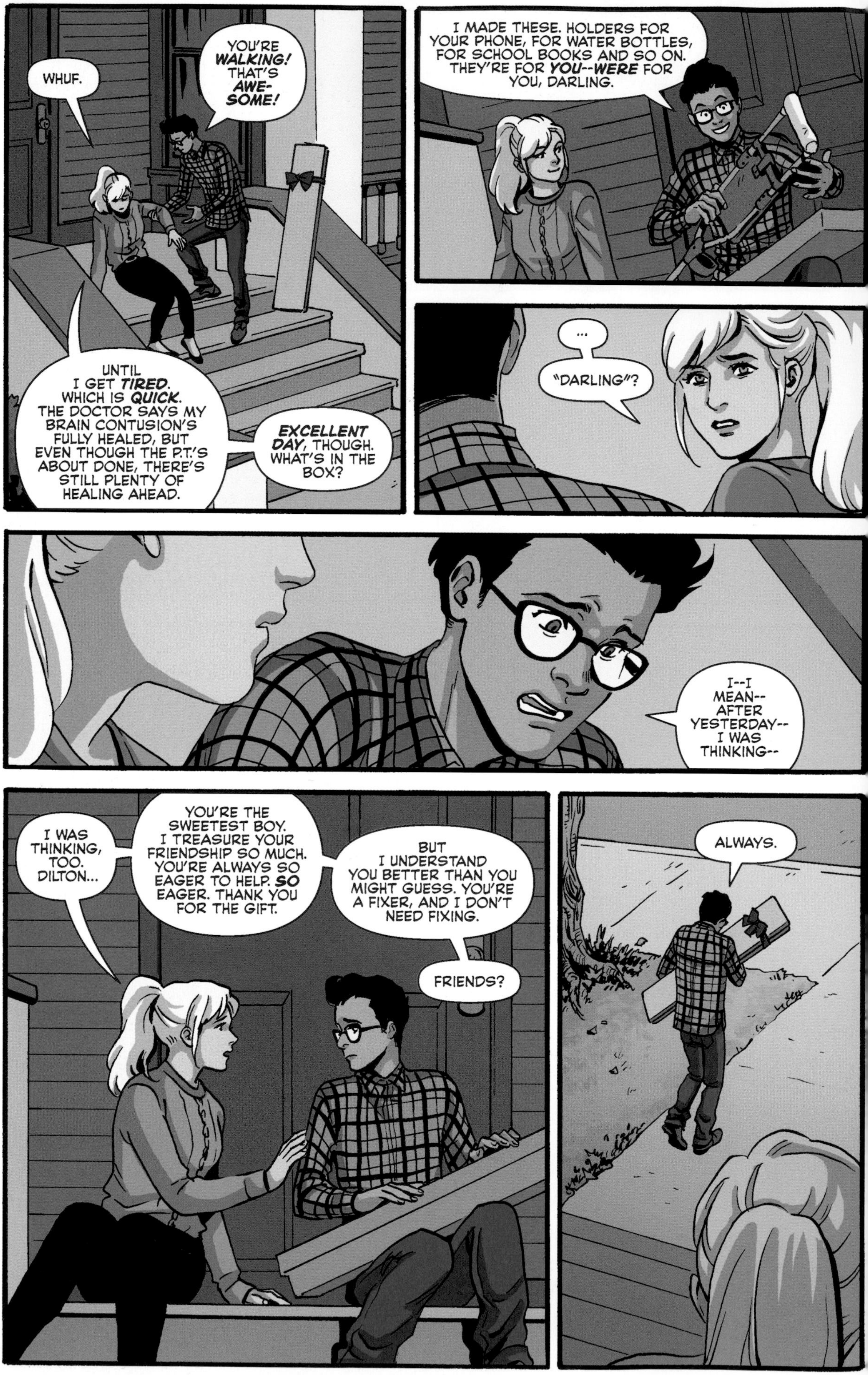
WHUF.
YOU'RE WALKING! THAT'S AWE-SOME!
UNTIL I GET TIRED. WHICH IS QUICK. THE DOCTOR SAYS MY BRAIN CONTUSION'S FULLY HEALED, BUT EVEN THOUGH THE P.T.'S ABOUT DONE, THERE'S STILL PLENTY OF HEALING AHEAD.
EXCELLENT DAY, THOUGH. WHAT'S IN THE BOX?
I MADE THESE. HOLDERS FOR YOUR PHONE, FOR WATER BOTTLES, FOR SCHOOL BOOKS AND SO ON. THEY'RE FOR YOU--WERE FOR YOU, DARLING.
...
"DARLING"?
I--I MEAN--AFTER YESTERDAY--I WAS THINKING--
I WAS THINKING, TOO. DILTON...
YOU'RE THE SWEETEST BOY. I TREASURE YOUR FRIENDSHIP SO MUCH. YOU'RE ALWAYS SO EAGER TO HELP. SO EAGER. THANK YOU FOR THE GIFT.
BUT I UNDERSTAND YOU BETTER THAN YOU MIGHT GUESS. YOU'RE A FIXER, AND I DON'T NEED FIXING.
FRIENDS?
ALWAYS.

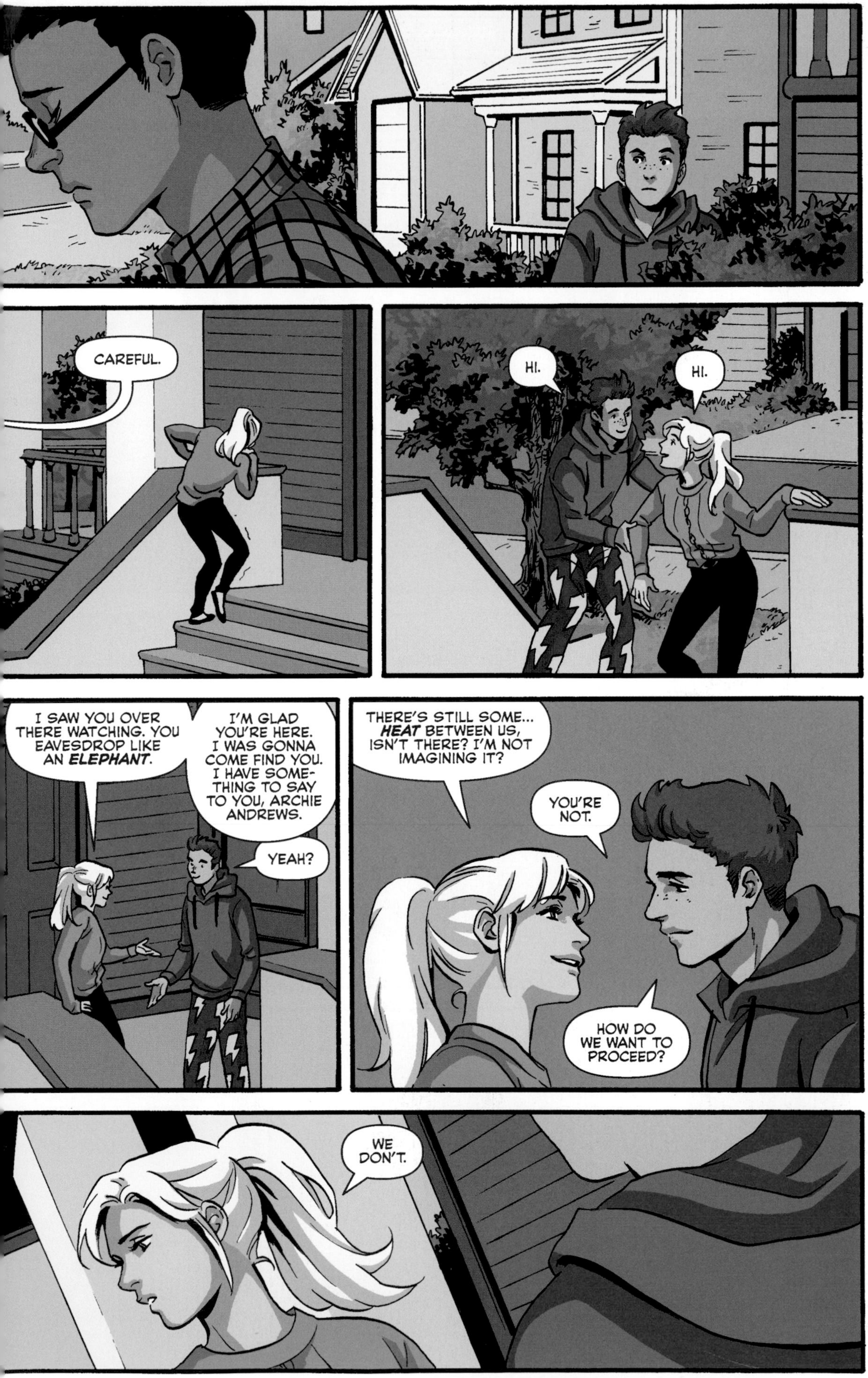
CAREFUL.
HI.
HI.
I SAW YOU OVER THERE WATCHING. YOU EAVESDROP LIKE AN ***ELEPHANT***.
I'M GLAD YOU'RE HERE. I WAS GONNA COME FIND YOU. I HAVE SOMETHING TO SAY TO YOU, ARCHIE ANDREWS.
YEAH?
THERE'S STILL SOME... ***HEAT*** BETWEEN US, ISN'T THERE? I'M NOT IMAGINING IT?
YOU'RE NOT.
HOW DO WE WANT TO PROCEED?
WE DON'T.

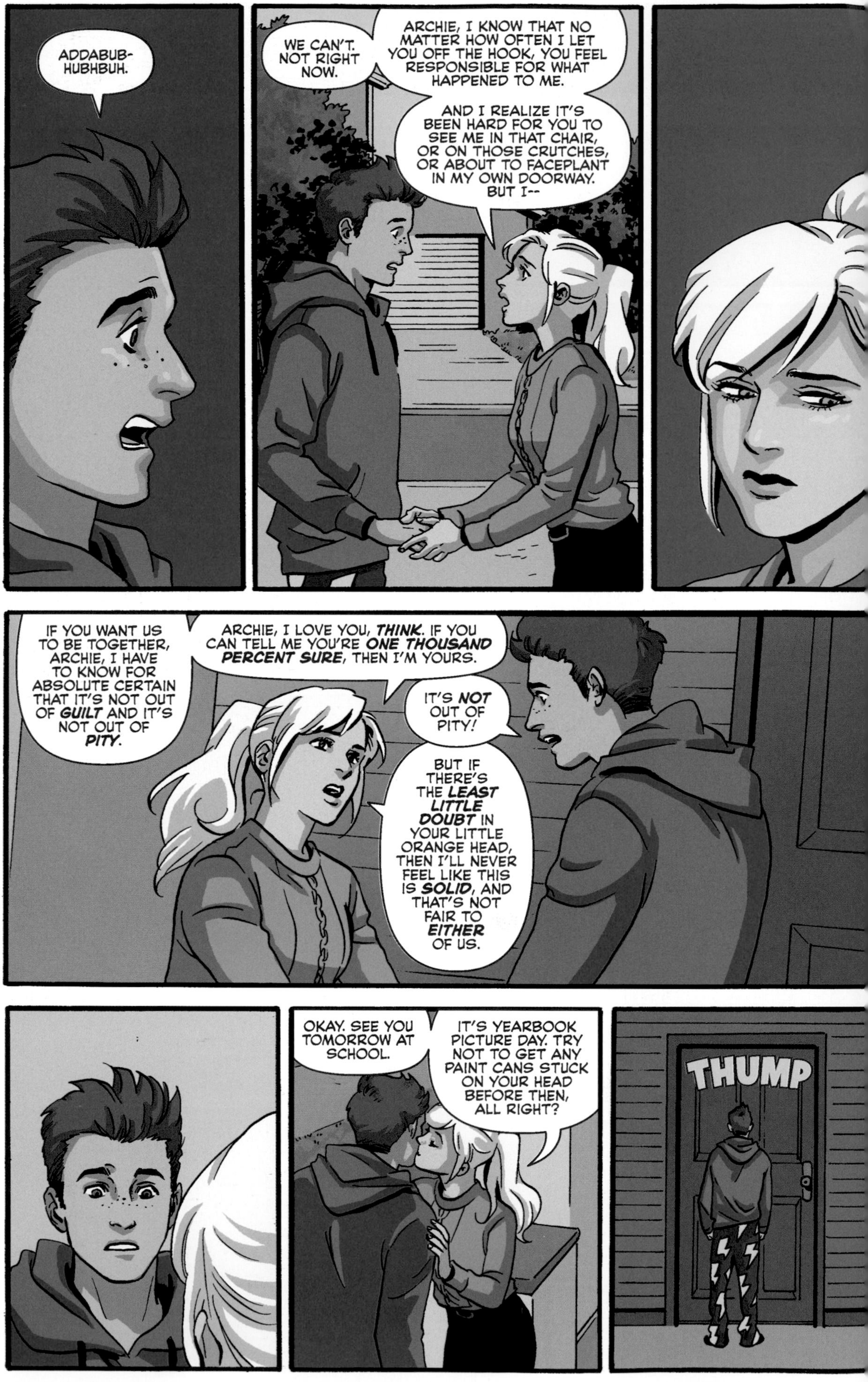
ADDABUB-HUBHBUH.
WE CAN'T. NOT RIGHT NOW.
ARCHIE, I KNOW THAT NO MATTER HOW OFTEN I LET YOU OFF THE HOOK, YOU FEEL RESPONSIBLE FOR WHAT HAPPENED TO ME.
AND I REALIZE IT'S BEEN HARD FOR YOU TO SEE ME IN THAT CHAIR, OR ON THOSE CRUTCHES, OR ABOUT TO FACEPLANT IN MY OWN DOORWAY. BUT I--
IF YOU WANT US TO BE TOGETHER, ARCHIE, I HAVE TO KNOW FOR ABSOLUTE CERTAIN THAT IT'S NOT OUT OF GUILT AND IT'S NOT OUT OF PITY.
ARCHIE, I LOVE YOU, THINK. IF YOU CAN TELL ME YOU'RE ONE THOUSAND PERCENT SURE, THEN I'M YOURS.
IT'S NOT OUT OF PITY!
BUT IF THERE'S THE LEAST LITTLE DOUBT IN YOUR LITTLE ORANGE HEAD, THEN I'LL NEVER FEEL LIKE THIS IS SOLID, AND THAT'S NOT FAIR TO EITHER OF US.
OKAY. SEE YOU TOMORROW AT SCHOOL.
IT'S YEARBOOK PICTURE DAY. TRY NOT TO GET ANY PAINT CANS STUCK ON YOUR HEAD BEFORE THEN, ALL RIGHT?
THUMP

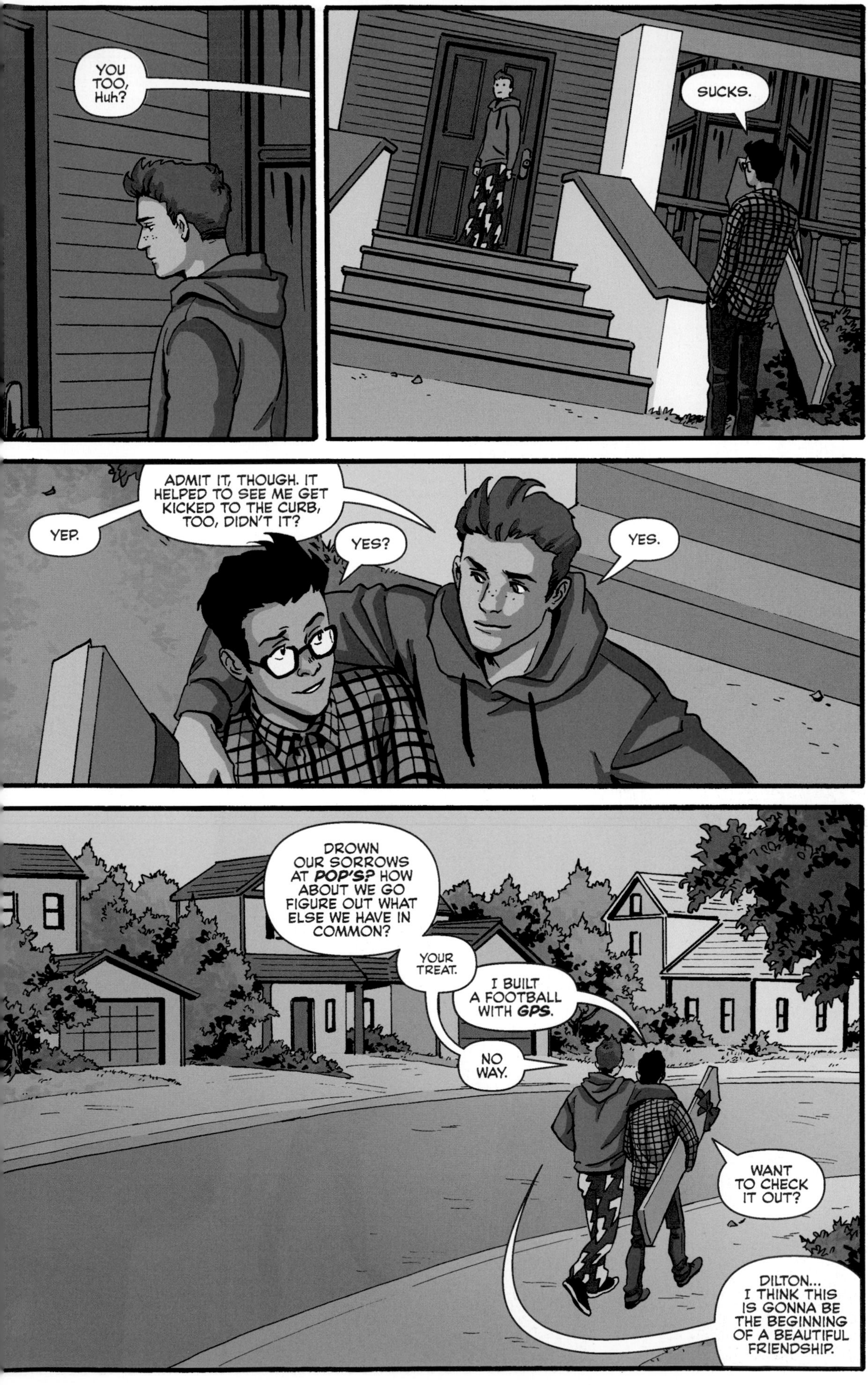
YOU TOO, Huh?
SUCKS.
YEP.
ADMIT IT, THOUGH. IT HELPED TO SEE ME GET KICKED TO THE CURB, TOO, DIDN'T IT?
YES?
YES.
DROWN OUR SORROWS AT POP'S? HOW ABOUT WE GO FIGURE OUT WHAT ELSE WE HAVE IN COMMON?
YOUR TREAT.
I BUILT A FOOTBALL WITH GPS.
NO WAY.
WANT TO CHECK IT OUT?
DILTON... I THINK THIS IS GONNA BE THE BEGINNING OF A BEAUTIFUL FRIENDSHIP.

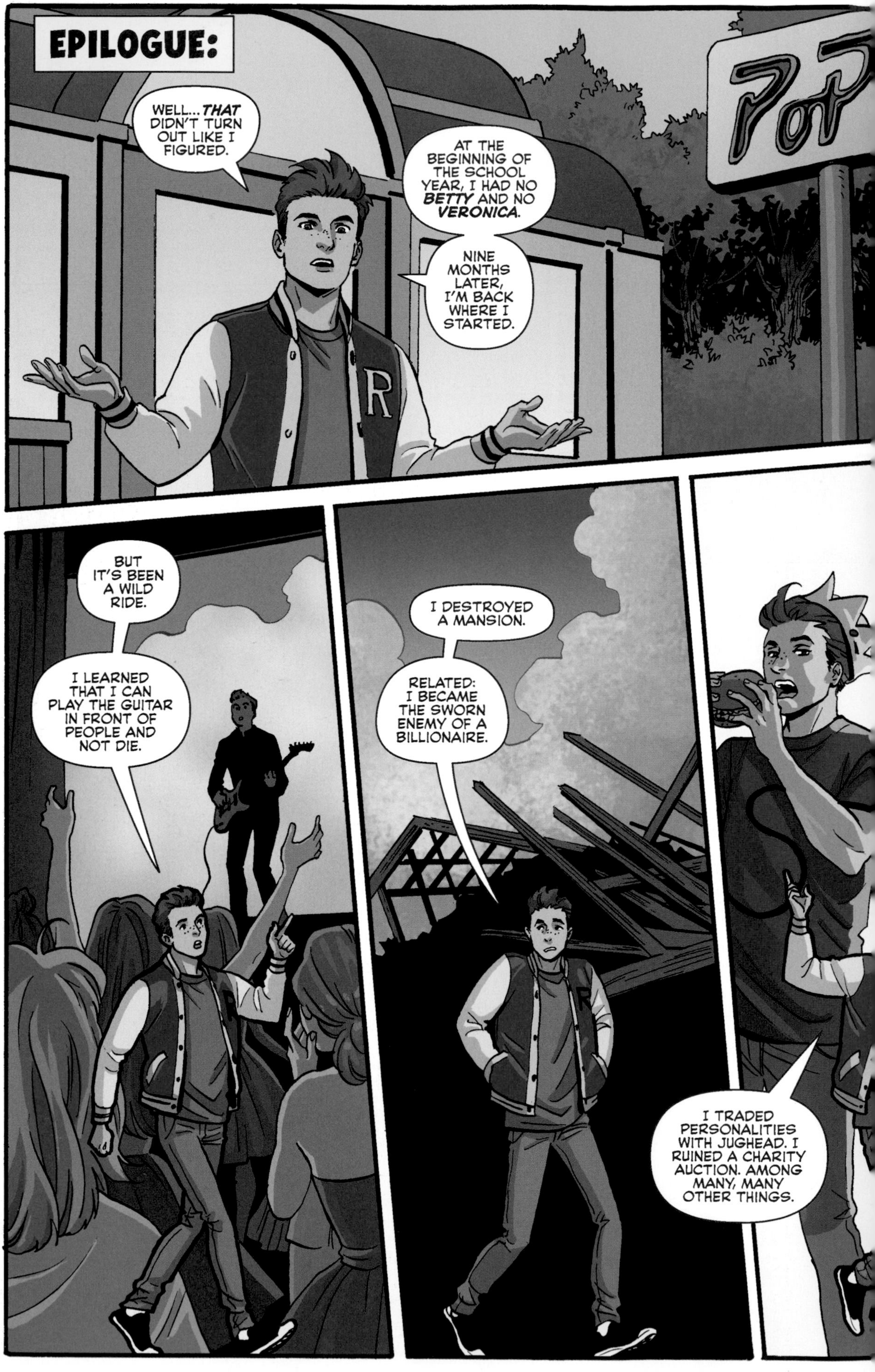
EPILOGUE:
WELL...THAT DIDN'T TURN OUT LIKE I FIGURED.
AT THE BEGINNING OF THE SCHOOL YEAR, I HAD NO BETTY AND NO VERONICA.
NINE MONTHS LATER, I'M BACK WHERE I STARTED.
BUT IT'S BEEN A WILD RIDE.
I LEARNED THAT I CAN PLAY THE GUITAR IN FRONT OF PEOPLE AND NOT DIE.
I DESTROYED A MANSION.
RELATED: I BECAME THE SWORN ENEMY OF A BILLIONAIRE.
I TRADED PERSONALITIES WITH JUGHEAD. I RUINED A CHARITY AUCTION. AMONG MANY, MANY OTHER THINGS.

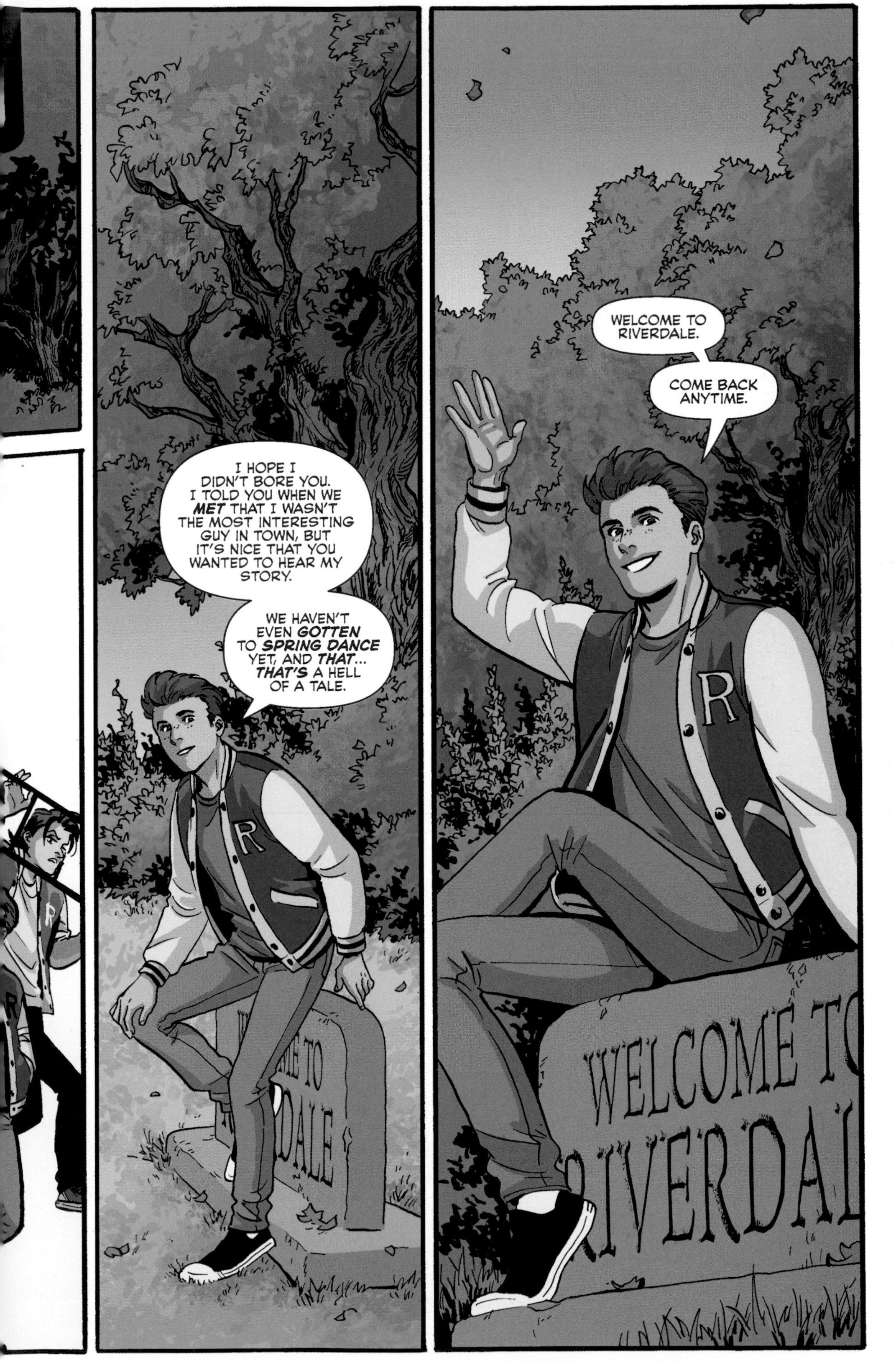
I HOPE I DIDN'T BORE YOU. I TOLD YOU WHEN WE MET THAT I WASN'T THE MOST INTERESTING GUY IN TOWN, BUT IT'S NICE THAT YOU WANTED TO HEAR MY STORY.
WE HAVEN'T EVEN GOTTEN TO SPRING DANCE YET, AND THAT... THAT'S A HELL OF A TALE.
WELCOME TO RIVERDALE.
COME BACK ANYTIME.
WELCOME TO
RIVERDAL

PROLOGUE:

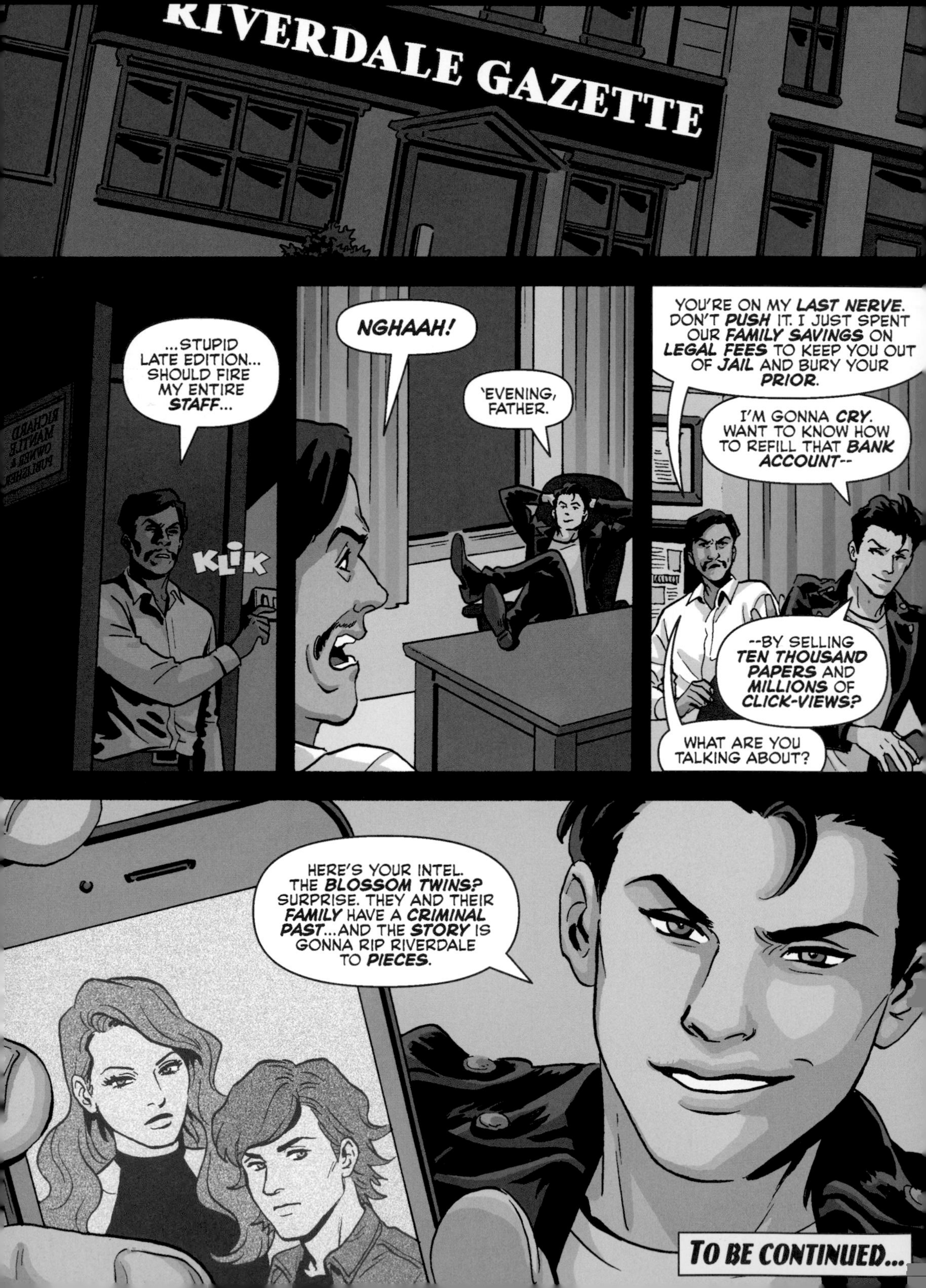
RIVERDALE GAZETTE
...STUPID LATE EDITION... SHOULD FIRE MY ENTIRE STAFF...
KLIK
NGHAAH!
'EVENING, FATHER.
YOU'RE ON MY LAST NERVE. DON'T PUSH IT. I JUST SPENT OUR FAMILY SAVINGS ON LEGAL FEES TO KEEP YOU OUT OF JAIL AND BURY YOUR PRIOR.
I'M GONNA CRY. WANT TO KNOW HOW TO REFILL THAT BANK ACCOUNT--
--BY SELLING TEN THOUSAND PAPERS AND MILLIONS OF CLICK-VIEWS?
WHAT ARE YOU TALKING ABOUT?
HERE'S YOUR INTEL. THE BLOSSOM TWINS? SURPRISE. THEY AND THEIR FAMILY HAVE A CRIMINAL PAST...AND THE STORY IS GONNA RIP RIVERDALE TO PIECES.
TO BE CONTINUED...

ARCHIE®

SPECIAL FEATURES

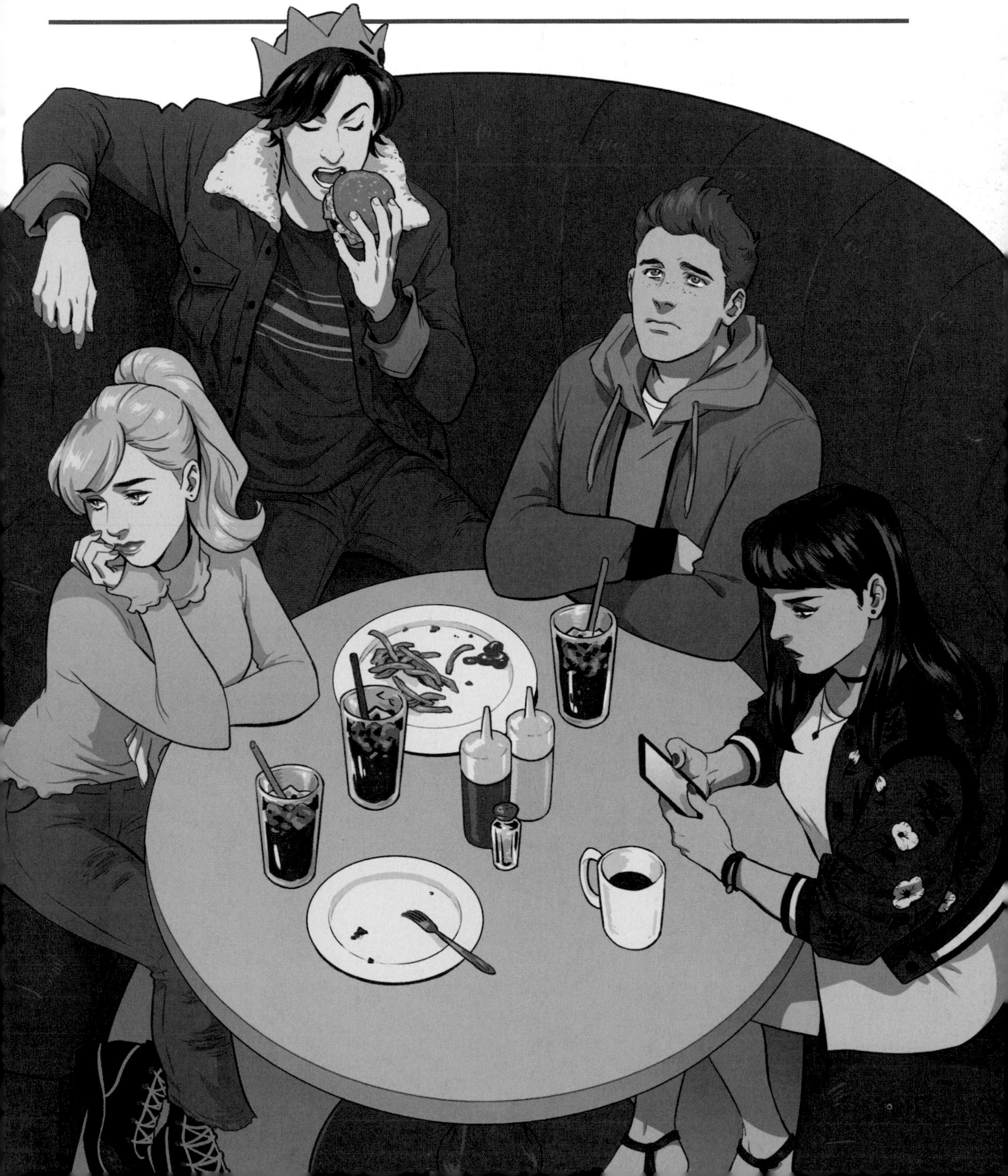

ARCHIE

COVER GALLERY

In addition to the amazing main covers we have for each issue, we also receive gorgeous artwork from an array of talented artists for our direct market exclusive covers. Here are all of the main and variant covers for each of the five issues in Archie Volume Five.

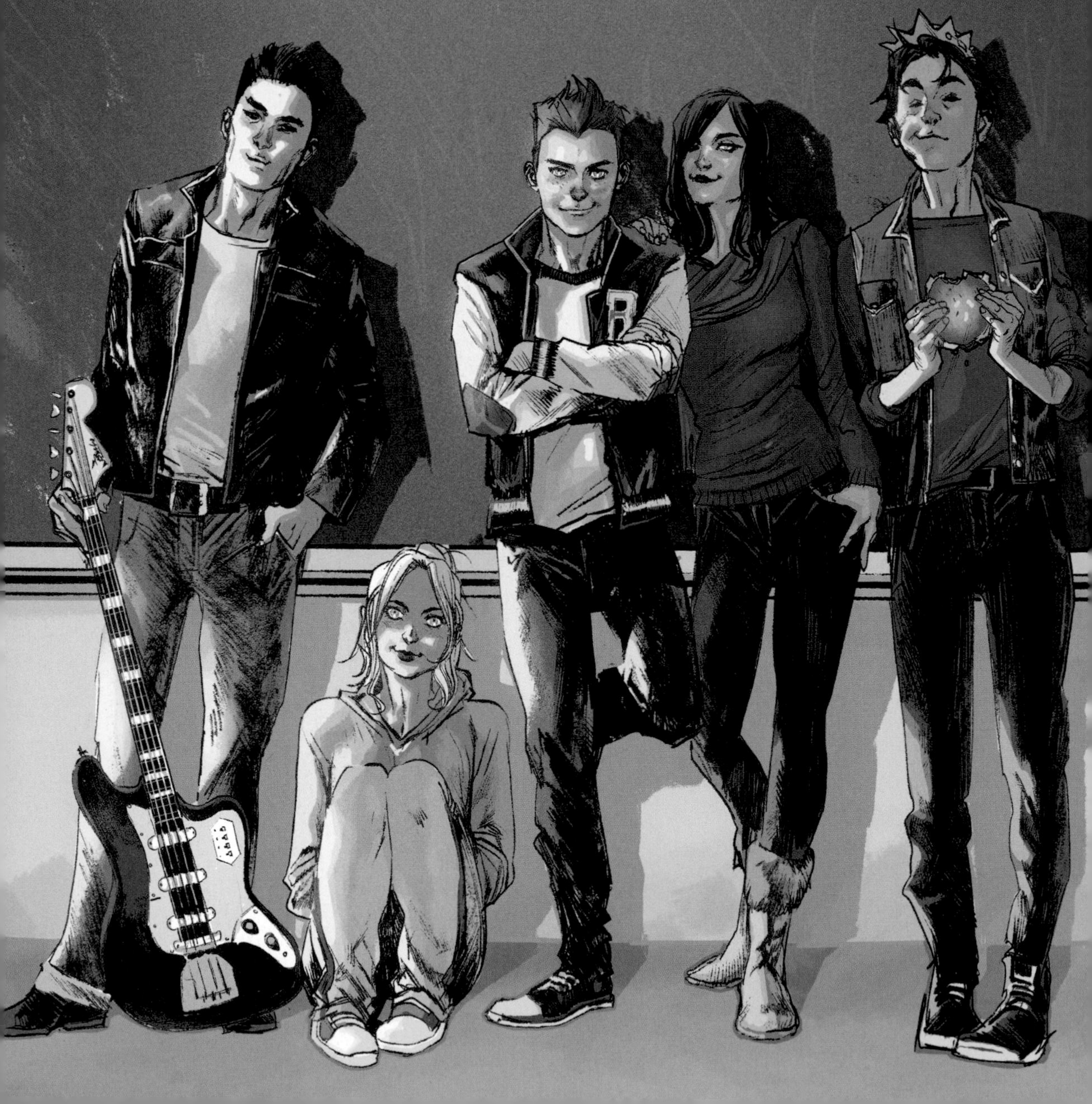

ISSUE TWENTY THREE

THOMAS PITILLI

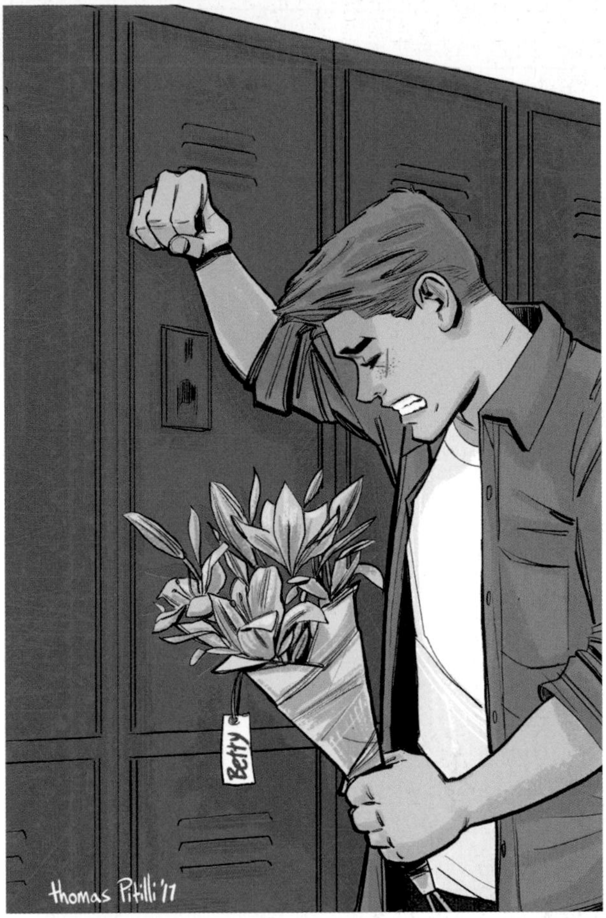
Betty
thomas Pitilli '17

GREG SMALLWOOD

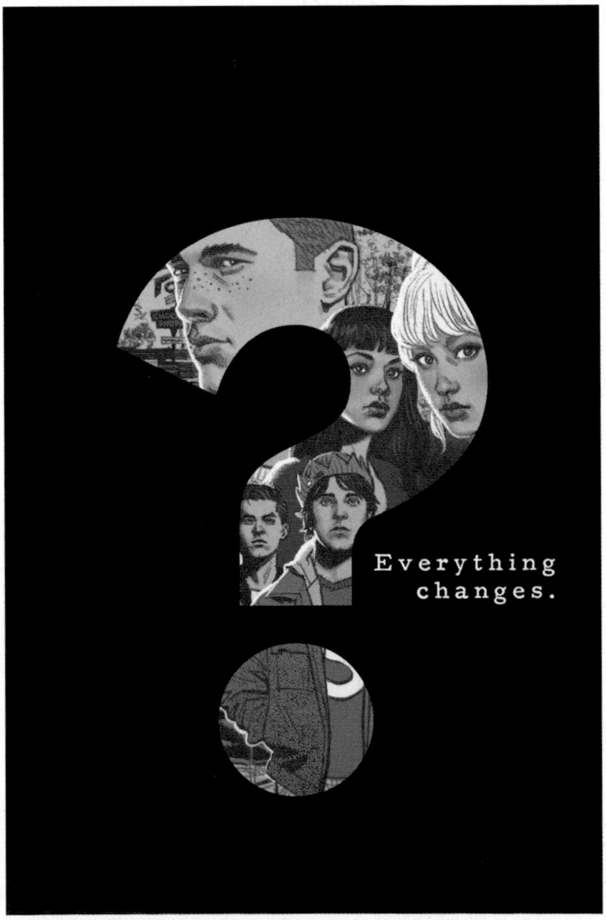
Everything changes.

ISSUE TWENTY FOUR

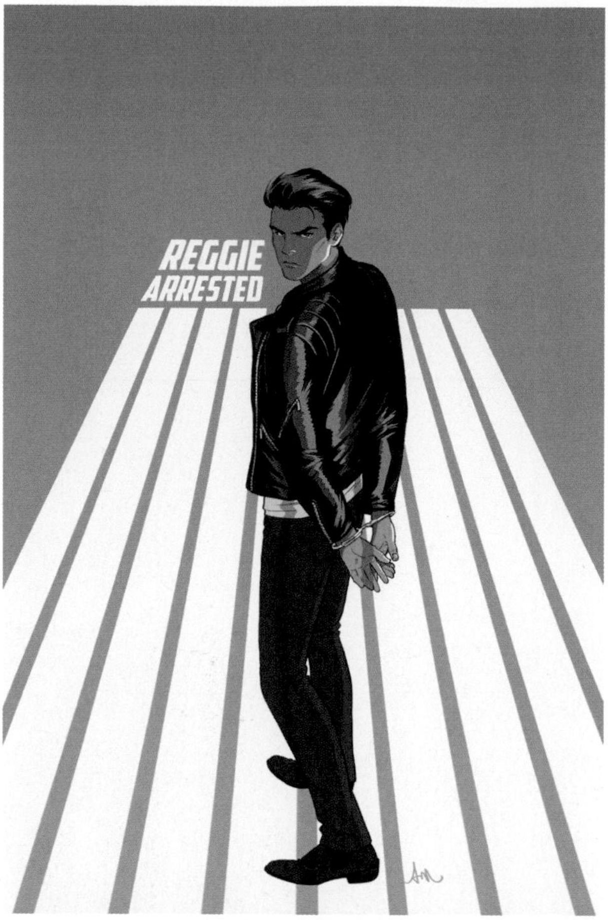
REGGIE
ARRESTED

AUDREY MOK

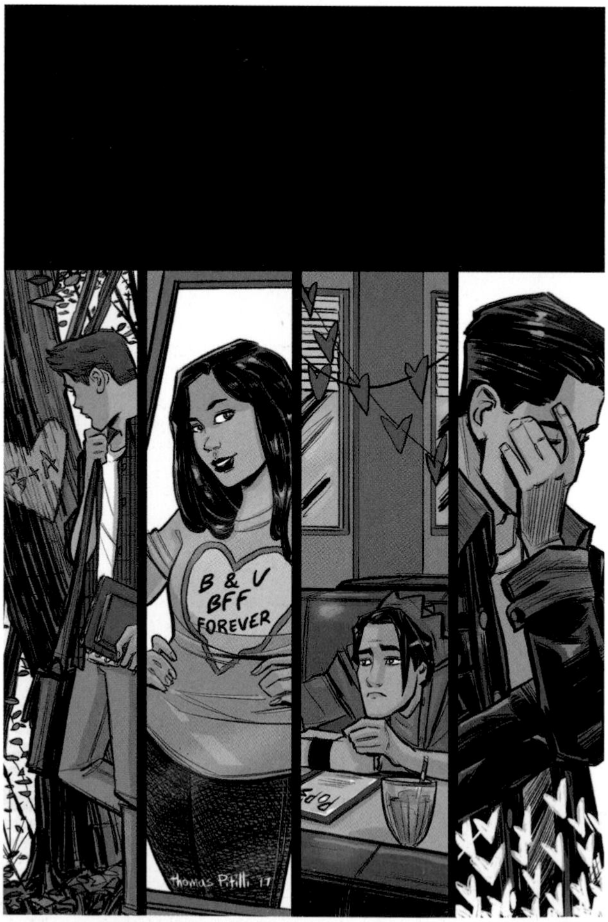
B & V
BFF
FOREVER

THOMAS PITILLI

ISSUE TWENTY FIVE

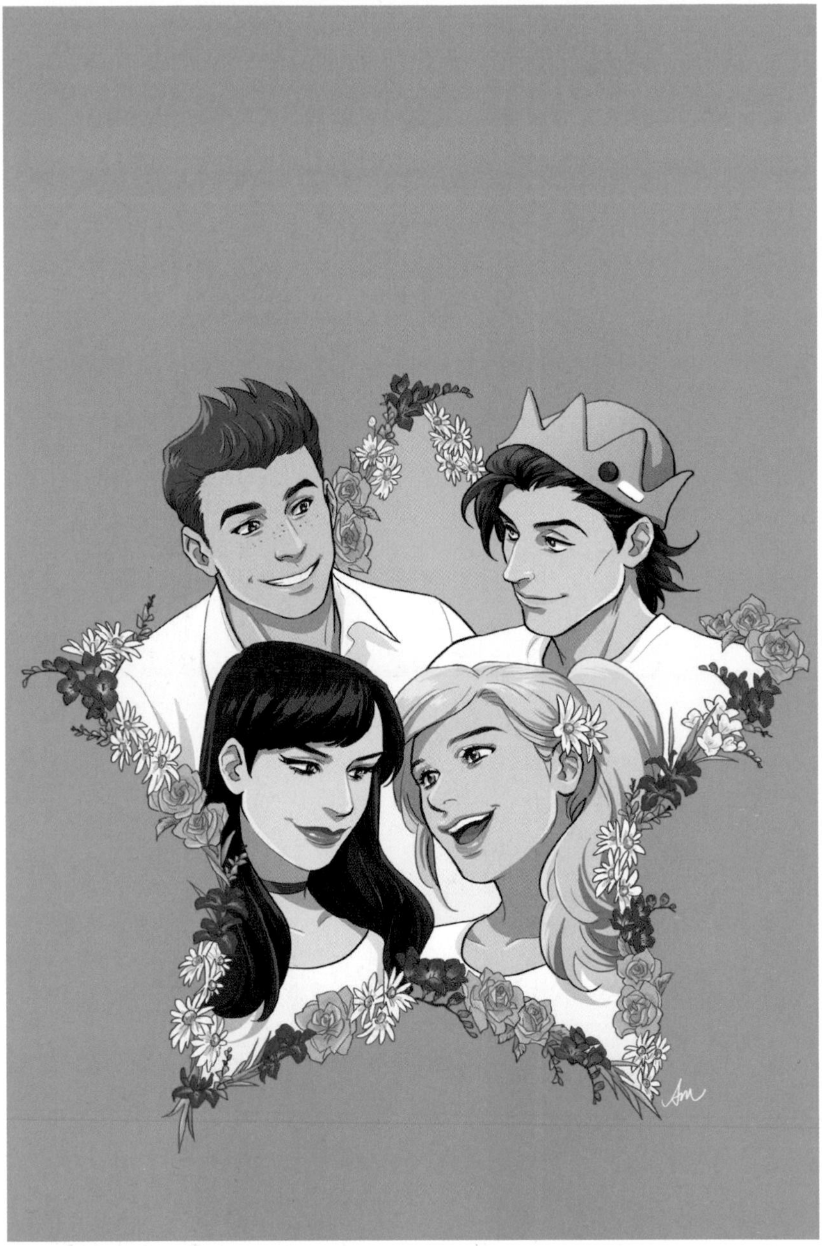

AUDREY
MOK

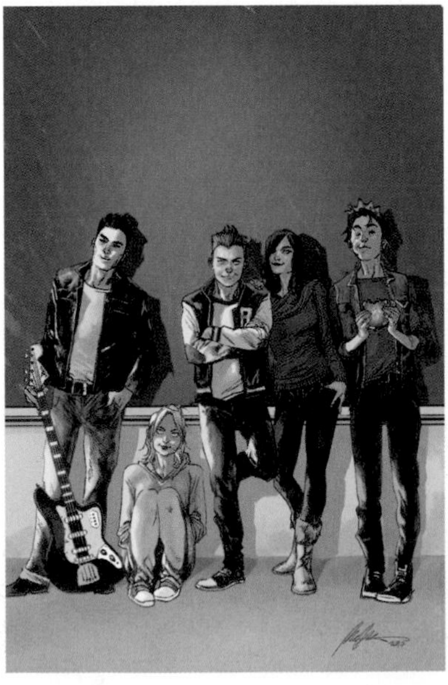

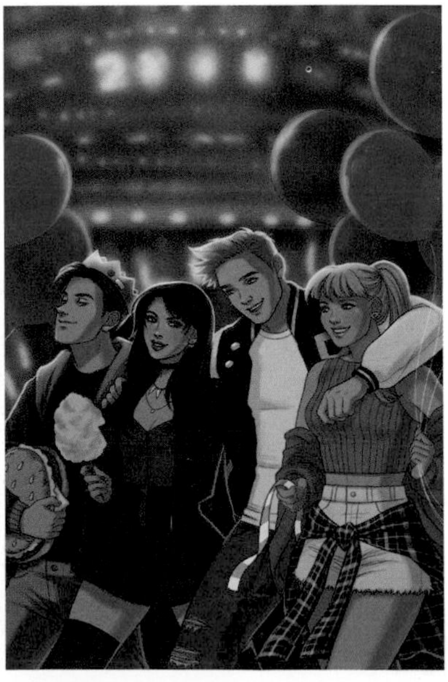

(L)
RAFAEL
ALBUQUERQUE

(R)
JEN
BARTEL

ISSUE TWENTY SIX

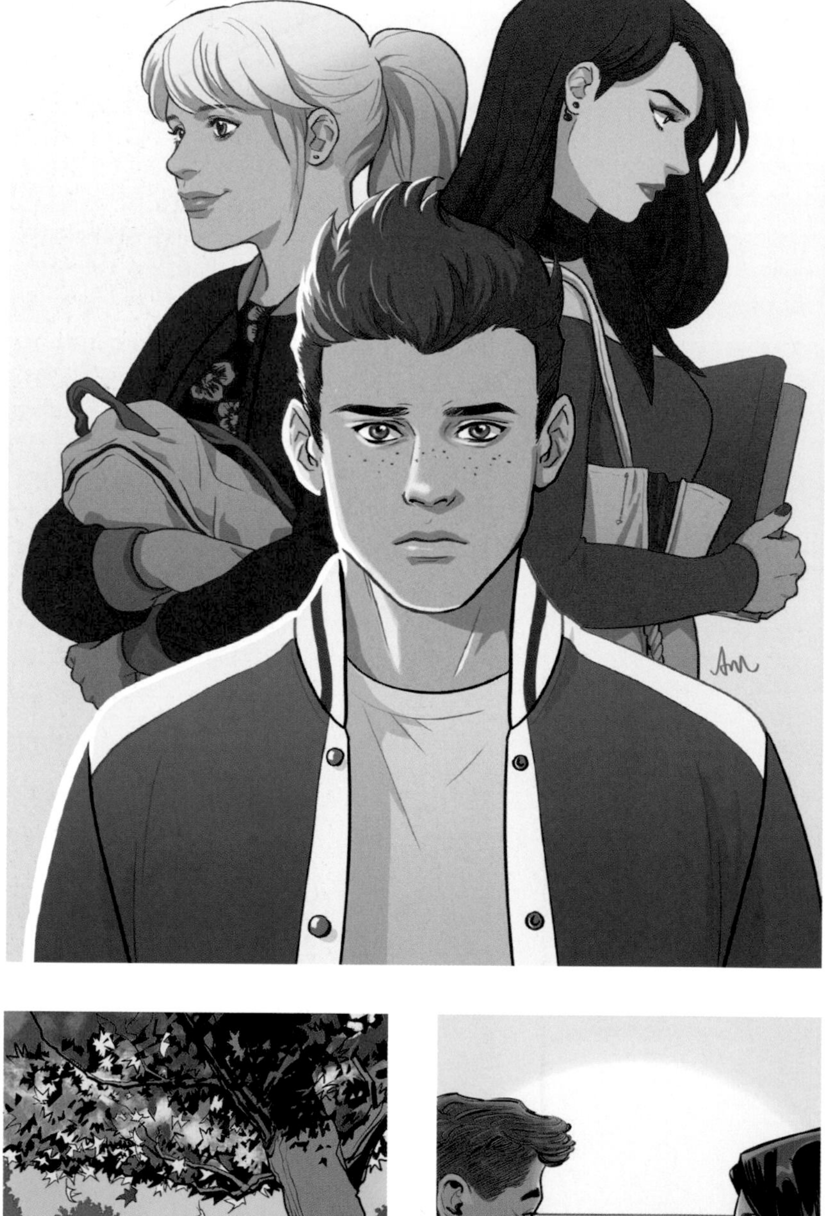

AUDREY MOK

(L) SANDY JARRELL

(R) THOMAS PITILLI

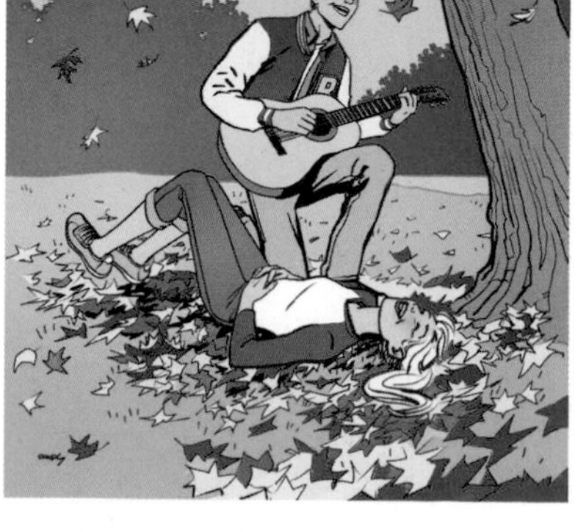

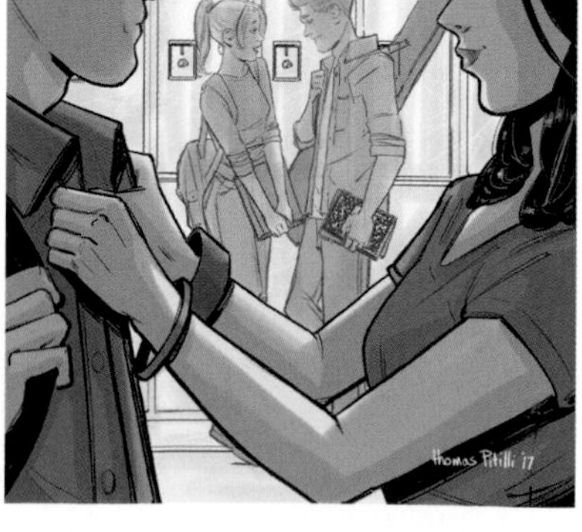

ISSUE TWENTY SEVEN

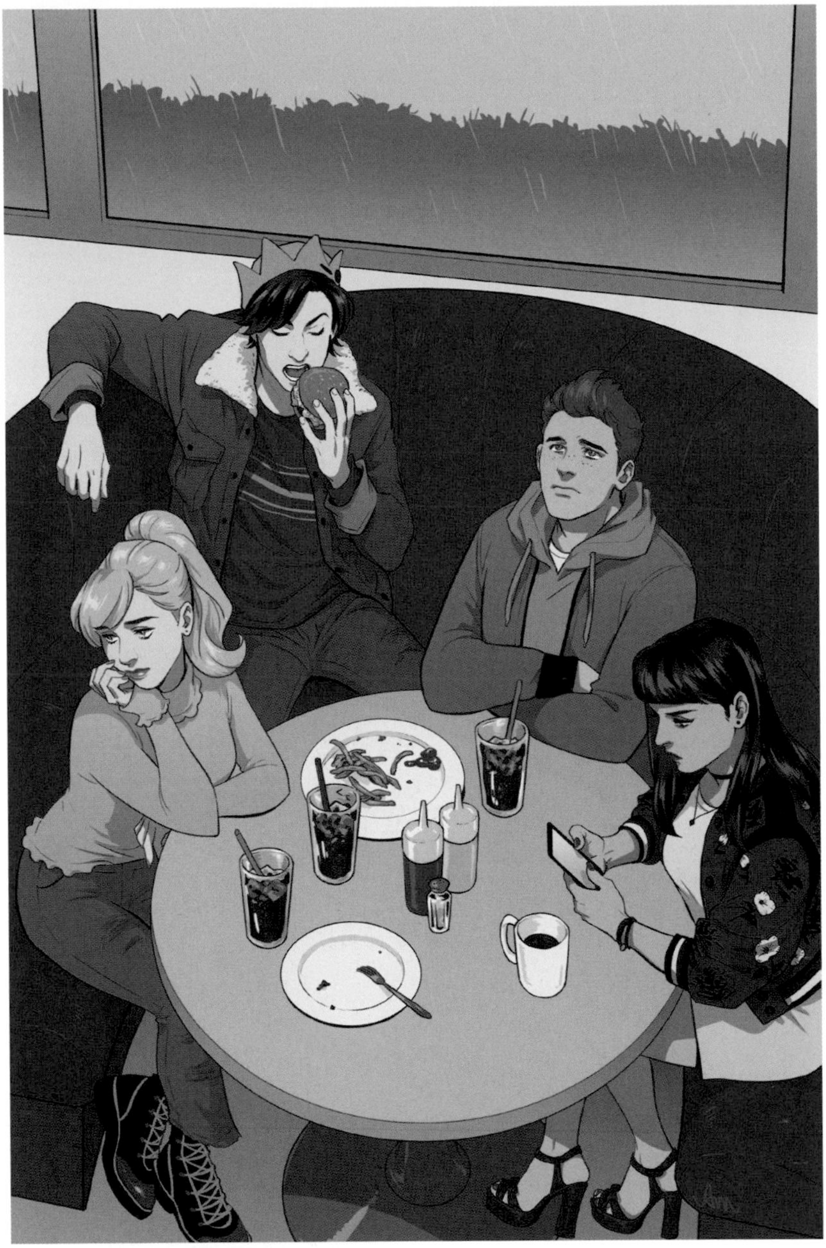

AUDREY MOK

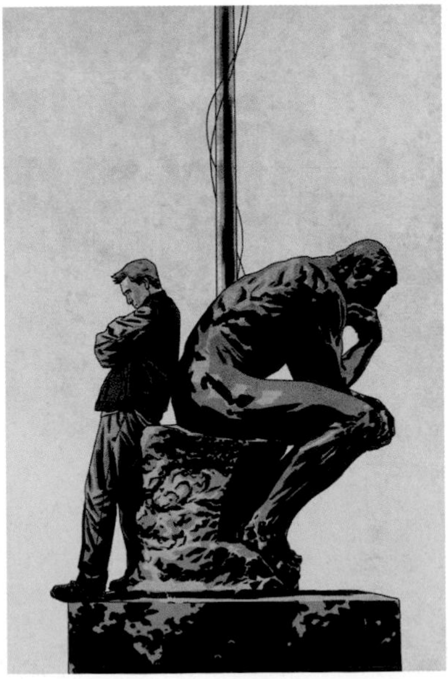

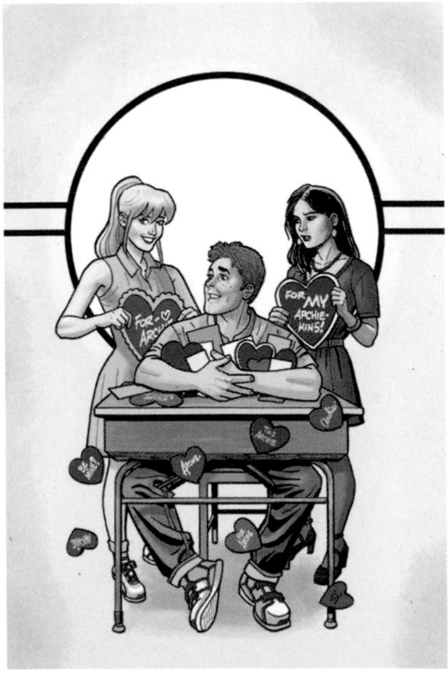
FOR MY ARCHIE-KINS!

(L) MATTHEW DOW SMITH

(R) TY TEMPLETON

ARCHIE

COVER SKETCHES

Before each issue goes through the solicitation process, our esteemed writer MARK WAID gives us a synopsis of what will occur in each upcoming issue, and from that our talented interior artist will come up with some main cover ideas and send in rough drafts of how they would like the cover to look. Here are a few of AUDREY MOK's brilliant cover sketches along with how they appeared in the final versions.

ISSUE TWENTY FOUR

ISSUE TWENTY FIVE

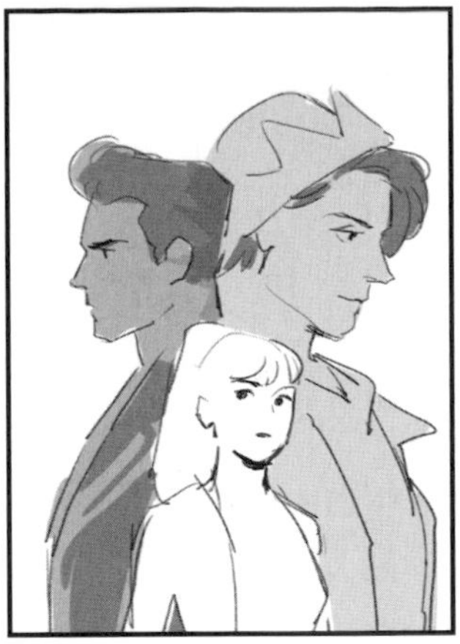

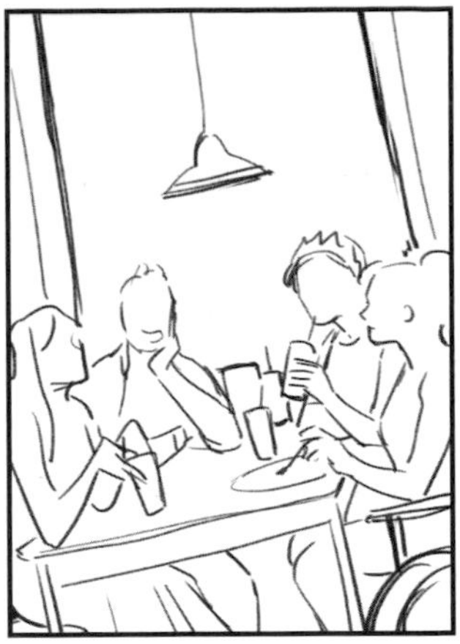

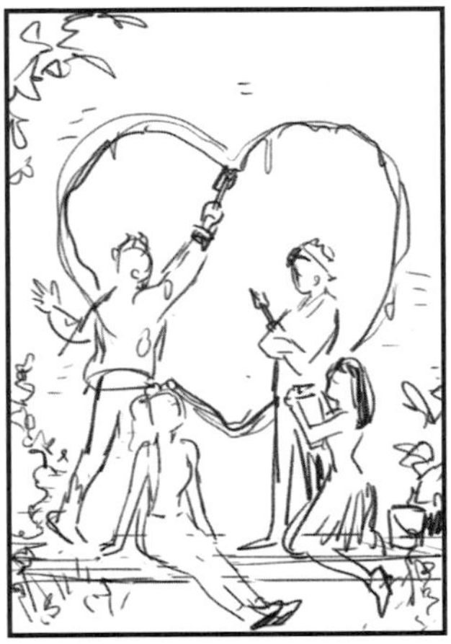

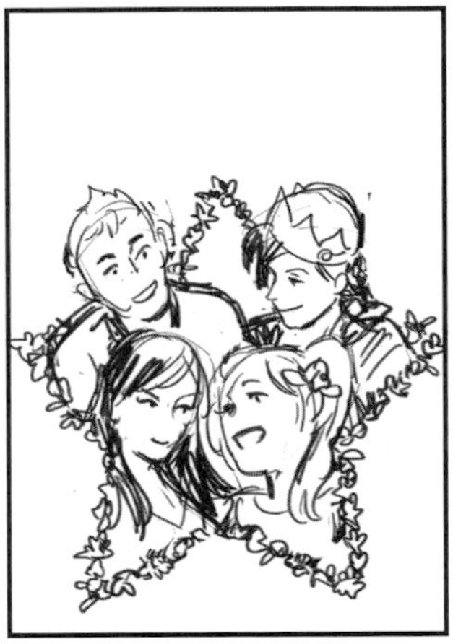

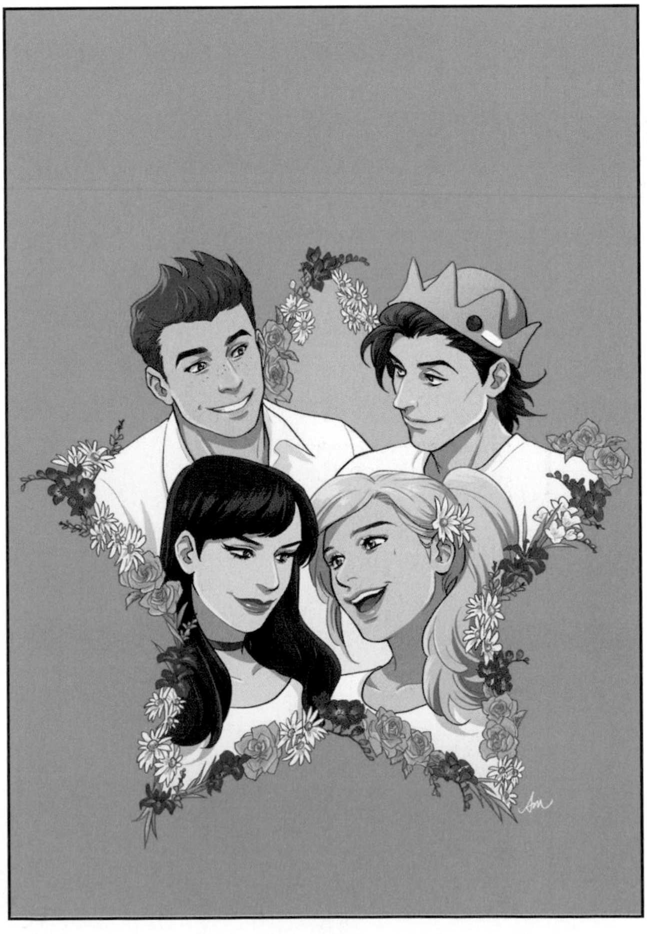

ISSUE
TWENTY
SEVEN

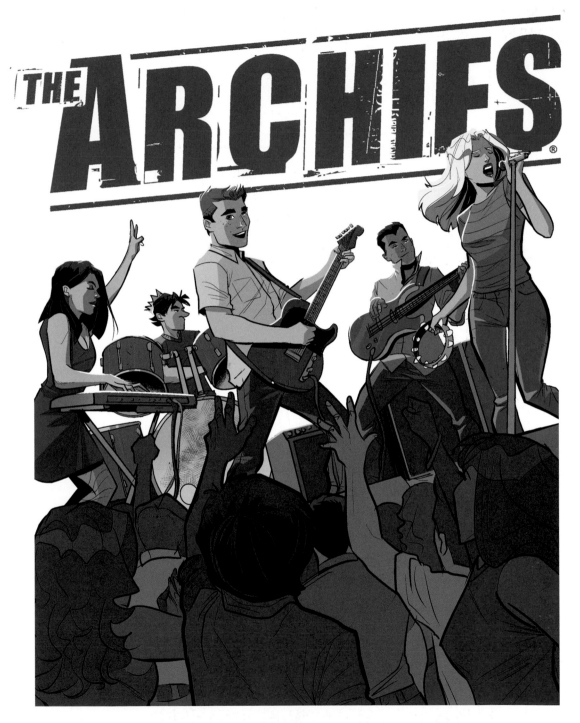

THE ARCHIES

STORY BY

ALEX SEGURA AND **MATTHEW ROSENBERG**

ART BY
JOE EISMA

COLORING BY
MATT HERMS

LETTERING BY
JACK MORELLI

ISSUE ONE

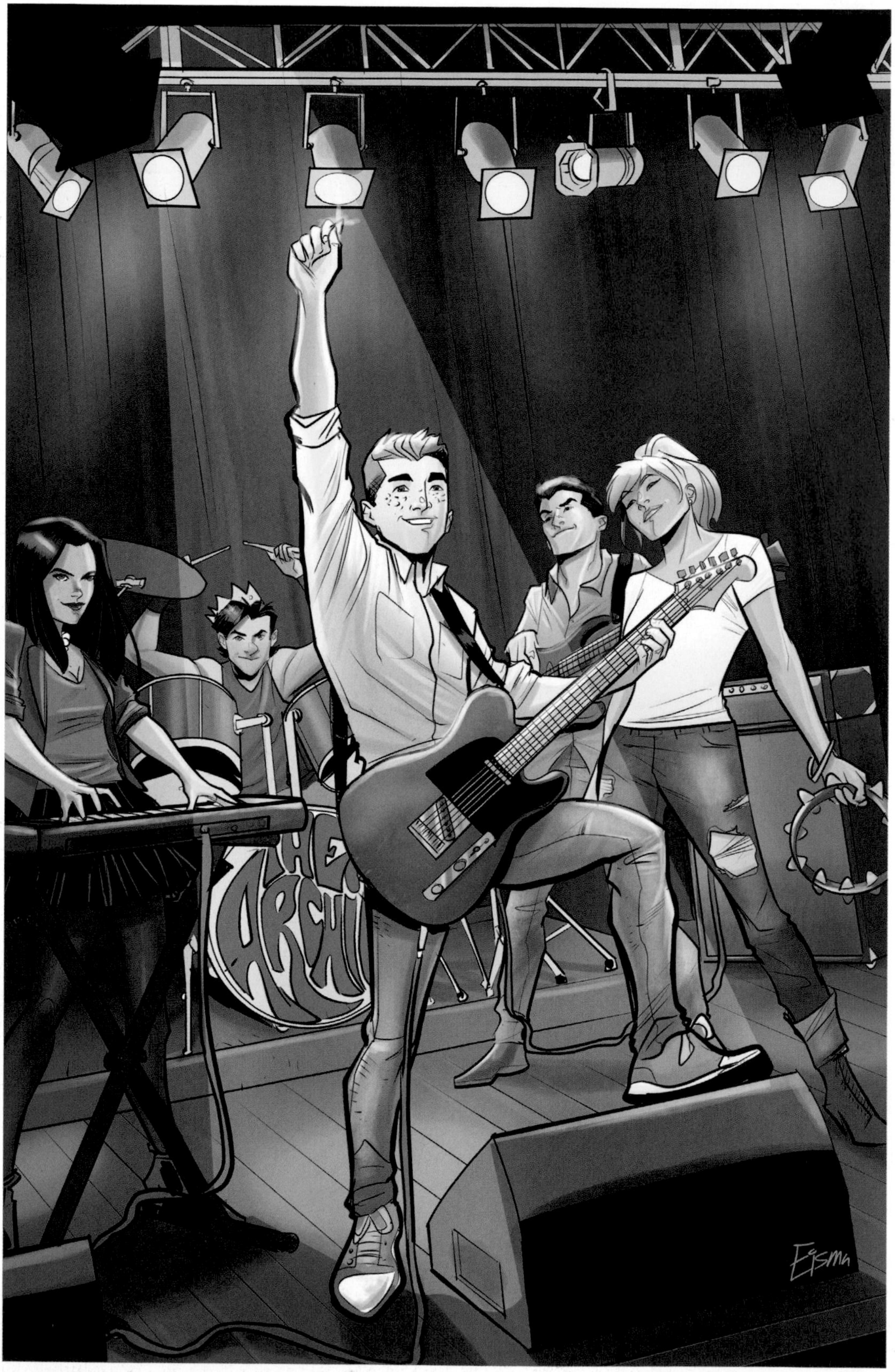
Eisma

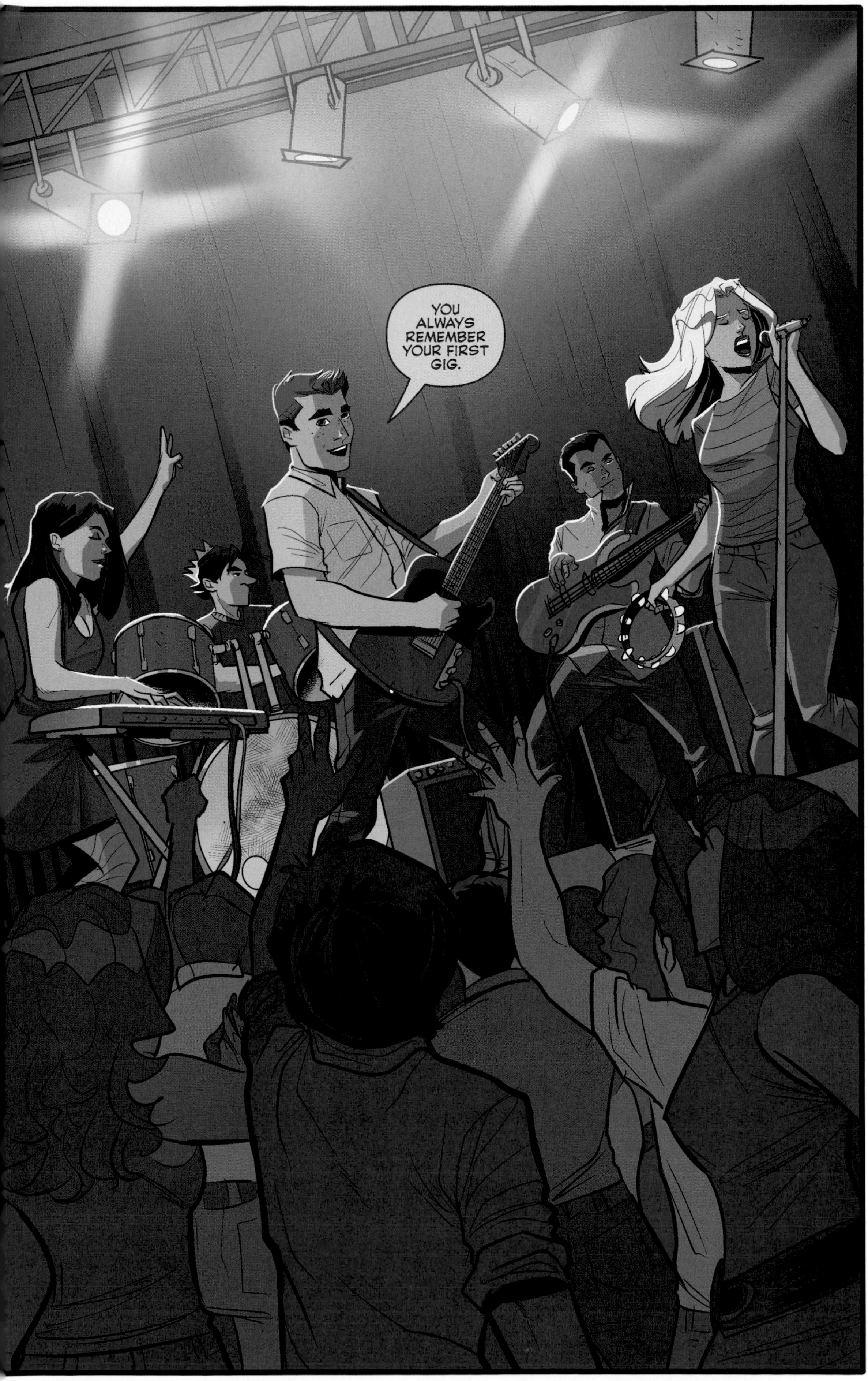
YOU ALWAYS REMEMBER YOUR FIRST GIG.

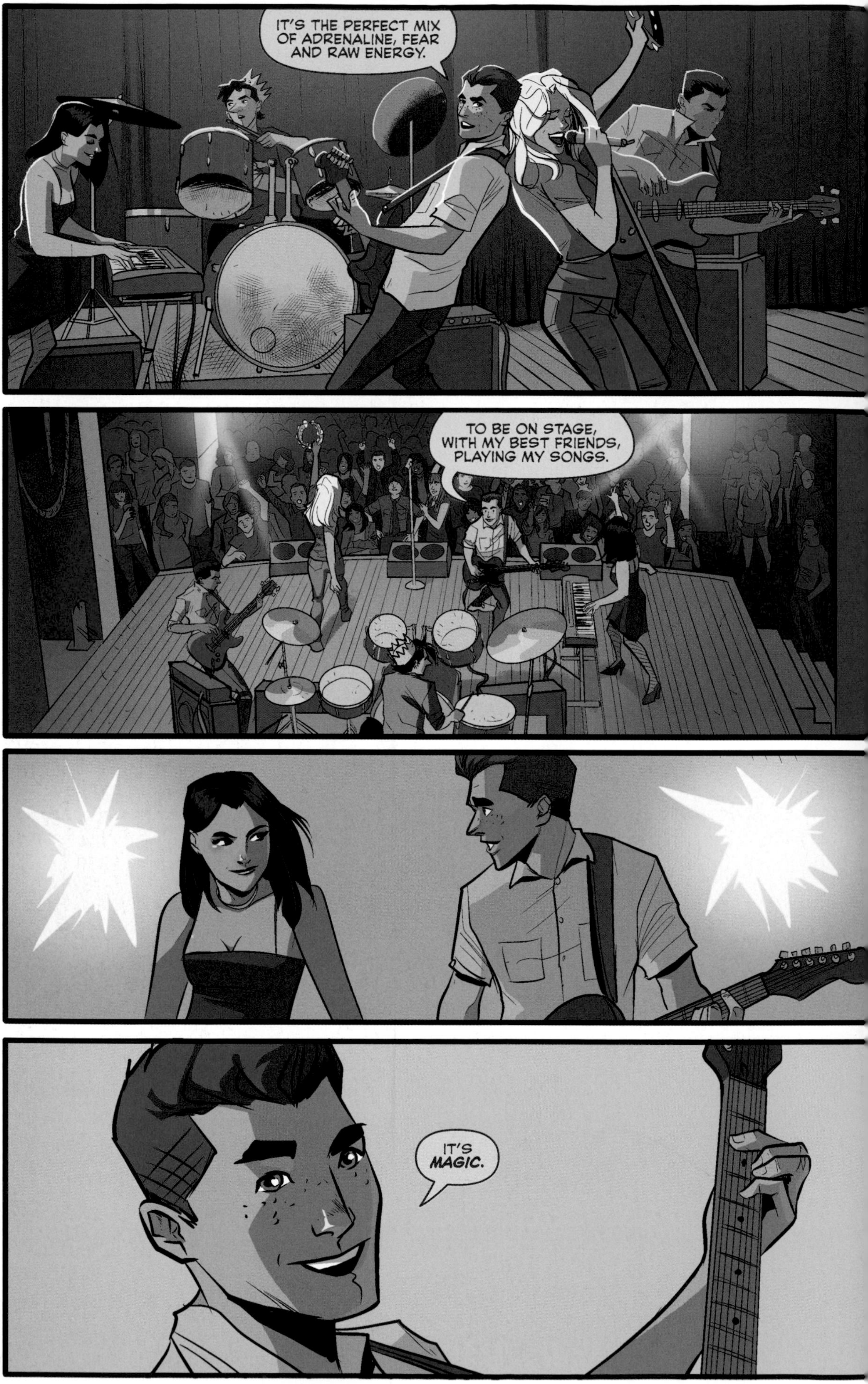
IT'S THE PERFECT MIX OF ADRENALINE, FEAR AND RAW ENERGY.
TO BE ON STAGE, WITH MY BEST FRIENDS, PLAYING MY SONGS.
IT'S *MAGIC.*

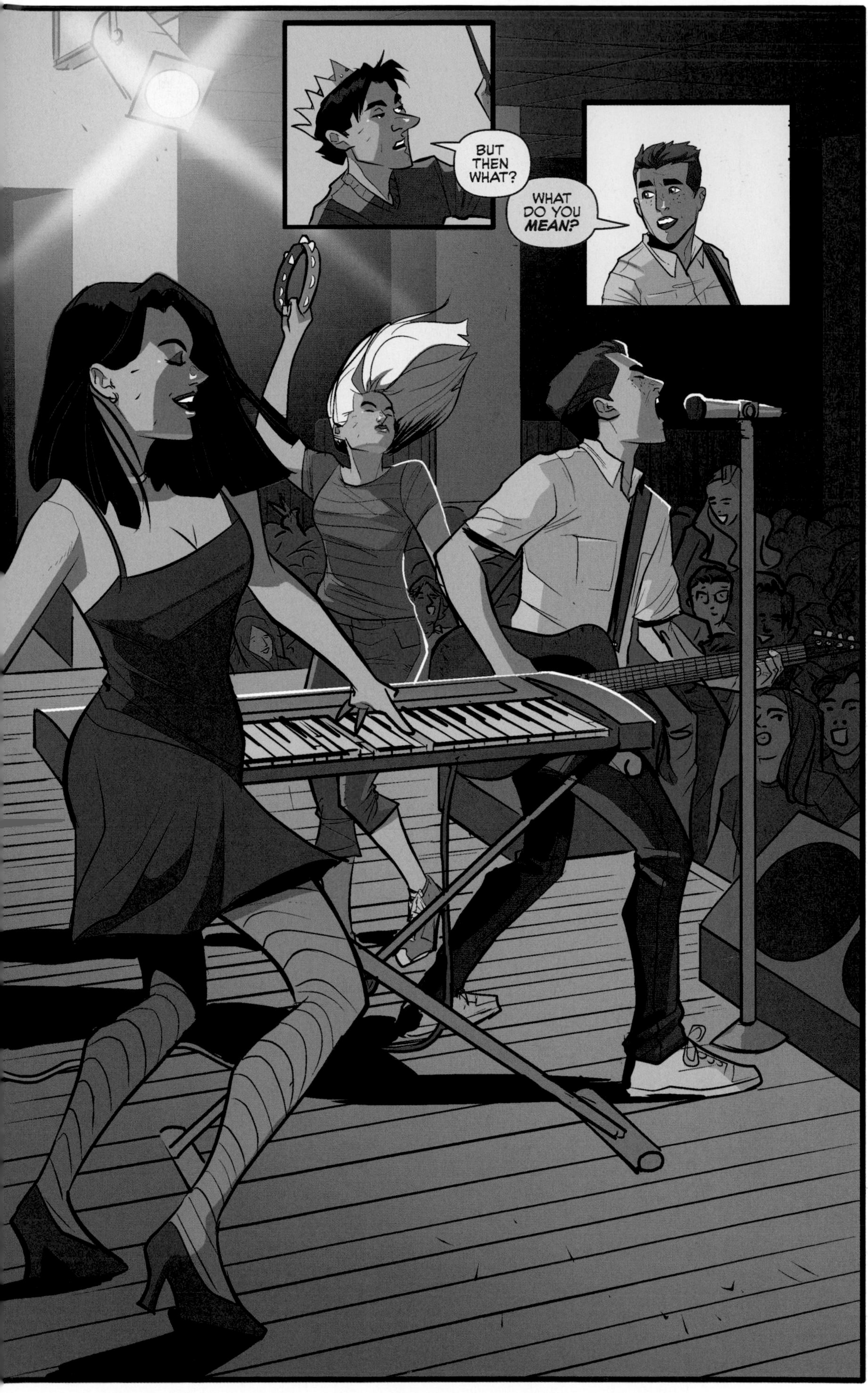
BUT THEN WHAT?
WHAT DO YOU *MEAN?*

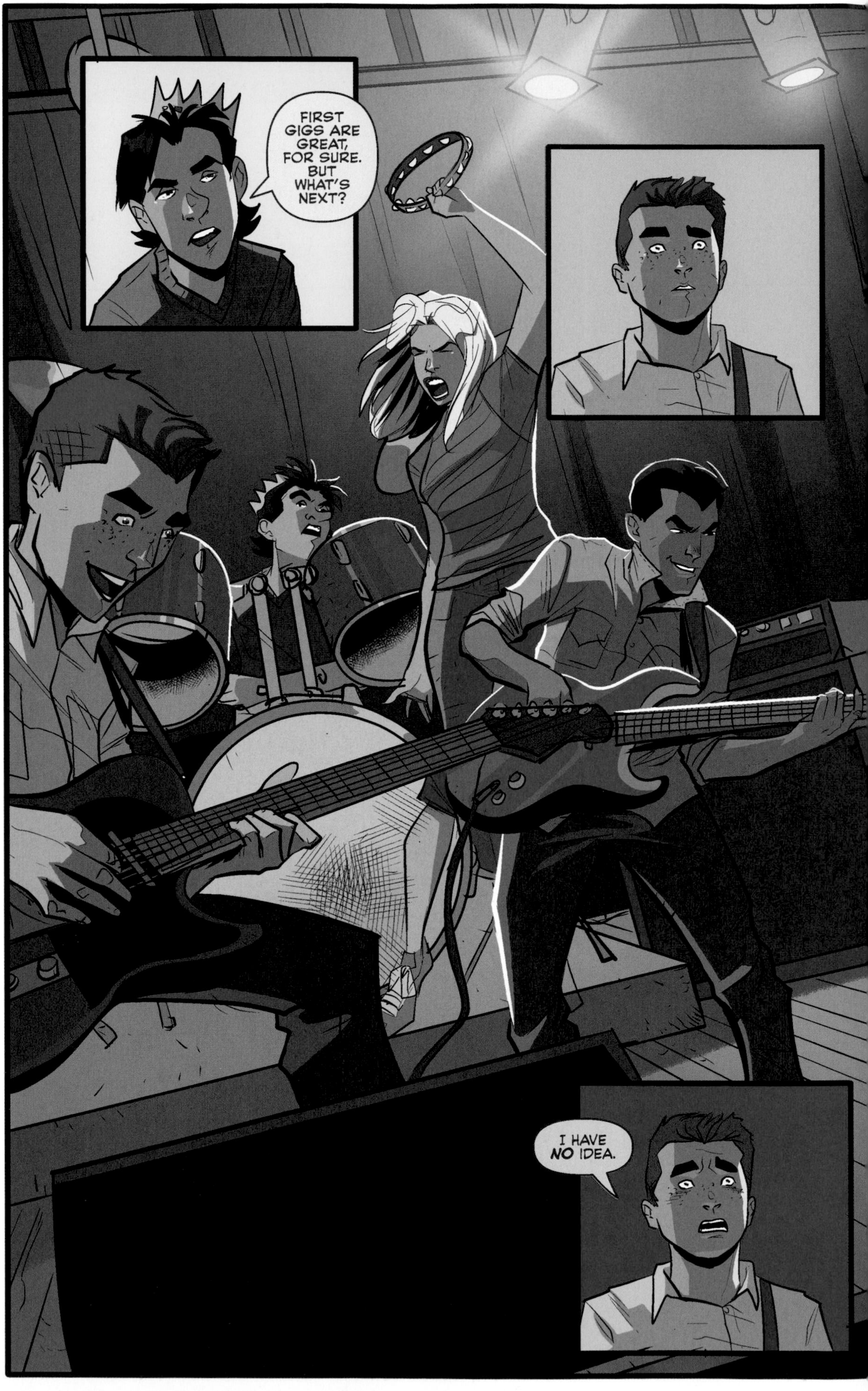
FIRST GIGS ARE GREAT, FOR SURE. BUT WHAT'S NEXT?
I HAVE **NO** IDEA.

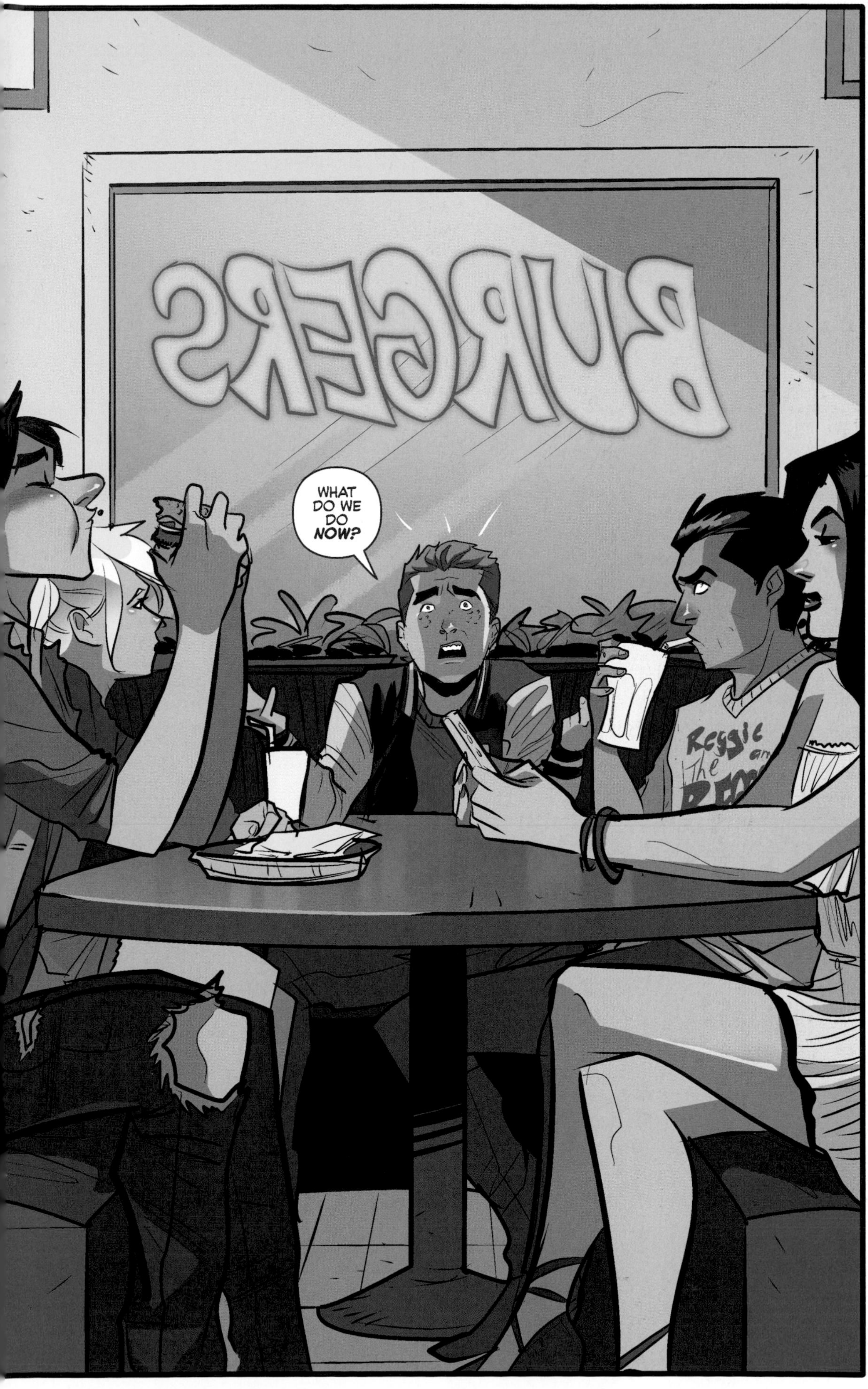
BURGERS
WHAT DO WE DO NOW?

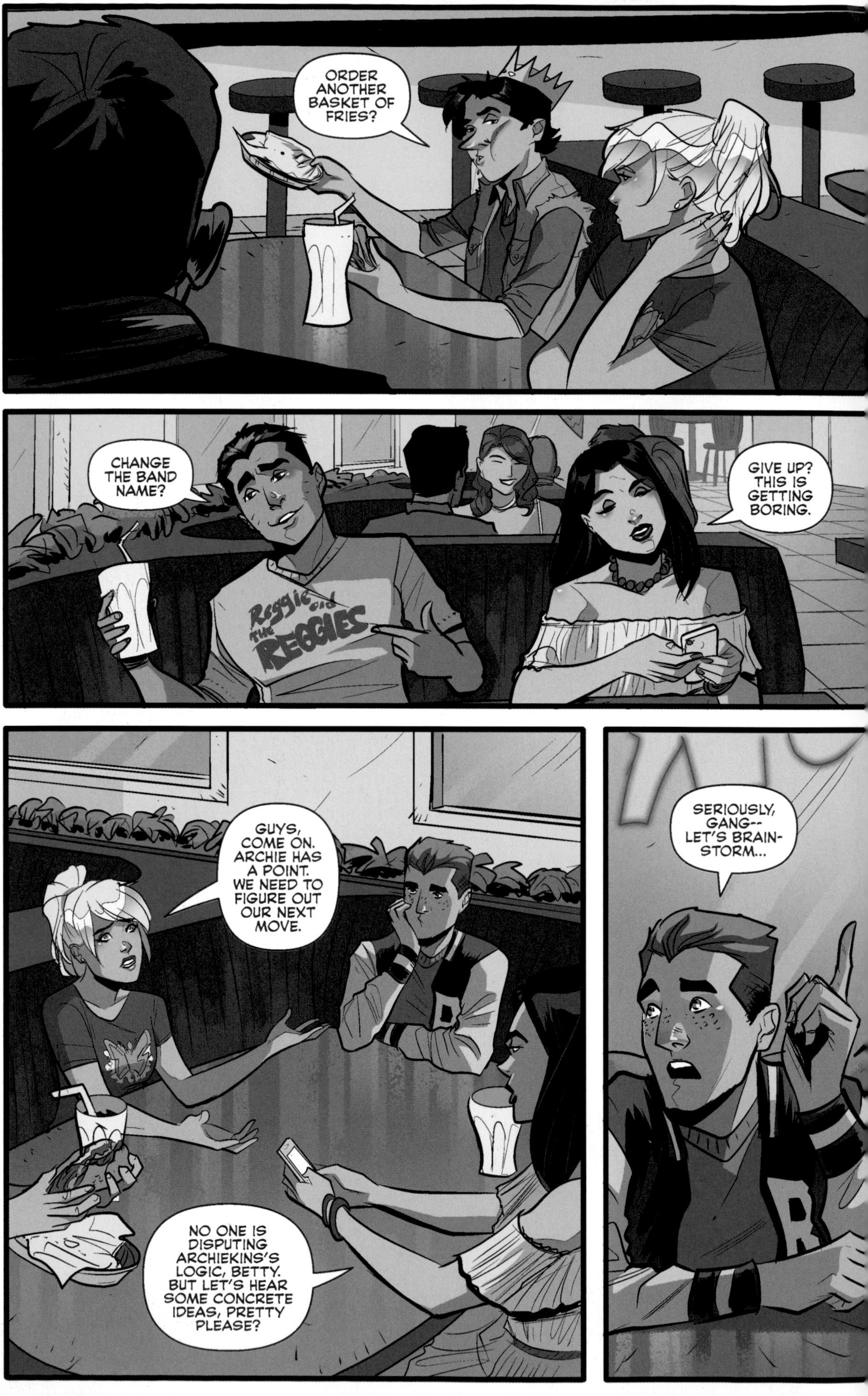
ORDER ANOTHER BASKET OF FRIES?
CHANGE THE BAND NAME?
Reggie and the REGGIES
GIVE UP? THIS IS GETTING BORING.
GUYS, COME ON. ARCHIE HAS A POINT. WE NEED TO FIGURE OUT OUR NEXT MOVE.
NO ONE IS DISPUTING ARCHIEKINS'S LOGIC, BETTY. BUT LET'S HEAR SOME CONCRETE IDEAS, PRETTY PLEASE?
SERIOUSLY, GANG-- LET'S BRAIN-STORM...

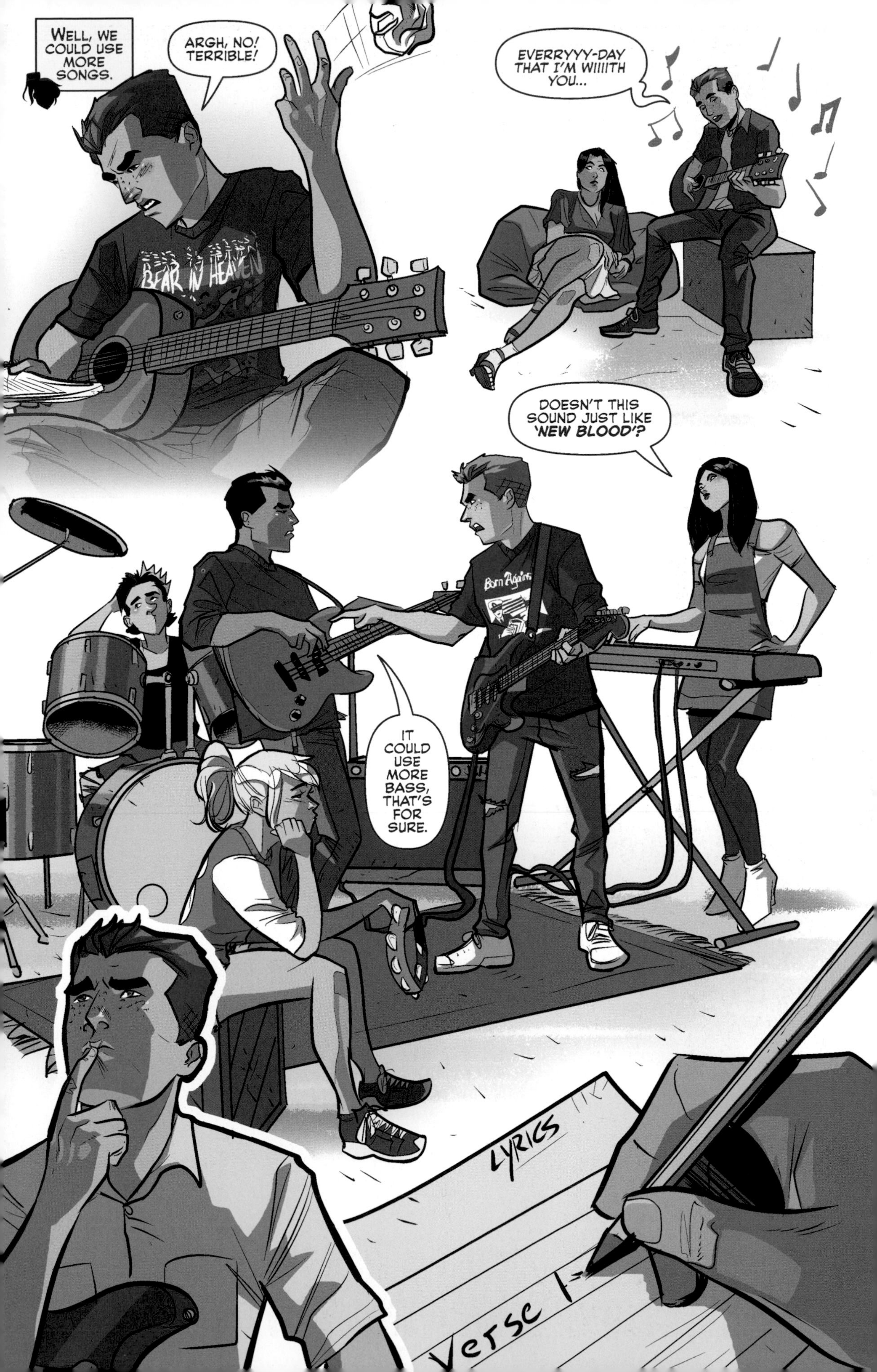
WELL, WE COULD USE MORE SONGS.
ARGH, NO! TERRIBLE!
BEAR IN HEAVEN
EVERRYYY-DAY THAT I'M WIIIITH YOU...
DOESN'T THIS SOUND JUST LIKE *'NEW BLOOD'*?
Born Agains
IT COULD USE MORE BASS, THAT'S FOR SURE.
LYRICS
Verse 1-

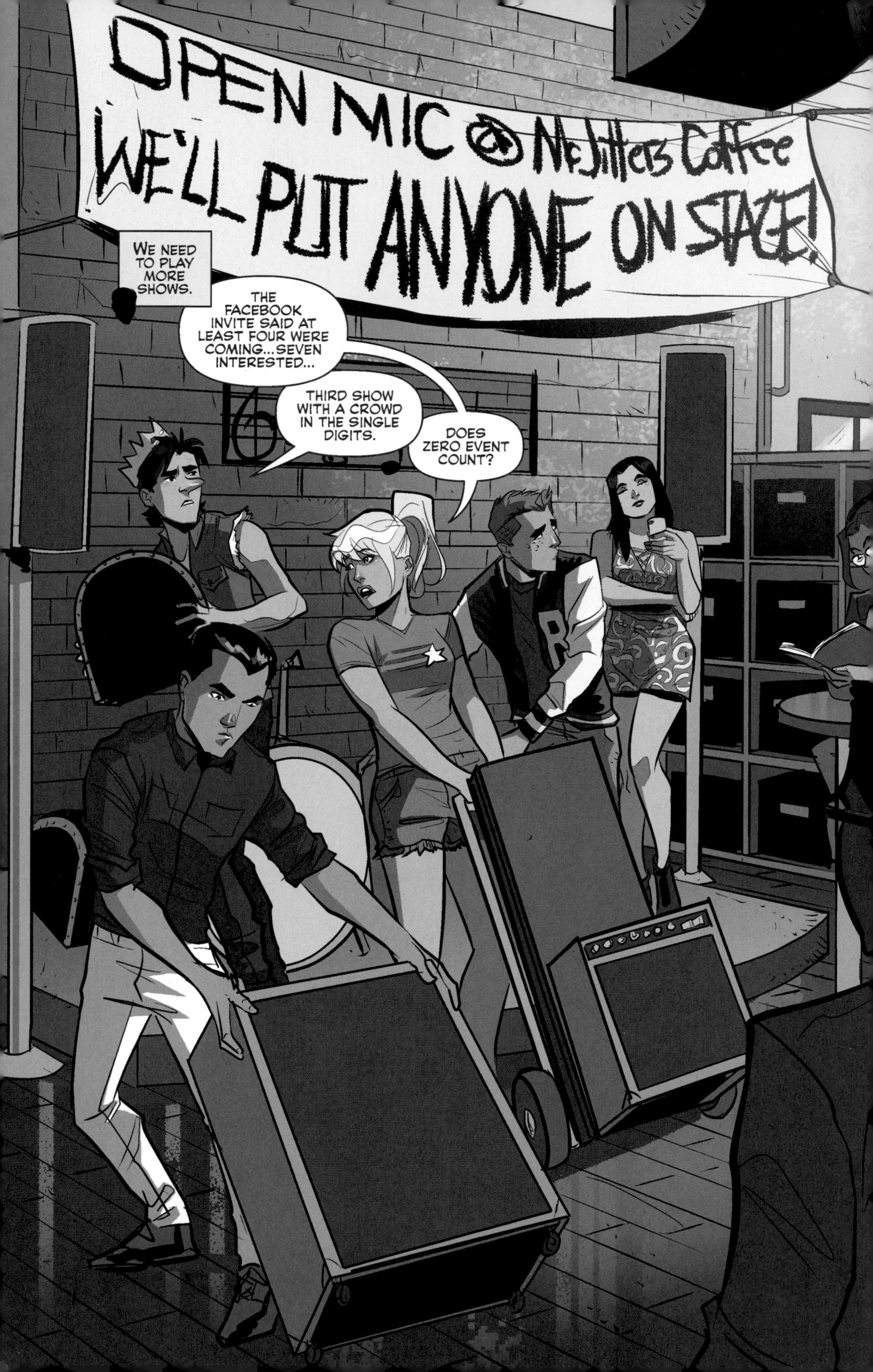
OPEN MIC @ Mr. Jitters Coffee
WE'LL PUT ANYONE ON STAGE!
WE NEED TO PLAY MORE SHOWS.
THE FACEBOOK INVITE SAID AT LEAST FOUR WERE COMING...SEVEN INTERESTED...
THIRD SHOW WITH A CROWD IN THE SINGLE DIGITS.
DOES ZERO EVENT COUNT?

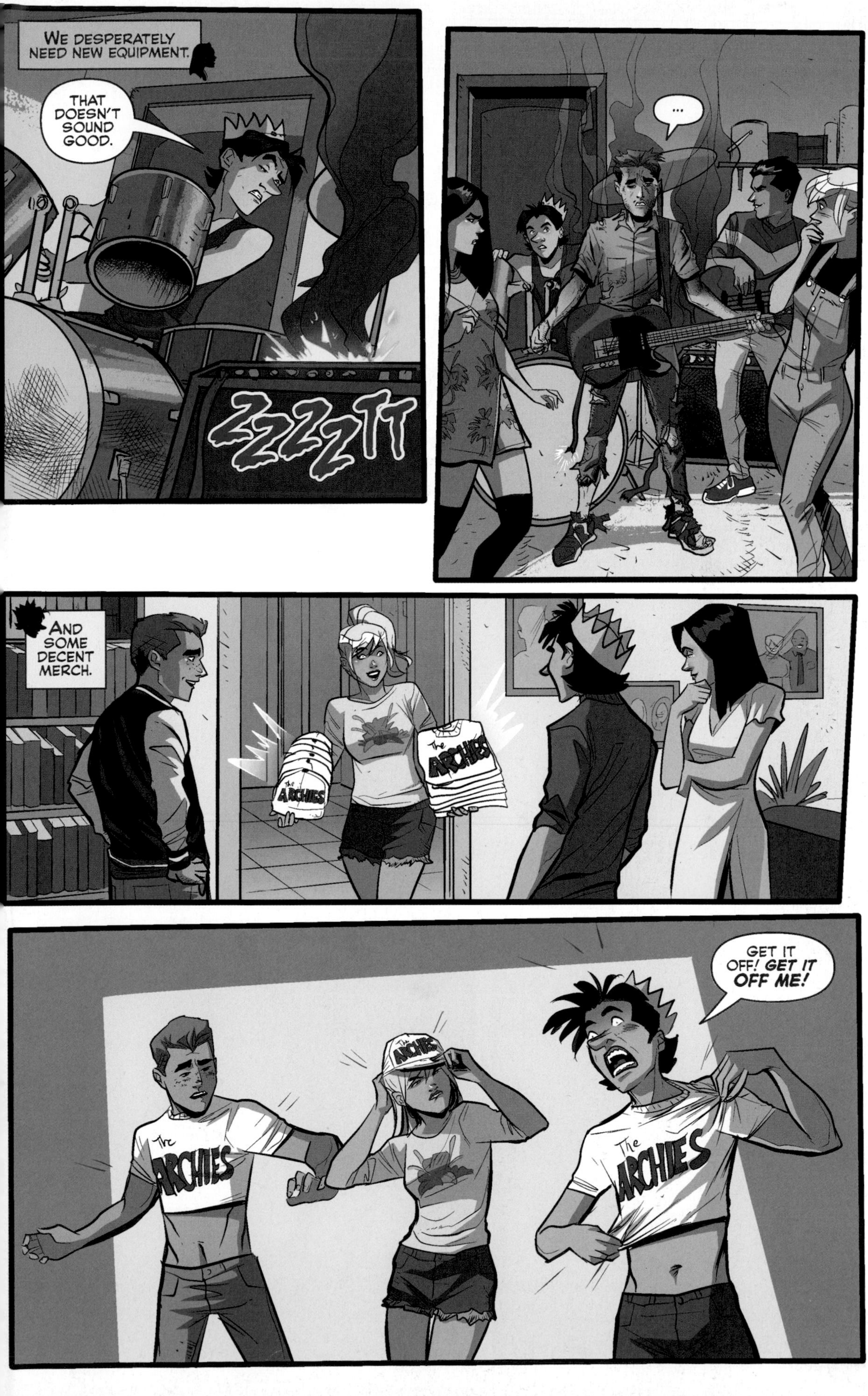

WE DESPERATELY NEED NEW EQUIPMENT.
THAT DOESN'T SOUND GOOD.
ZZZZTT
...
AND SOME DECENT MERCH.
The ARCHIES
The ARCHIES
GET IT OFF! GET IT OFF ME!
The ARCHIES
The ARCHIES
The ARCHIES

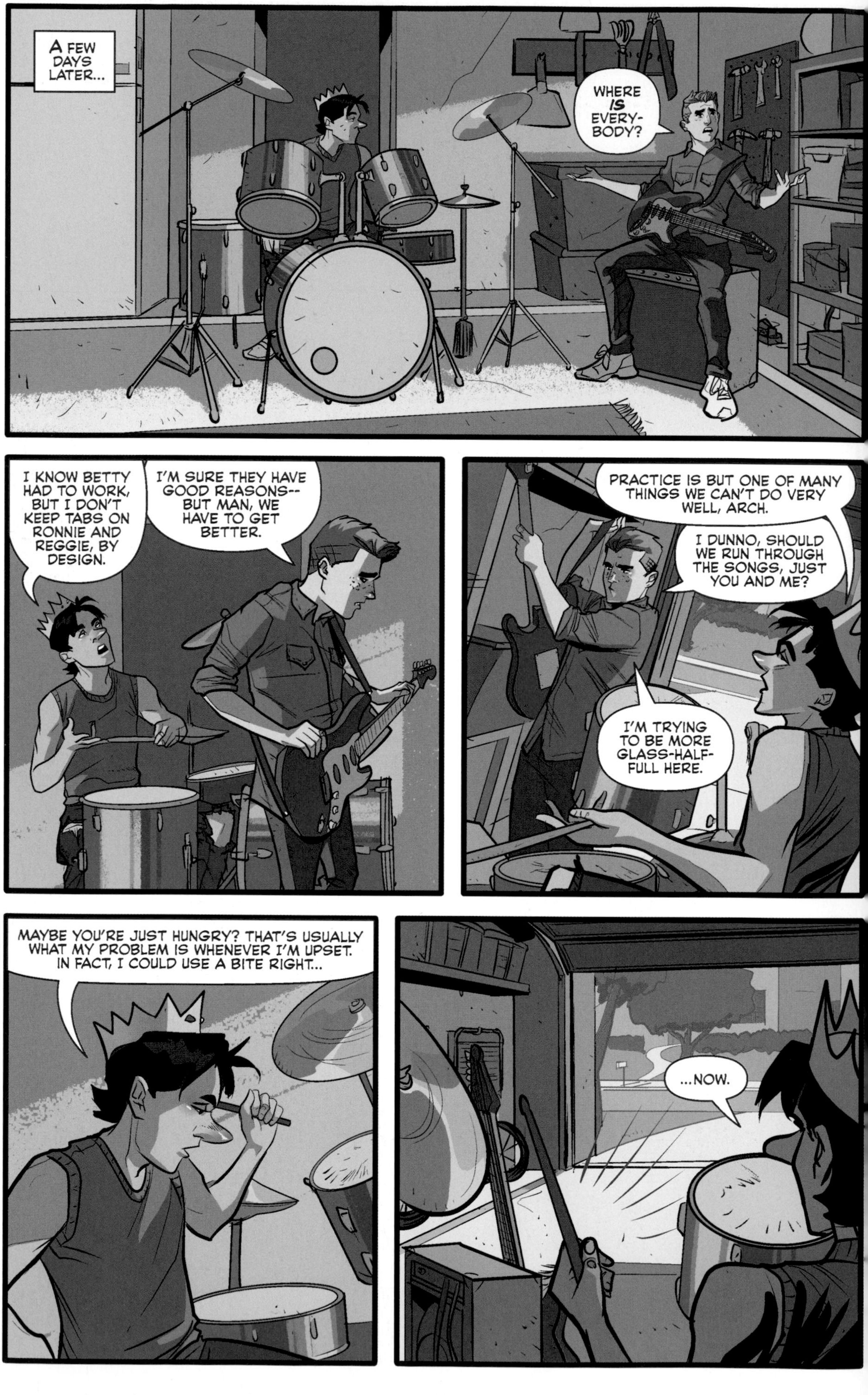
A FEW DAYS LATER...
WHERE *IS* EVERY-BODY?
I KNOW BETTY HAD TO WORK, BUT I DON'T KEEP TABS ON RONNIE AND REGGIE, BY DESIGN.
I'M SURE THEY HAVE GOOD REASONS-- BUT MAN, WE HAVE TO GET BETTER.
PRACTICE IS BUT ONE OF MANY THINGS WE CAN'T DO VERY WELL, ARCH.
I DUNNO, SHOULD WE RUN THROUGH THE SONGS, JUST YOU AND ME?
I'M TRYING TO BE MORE GLASS-HALF-FULL HERE.
MAYBE YOU'RE JUST HUNGRY? THAT'S USUALLY WHAT MY PROBLEM IS WHENEVER I'M UPSET. IN FACT, I COULD USE A BITE RIGHT...
...NOW.

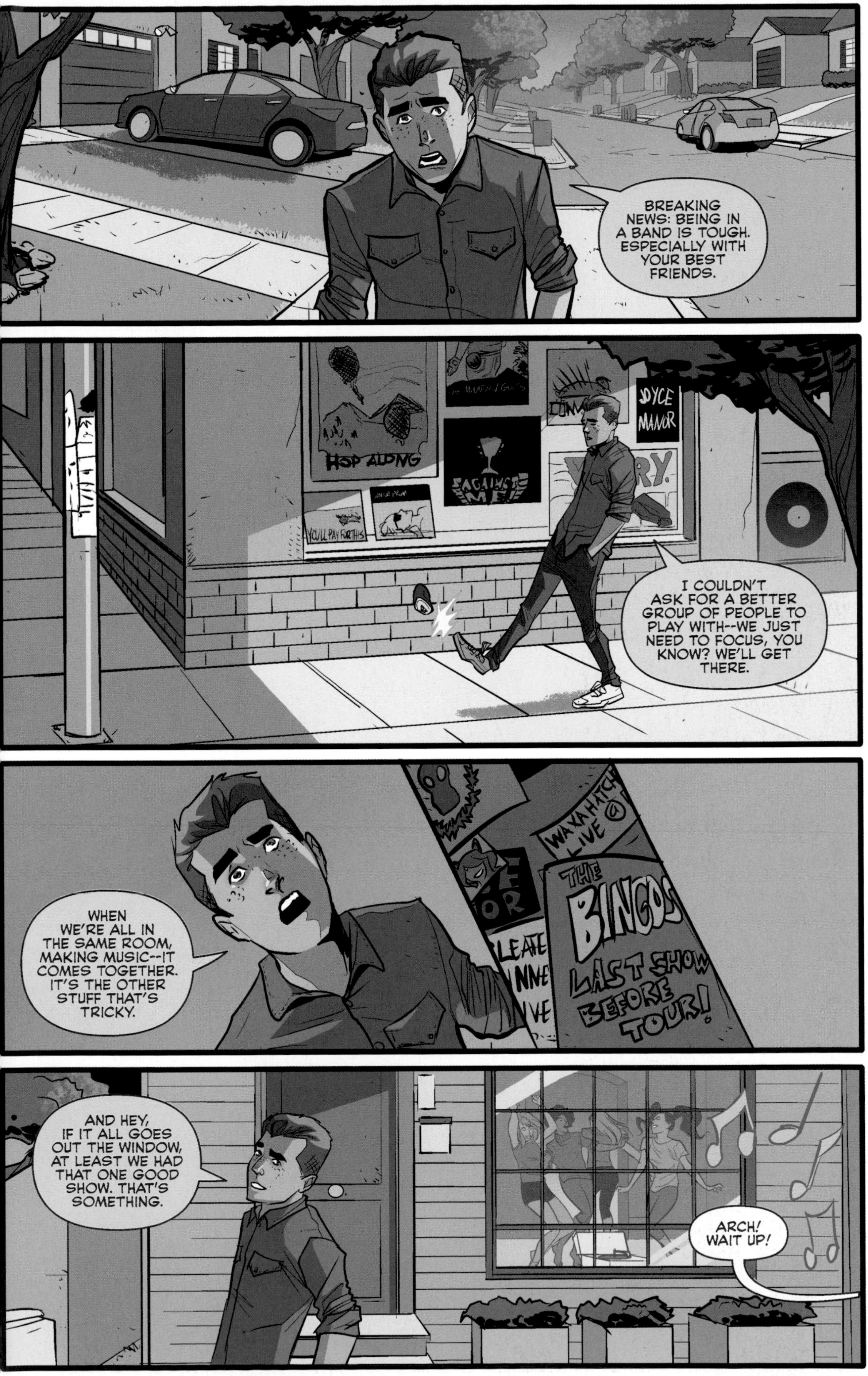
BREAKING NEWS: BEING IN A BAND IS TOUGH. ESPECIALLY WITH YOUR BEST FRIENDS.
HOP ALONG
AGAINST ME!
YOU'LL PAY FOR THIS
JOYCE MANOR
I COULDN'T ASK FOR A BETTER GROUP OF PEOPLE TO PLAY WITH--WE JUST NEED TO FOCUS, YOU KNOW? WE'LL GET THERE.
WHEN WE'RE ALL IN THE SAME ROOM, MAKING MUSIC--IT COMES TOGETHER. IT'S THE OTHER STUFF THAT'S TRICKY.
THE BINGOS LAST SHOW BEFORE TOUR!
AND HEY, IF IT ALL GOES OUT THE WINDOW, AT LEAST WE HAD THAT ONE GOOD SHOW. THAT'S SOMETHING.
ARCH! WAIT UP!

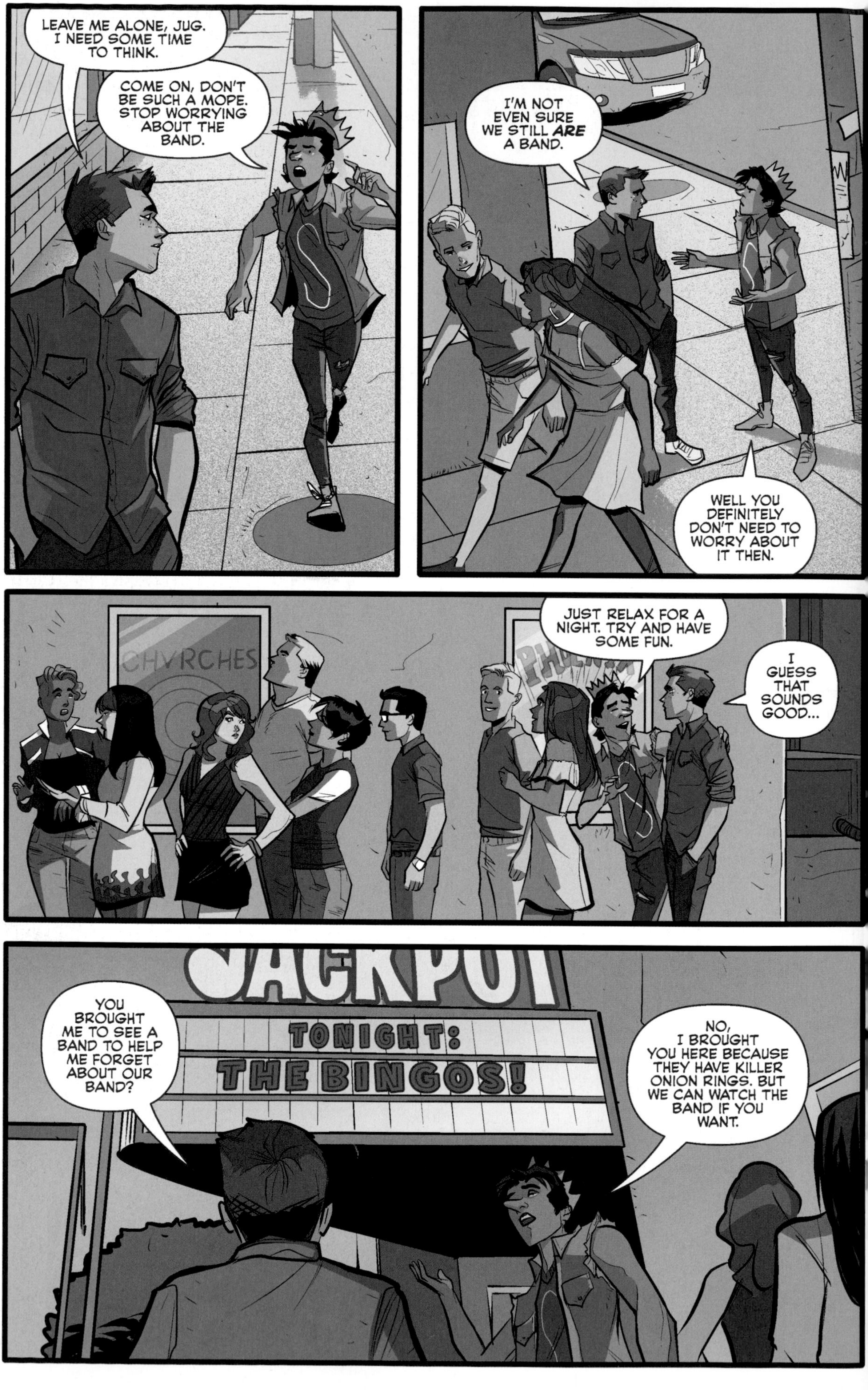

LEAVE ME ALONE, JUG. I NEED SOME TIME TO THINK.
COME ON, DON'T BE SUCH A MOPE. STOP WORRYING ABOUT THE BAND.
I'M NOT EVEN SURE WE STILL *ARE* A BAND.
WELL YOU DEFINITELY DON'T NEED TO WORRY ABOUT IT THEN.
CHVRCHES
JUST RELAX FOR A NIGHT. TRY AND HAVE SOME FUN.
I GUESS THAT SOUNDS GOOD...
JACKPOT
TONIGHT: THE BINGOS!
YOU BROUGHT ME TO SEE A BAND TO HELP ME FORGET ABOUT OUR BAND?
NO, I BROUGHT YOU HERE BECAUSE THEY HAVE KILLER ONION RINGS. BUT WE CAN WATCH THE BAND IF YOU WANT.

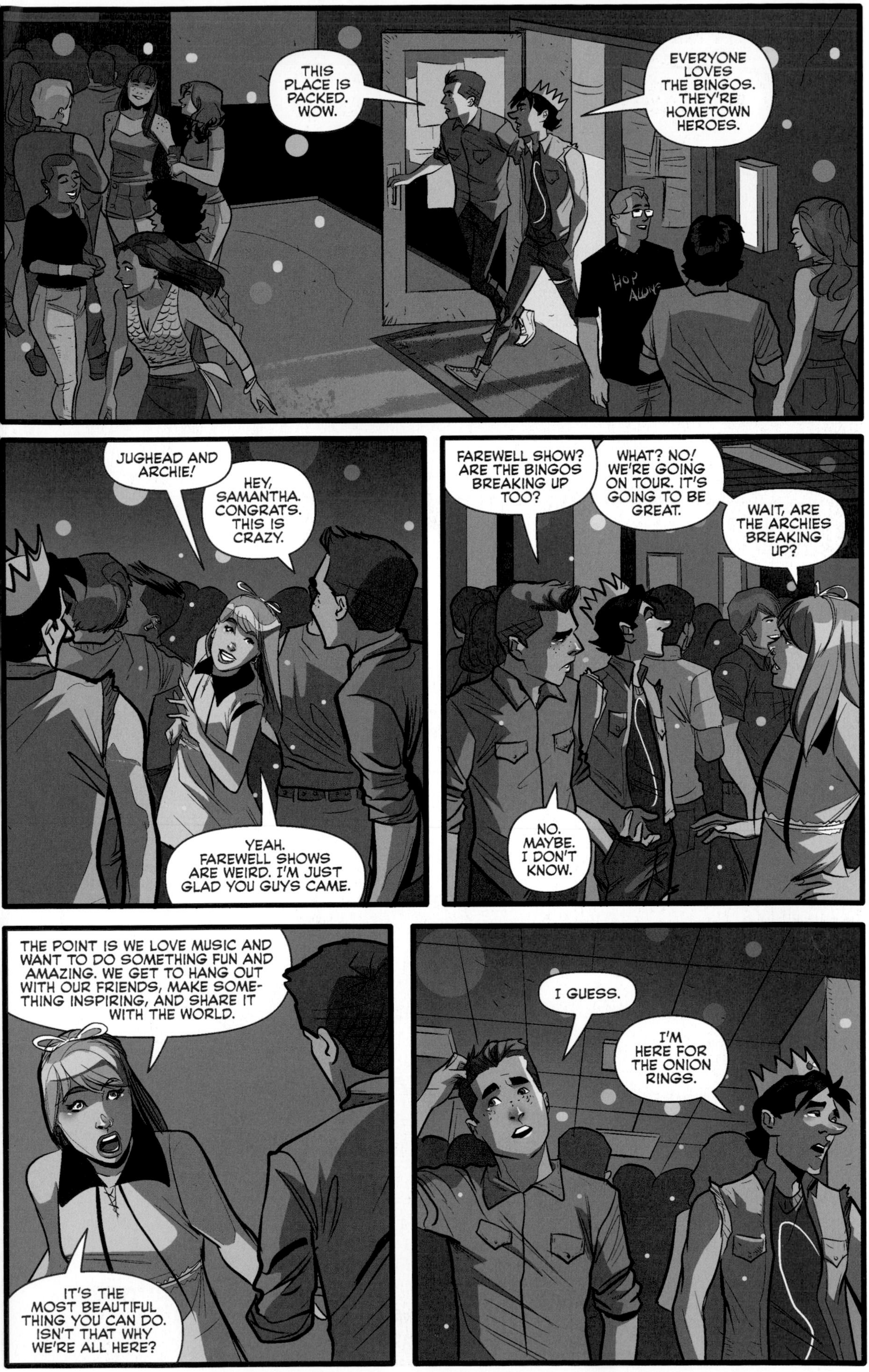
THIS PLACE IS PACKED. WOW.
EVERYONE LOVES THE BINGOS. THEY'RE HOMETOWN HEROES.
HOP ALONG
JUGHEAD AND ARCHIE!
HEY, SAMANTHA. CONGRATS. THIS IS CRAZY.
YEAH. FAREWELL SHOWS ARE WEIRD. I'M JUST GLAD YOU GUYS CAME.
FAREWELL SHOW? ARE THE BINGOS BREAKING UP TOO?
WHAT? NO! WE'RE GOING ON TOUR. IT'S GOING TO BE GREAT.
WAIT, ARE THE ARCHIES BREAKING UP?
NO. MAYBE. I DON'T KNOW.
THE POINT IS WE LOVE MUSIC AND WANT TO DO SOMETHING FUN AND AMAZING. WE GET TO HANG OUT WITH OUR FRIENDS, MAKE SOME-THING INSPIRING, AND SHARE IT WITH THE WORLD.
IT'S THE MOST BEAUTIFUL THING YOU CAN DO. ISN'T THAT WHY WE'RE ALL HERE?
I GUESS.
I'M HERE FOR THE ONION RINGS.

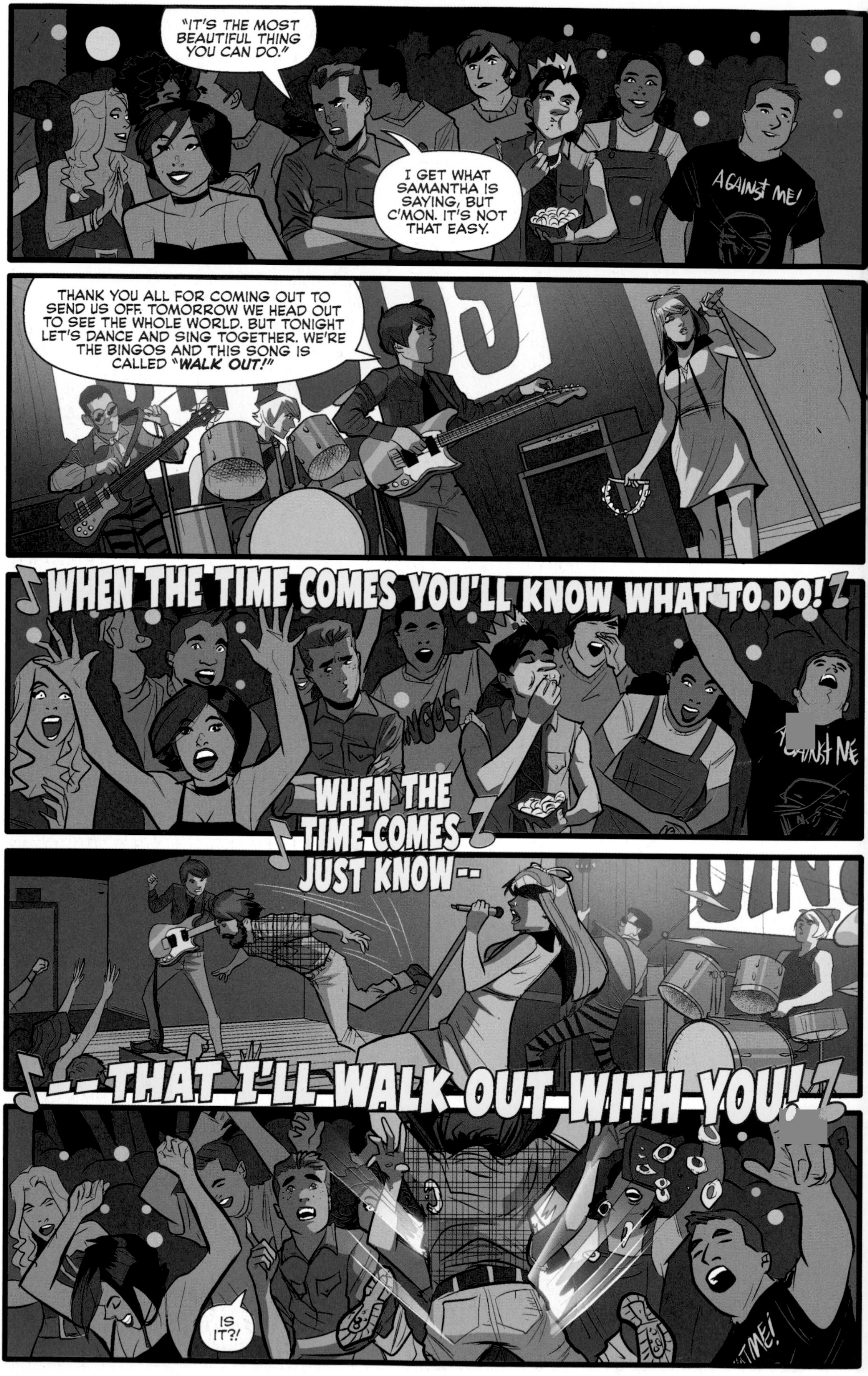
"IT'S THE MOST BEAUTIFUL THING YOU CAN DO."
I GET WHAT SAMANTHA IS SAYING, BUT C'MON. IT'S NOT THAT EASY.
AGAINST ME!
THANK YOU ALL FOR COMING OUT TO SEND US OFF. TOMORROW WE HEAD OUT TO SEE THE WHOLE WORLD. BUT TONIGHT LET'S DANCE AND SING TOGETHER. WE'RE THE BINGOS AND THIS SONG IS CALLED "WALK OUT!"
WHEN THE TIME COMES YOU'LL KNOW WHAT TO DO!
WHEN THE TIME COMES JUST KNOW--
--THAT I'LL WALK OUT WITH YOU!
IS IT?!

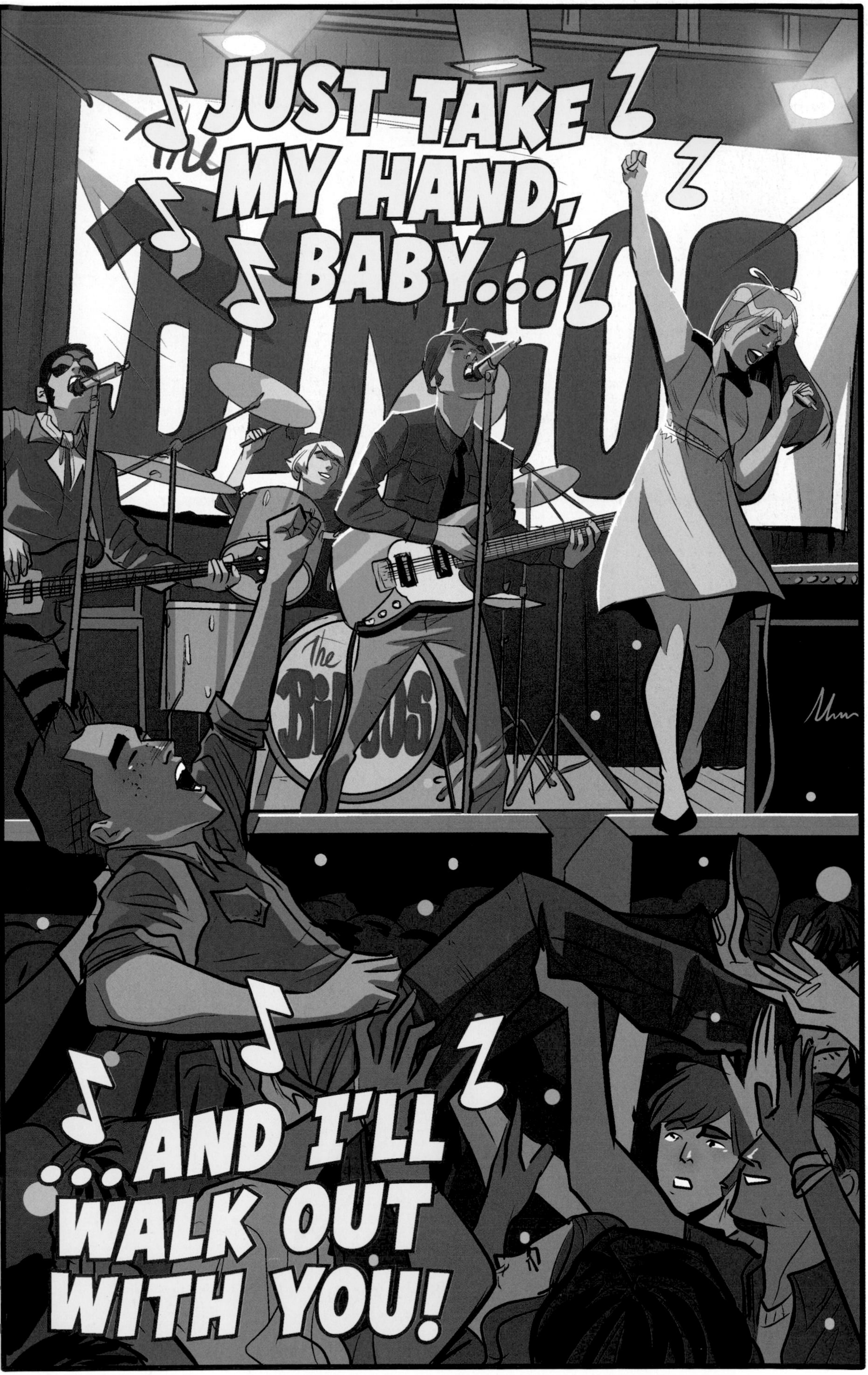
JUST TAKE MY HAND, BABY...
...AND I'LL WALK OUT WITH YOU!

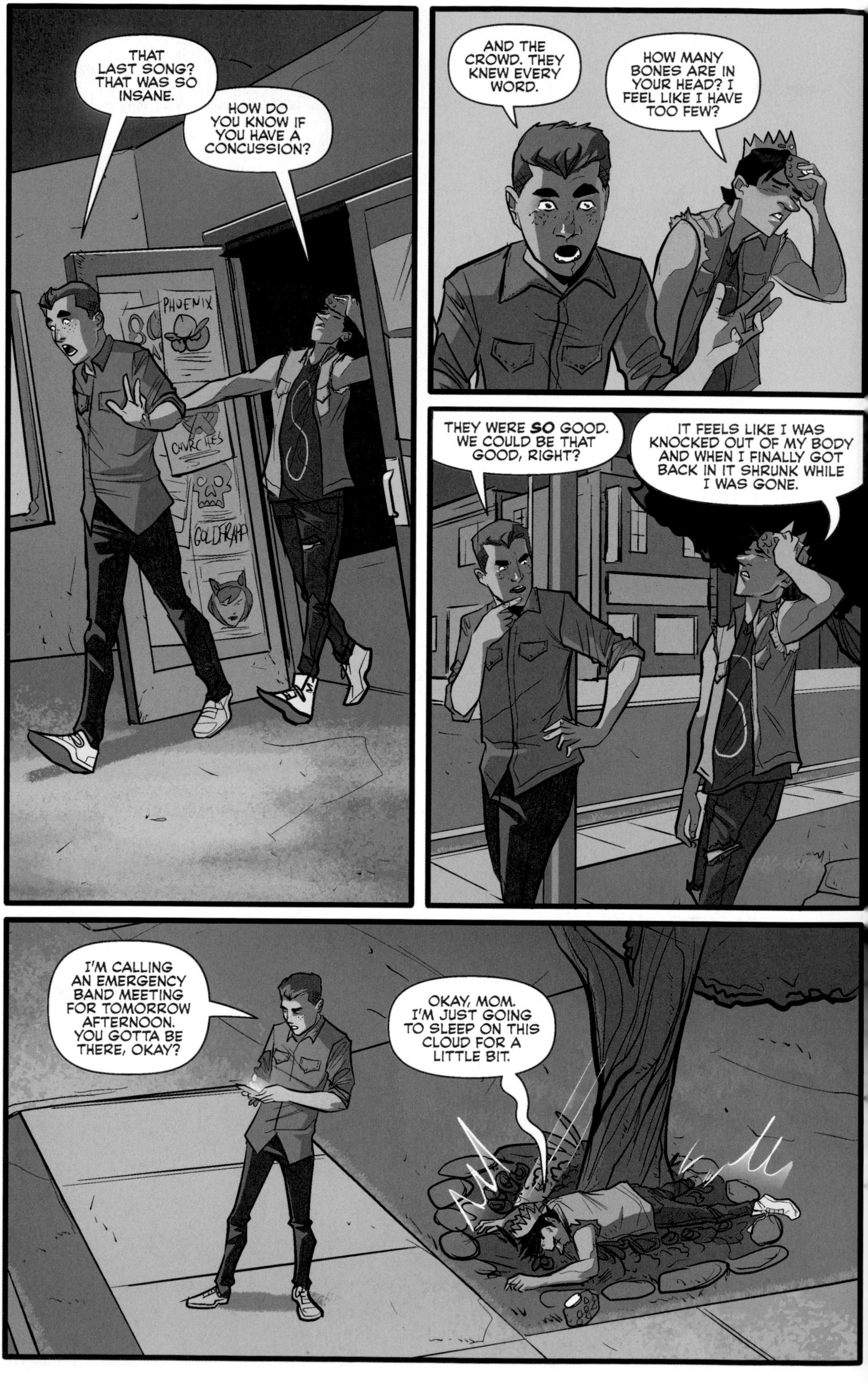
THAT LAST SONG? THAT WAS SO INSANE.
HOW DO YOU KNOW IF YOU HAVE A CONCUSSION?
PHOENIX
CHURCHES
GOLDFRAPP
AND THE CROWD. THEY KNEW EVERY WORD.
HOW MANY BONES ARE IN YOUR HEAD? I FEEL LIKE I HAVE TOO FEW?
THEY WERE **SO** GOOD. WE COULD BE THAT GOOD, RIGHT?
IT FEELS LIKE I WAS KNOCKED OUT OF MY BODY AND WHEN I FINALLY GOT BACK IN IT SHRUNK WHILE I WAS GONE.
I'M CALLING AN EMERGENCY BAND MEETING FOR TOMORROW AFTERNOON. YOU GOTTA BE THERE, OKAY?
OKAY, MOM. I'M JUST GOING TO SLEEP ON THIS CLOUD FOR A LITTLE BIT.

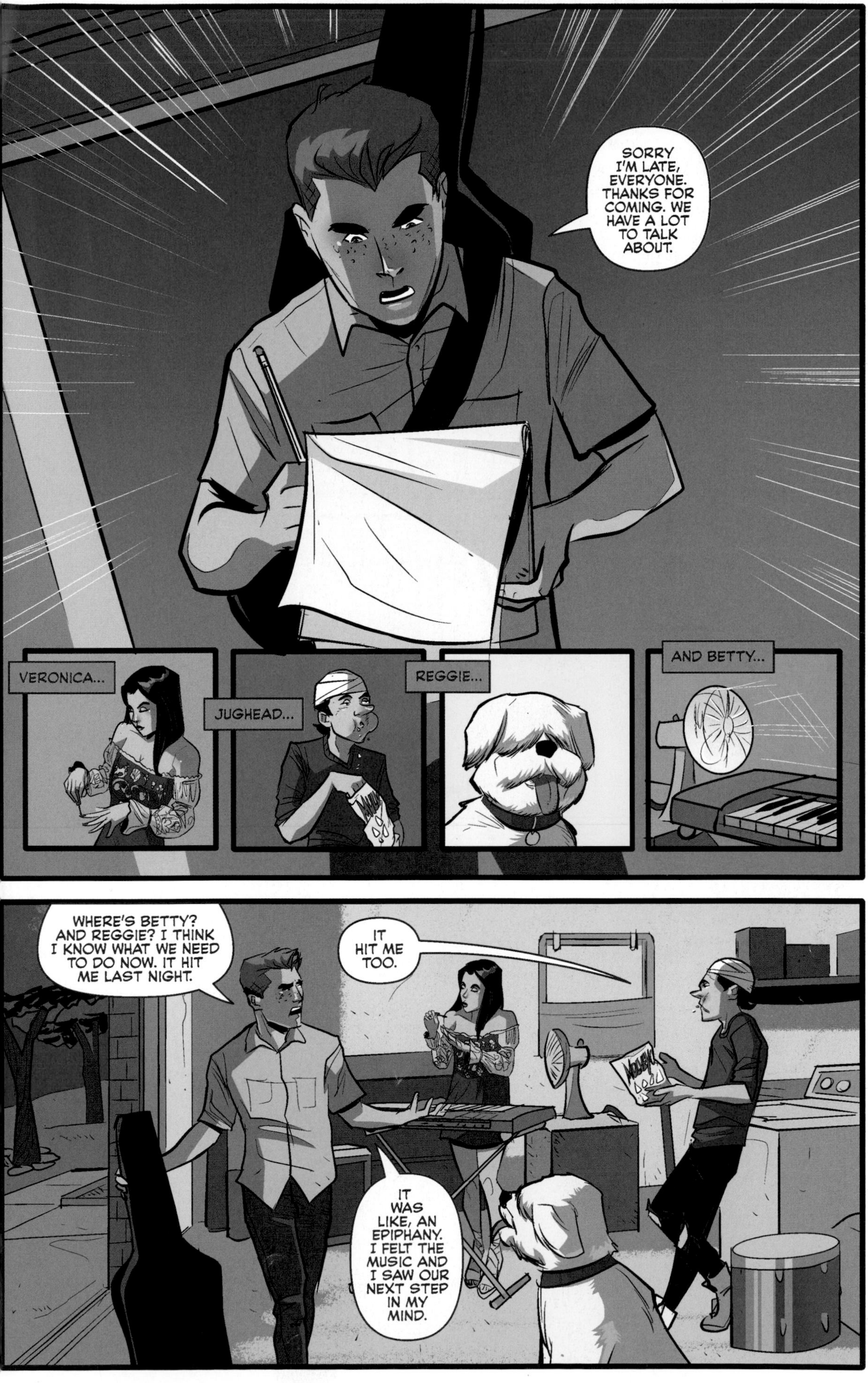
SORRY I'M LATE, EVERYONE. THANKS FOR COMING. WE HAVE A LOT TO TALK ABOUT.
VERONICA...
JUGHEAD...
REGGIE...
AND BETTY...
WHERE'S BETTY? AND REGGIE? I THINK I KNOW WHAT WE NEED TO DO NOW. IT HIT ME LAST NIGHT.
IT HIT ME TOO.
IT WAS LIKE, AN EPIPHANY. I FELT THE MUSIC AND I SAW OUR NEXT STEP IN MY MIND.

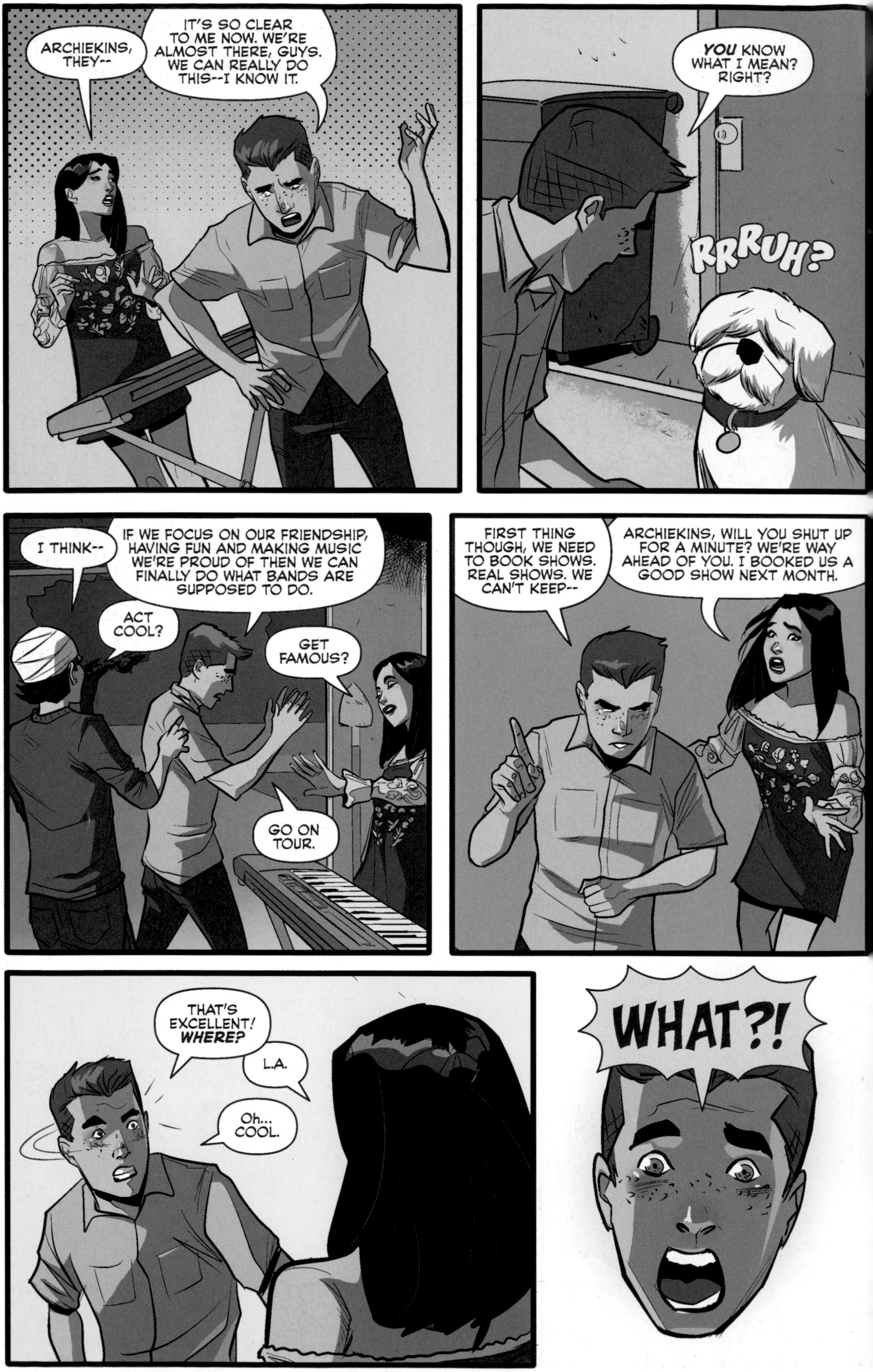
ARCHIEKINS, THEY--
IT'S SO CLEAR TO ME NOW. WE'RE ALMOST THERE, GUYS. WE CAN REALLY DO THIS--I KNOW IT.
YOU KNOW WHAT I MEAN? RIGHT?
RRRUH?
I THINK--
IF WE FOCUS ON OUR FRIENDSHIP, HAVING FUN AND MAKING MUSIC WE'RE PROUD OF THEN WE CAN FINALLY DO WHAT BANDS ARE SUPPOSED TO DO.
ACT COOL?
GET FAMOUS?
GO ON TOUR.
FIRST THING THOUGH, WE NEED TO BOOK SHOWS. REAL SHOWS. WE CAN'T KEEP--
ARCHIEKINS, WILL YOU SHUT UP FOR A MINUTE? WE'RE WAY AHEAD OF YOU. I BOOKED US A GOOD SHOW NEXT MONTH.
THAT'S EXCELLENT! WHERE?
L.A.
Oh... COOL.
WHAT?!

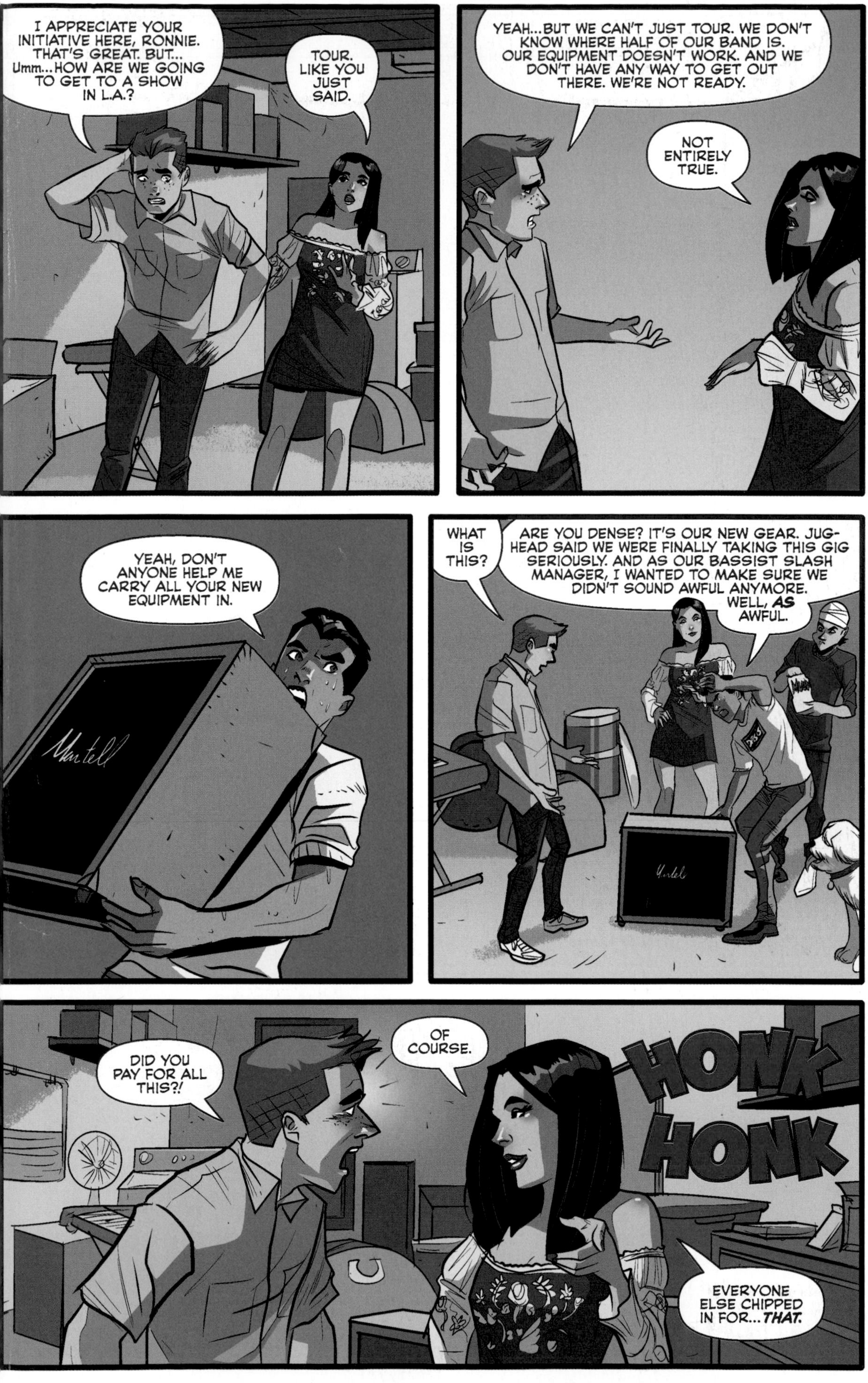
I APPRECIATE YOUR INITIATIVE HERE, RONNIE. THAT'S GREAT. BUT... Umm...HOW ARE WE GOING TO GET TO A SHOW IN L.A.?
TOUR. LIKE YOU JUST SAID.
YEAH...BUT WE CAN'T JUST TOUR. WE DON'T KNOW WHERE HALF OF OUR BAND IS. OUR EQUIPMENT DOESN'T WORK. AND WE DON'T HAVE ANY WAY TO GET OUT THERE. WE'RE NOT READY.
NOT ENTIRELY TRUE.
YEAH, DON'T ANYONE HELP ME CARRY ALL YOUR NEW EQUIPMENT IN.
WHAT IS THIS?
ARE YOU DENSE? IT'S OUR NEW GEAR. JUG-HEAD SAID WE WERE FINALLY TAKING THIS GIG SERIOUSLY. AND AS OUR BASSIST SLASH MANAGER, I WANTED TO MAKE SURE WE DIDN'T SOUND AWFUL ANYMORE.
WELL, AS AWFUL.
DID YOU PAY FOR ALL THIS?!
OF COURSE.
HONK HONK
EVERYONE ELSE CHIPPED IN FOR...THAT.

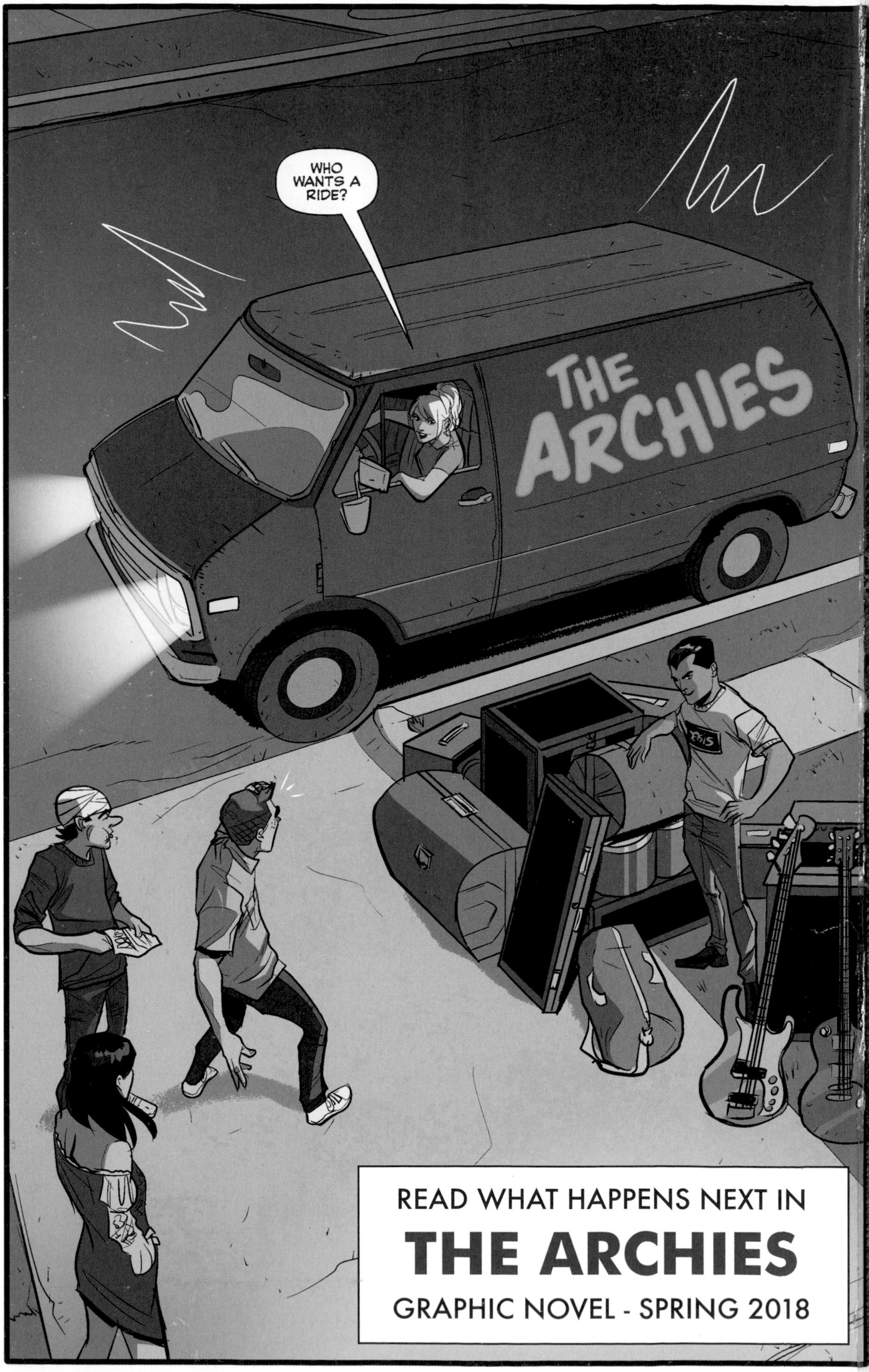
WHO WANTS A RIDE?
THE ARCHIES
READ WHAT HAPPENS NEXT IN
THE ARCHIES
GRAPHIC NOVEL - SPRING 2018